ON DRUGS

ON DRUGS

PSYCHEDELICS, PHILOSOPHY, AND THE NATURE OF REALITY

JUSTIN SMITH-RUIU

LIVERIGHT PUBLISHING CORPORATION
A Division of W. W. Norton & Company
Independent Publishers Since 1923

The names of certain people referred to in this book have been changed.

Copyright © 2025 by Justin Smith-Ruiu

All rights reserved
Printed in the United States of America
First Edition

For information about permission to reproduce selections from this book, write to Permissions, Liveright Publishing Corporation, a division of W. W. Norton & Company, Inc., 500 Fifth Avenue, New York, NY 10110

For information about special discounts for bulk purchases, please contact W. W. Norton Special Sales at specialsales@wwnorton.com or 800-233-4830

Manufacturing by Lakeside Book Company
Book design by Chris Welch
Production manager: Daniel Van Ostenbridge

ISBN 978-1-324-09497-5

Liveright Publishing Corporation, 500 Fifth Avenue, New York, NY 10110
www.wwnorton.com

W. W. Norton & Company Ltd., 15 Carlisle Street, London W1D 3BS

10 9 8 7 6 5 4 3 2 1

There are more things in Heaven and Earth, Horatio,
Than are dreamt of in your philosophy.

—William Shakespeare, *Hamlet* (c. 1600)

Now this connection or adaptation of all created things to each and of each to all, means that each simple substance has relations which express all the others, and, consequently, that it is a perpetual living mirror of the universe.

—G. W. Leibniz, *Monadology* (1714)

Along came LSD and . . . the whole world just went kablooey.

—Jerry Garcia, interviewed in *Rolling Stone* (1972)

CONTENTS

INTRODUCTION ... ix

CHAPTER ONE: **What It's Like** ... 1

CHAPTER TWO: **Articulate Guinea Pigs** ... 41

CHAPTER THREE: **Psychedelic Meditations** ... 63

CHAPTER FOUR: **What *Are* Drugs?** ... 89

CHAPTER FIVE: **More Than a Feeling?** ... 125

CHAPTER SIX: **Galaxy Brains** ... 159

CHAPTER SEVEN: **Seeing God** ... 199

ACKNOWLEDGMENTS ... 233
NOTES ... 235
BIBLIOGRAPHY ... 241
INDEX ... 247

INTRODUCTION

I'm standing in an open field with my new friends, Dasha, Lena, and Sveta. It's the early fall of 1991, and I am nineteen years old. There has just been a failed coup attempt by communist hardliners, and all of Russia is still in chaos, but that great commotion seems as if it's a world away today. We've taken a regional train an hour or so outside of Saint Petersburg for a day of mushroom hunting.

Dasha calls from a grove off in the distance, announcing she's found some of the "special" ones. The rest of us run over, and I naïvely ask what makes them so special. They tell me these are the ones with the power to "make you see things differently." I ask whether they mean these are psilocybin mushrooms, or fly agaric, or what. They say they have no idea what the scientific name for them is, but that I should just trust them. We stop by an old lady's remote dacha and ask if we can use her modest facilities to freshen up before heading back. The girls tell her about our special find, and she laughs knowingly, a facial contortion that almost bursts the knot of the headscarf below her chin. Around here these special mushrooms, evidently, if not their Linnean nomenclature, are well known across the generations.

When we get back to Saint Petersburg, we boil them up and make a tea, and then we drink it. I don't recall much of what happened next, but one scene stands out to me. The sun has gone down and I'm sitting on a log, Sveta beside me, on the trash-strewn beach of the Gulf of Finland. I dig a hole in the wet sand with my foot, and at some point she throws a cigarette into it. I look at the glowing ember and it horrifies me. I tell her I can't bear to look any longer, that what I am seeing appears to me as the pit of hell. "Keep looking then," Sveta says. "It will turn into something else soon enough. Everything always does."

It may disappoint at least some readers to learn that I am not, as I write this, on drugs. I am not that kind of author, and this is not that kind of book. I am, as I write, sober, lucid, and entirely focused on the task at hand.

I have never been a great fan of the gonzo approach to writing, as when, in the 1960s, Hunter S. Thompson used to dash off chaotic jumbles of words, under the simultaneous influence of multiple mind-altering substances, and sought to pass this work off to his editors as an expression of the freewheeling spirit of the era. Still less do I take my cue from Timothy Leary, the counterculture icon and disgraced Harvard psychologist who was known not only to champion the use of LSD but even to administer it to undergraduate students without their consent or knowledge. The great majority of my intellectual and philosophical heroes have never used drugs at all, or, if they did, it did not subsequently have a noticeable effect on their work. I generally agree with the eighteenth-century African philosopher Anton Wilhelm Amo, to cite the title of a 1738 treatise of his, that philosophy is an activity that can only be pursued "soberly and accurately."[1] Even if Amo was not thinking of sobriety narrowly here as the opposite of drunkenness, intoxication, or psychedelic ecstasy, in a broad sense we may agree that it is simply intrinsic to the project of philosophy that one must be eminently clearheaded at least at the moment one is seeking to make a contribution to it in writing. Whether one might also be permitted to *prepare* for that clearheaded philosophical thinking by the use of psychedelic drugs is a very thorny question, and one that this book aims to go some distance toward resolving.

So far am I from the freewheeling and gonzo world of the 1960s acid gurus as to feel the need to stress at the very opening of this book that nowhere in it will you find any straightforward defense of recreational drug use, let alone for any violation of existing law. My own use of illegal substances is far enough in the past now that I can acknowledge it without so much as the appearance of advocacy. My experience of what are now, in some jurisdictions, legal psychedelics, notably psilocybin, is rather more recent. Indeed, this experience has constituted part of the research, in the broad sense, for this book. So prudent am I, moreover, that I feel the need to stress at the outset, with the psychedelics scholar Daniel M. Perrine, "that entheogenic experiences do not necessarily involve the violation of any law, even laws which are arguably adjudged as excessive and immoral."[2]

And even the newly legal use of psychedelics, and the account here of my experience under their influence, does not amount to advocacy. The choice, obviously, is *entirely up to you*. If you are well-informed as to the risks, and if you nonetheless find compelling reasons to try anyway; if you are an adult and you have several hours open with no significant responsibilities to others and no need to drive a car or operate heavy machinery, then psychedelics may be for you.

Or not. Perhaps it's best to hold off just a while longer. Read this book to the end, reflect with me on all dimensions of the psychedelic experience, both good and bad, and then decide how you would like to proceed.

Caveats offered, it is nonetheless true that for most of my adult life I have considered that it would be good for everyone to have the opportunity to use psychedelic drugs at some point in their lives. Like falling in love, or having children, or swimming, or looking a wild animal in the eyes at close range, such an experience can be a significant part of what we rightly take to be the fullness of a life. It has moreover seemed to me that there is nothing intrinsically shameful about psychedelics. And yet clearly psychedelic drug use is often surrounded with shame. It's worth asking why.

One possible reason for the shame is that psychedelic drug use is often conflated with other forms of drug use in which addiction, and in consequence diminution of a person's full moral agency, is a greater danger. It is practically a tautology to say that addiction is bad, since by definition it limits one's autonomy and causes the addict to live in a way that he or she would rather not live. But psychedelic drugs are not like that. No one joneses for acid or gets the D.T.'s from sudden cessation of psilocybin.

Another reason, of more philosophical interest, is that the dimensions of ourselves that are churned up while under the influence of psychedelics are ones that we often have difficulty squaring with the persons endowed with moral agency that we ordinarily take ourselves to be. It is normal to recoil from some of what we find within ourselves, to seek to disavow it once the trip is over. But the fact that we *are* able to find hidden dimensions of ourselves that seem to have a life of their own, whether we like what we find or not, while under the influence of certain substances is itself of interest, or should be, to anyone who wants to understand what it is to live in this world, with a human mind and a sense of wonder.

If I have generally thought that it would be good for every adult to have the opportunity to use psychedelics, I have also supposed that there should be laws and institutions that make this possible. I have supported the moves toward broad legalization of cannabis in the United States, and the much smaller-scale beginnings of a similar trend for psilocybin, MDMA, peyote, and other drugs. It has seemed to me for these latter that the most suitable approach might be to create special clinics—or, perhaps more appealingly, "resorts" or "retreats"—where people can go to consume these substances in a safe and comfortable setting under the supervision of trained attendants. This is the model that is currently being adopted for the use of psilocybin in the state of Oregon, and it is one option in the Netherlands where (much to the benefit of the research for this book) a curious loophole brought it about that the "truffles" of psychedelic mushrooms (more technically, the sclerotia) remained legal after the 2008 prohibition on all other parts of the same species of fungus, even though these truffles contain exactly the same chemical compound responsible for their psychedelic effect. In essence, the Dutch legal system permits psilocybin trips, as long as they draw only on one part of the mushroom's anatomy—one instance among many in which the law fails to keep up with the complexities of botany, mycology, and organic chemistry.

Because I am neither an advocate nor an activist, questions concerning the law do not interest me all that much, except to the extent that I would prefer not to find myself on the wrong side of it. I think it is interesting that human societies try to suppress certain substances, even naturally occurring ones, and as a scholar and historian of science I am concerned to understand why this happens. But my suspicion is that it always will happen, for better or worse, and that any future psychedelic utopia activists may succeed in bringing about in part through legal reforms will in any case be short-lived. There will always be cycles of liberality and prohibition, just as there always have been.

Another aspect of this book that positions it far, far away from the world of Thompson and Leary is that the science of psychedelics is in a very different place in the 2020s than it was in the 1960s. This is particularly so in medical research, where a growing mountain of evidence suggests that psychedelic drugs show considerable promise for the treatment of depression, post-traumatic stress disorder, opiate addiction, and other conditions—indeed, far greater promise than the standard gamut of antidepressants and anxiolytics. At the same time, there is significantly broader cultural interest today in the practice of microdosing, which is to say the therapeutic use of small quantities of psychedelics intended to enhance one's daily thriving, rather than fundamentally to transform one's perception of reality for a short period of time.

In this book I will primarily focus on "macrodosing," or at least the consumption of psychedelic substances in sufficient quantities as to alter, at least temporarily and perhaps for much longer, our most basic understanding of who we are and of the nature of external reality. Nonetheless, there can be no sharp distinction between these sorts of experience—micro- and macrodosing, the objective of improved wellness and the objective of the total overhaul of the psyche—as indeed cultural attitudes about the one sort of practice inevitably shape attitudes about the other.

Philosophically and neuroscientifically, moreover, we must face up to the fact that whatever the quantity taken and whatever the circumstances, it is always a human brain, and a human consciousness, that are being worked upon. It is that brain and that consciousness, under the influence of supplementary substances or not, that are the real wonder, and the real object of this book's attention. How is it that we perceive reality the way we do? And what does it say about our perception of reality that it can be so fundamentally altered through an intentional alteration of our internal chemistry? Do psychedelics warp our perception of reality, drawing us further than in our ordinary lucid state from the actual way things are? Or do they rather reveal something to us about the way things are that we ordinarily cannot perceive? How, moreover, can we answer these questions with any real confidence? It seems that to answer in favor of the view that psychedelics push us further from apprehension of the world as it is presupposes that our mind is, in its default state, naturally and adequately constituted so as to know reality itself. But philosophy has spent the last few millennia coming up with some pretty good reasons why we should be skeptical of the idea that the mind is so constituted. Something therefore seems a bit off, a bit fishy, when philosophers, along with the surrounding culture, shy away from psychedelics, whether taking them or studying their effects, on the grounds that they distance you from reality. Philosophy is born of the realization that we already *are*, or seem to be, at some distance from reality even in our default mode of consciousness. Why not, then, explore all the modes of consciousness available to us, considering what each of them might have to tell us about the relationship between mind and world? That is what I propose to do in this book.

ON DRUGS

CHAPTER ONE

※

WHAT IT'S LIKE

Not so long ago I was in a city in the Netherlands for three nights, not at all far from Leiden and Utrecht and the other Dutch cities where René Descartes had, centuries earlier, spent some of the most productive years of his life living in exile from the Inquisition that still had considerable sway in France. I had been invited to give a public lecture, and I decided to stay on over the weekend to conduct some research for the present book.

The city had one prominent "smart shop," as these are called in the local parlance, offering a wide range of psilocybin-truffle products, as well as seeds for those who wish to grow their own mushrooms at home. The ambience at this establishment was closer to that of a dentist's office than of a classic headshop of the sort I had known from my California youth, with their bongs and pipes and drug-themed alien-head paraphernalia. There was one employee working and a short line of customers. Each customer had to consult with the employee and answer a set of questions concerning their reasons for wishing to take psilocybin and what sort of psilocybin experience they were hoping to have. I was struck, when my turn came, by the inadequacy of the available vocabulary for my impending interview, and even though I had not yet tried any of his goods, I already anticipated that no matter what adjectives I came up with on the spot (heady, cosmic, etc.), the particular strain that the shopkeeper was going to deliver was not really going to fit those adjectives in any precise way.

He asked me whether I had taken mushrooms before, and I told him yes, but it had been some years since the last time. He said taking them again will be like going back into a home from which you have been long absent. You will still know where everything is, he said, by which I think he meant you will feel "at home." The experience will be familiar, even if it is an experience whose precise nature has not been directly accessible to your conscious mind throughout the intervening period. He asked me why I wanted to take mushrooms, and for some reason, in that moment, it made sense to me to tell him the whole truth. I am an academic philosopher, I said, and I am writing a book on the potential lessons psychedelic drugs might hold for philosophical inquiry.

He winced. It was not the "philosophy" part he found offensive, as I suspected at first. What made him wince is that he did not at all like hearing that other key word, "drugs," and in his gesture he seemed to indicate that I really should not have said it so loud. He told me he always bristled when his own family members described him as being in the business of "selling drugs." These are not "drugs," he was in the habit of explaining to them; they are *plants*, they grow right out of the earth, and there is nothing more natural in the world than for us to consume them. I did not superciliously object to him, as I could have, that his taxonomic lumping of plants and fungi together was disappointingly imprecise. I was more struck, in the instant, by his peculiar lexical taboo on the word "drug." After all, this is a word of Dutch origin, coming from *droog*, meaning "dry," and used originally in the context of the global trade in dried plants as pharmaceutical commodities in the Dutch Golden Age of the seventeenth century. So a "drug" is just a dried plant, or perhaps also a fungus, and that is exactly what I was there to buy. Everything we were doing was legal, and yet the vigilance with which my tabooed language was corrected vividly reminded me that simply legalizing an activity does not immediately deprive it of its illicit charge.

This drug merchant, anyhow, was not at all interested in the book project. I had the strong impression, in fact, that he disliked me, and I was relieved when he consented to sell me two containers of truffles, after which I got out of there as quickly as I could. That evening I followed the instructions on the packaging and chewed them slowly. They tasted much sourer than I had expected, and it was long, hard work to get them down. I took abundant notes over the next few hours, as any rigorous autoexperimenter does. Among the observations I find most amusing now, when I go over them, is this remark on the similarities and differences between cannabis and psilocybin: "For one thing," I wrote, "cannabis never made me want to take notes!" I was, indeed, for at least the first two hours, unusually wordy. I felt as if I was at the height of my expressive power, and for some time I was able to write down extremely minute observations that ordinarily would have escaped my attention.

My notes reflect considerable uncertainty as to what was causing what, and whether my expectations, and my prior priming as a philosopher, were not shaping the quality of the experiences I was having. Thirty minutes or so in, I got up from the bed to use the restroom and noticed unmistakable auras around the edges of objects, as well as pareidolia, or hallucinated face-like patterns, in the light sockets, in the screws on the knobs of the towel rack, and so on. These, my notes indicate, were the first certain announcements of the drug's effects, rather than of my own impatient expectations. After returning to the bed, I wrote: "Things in my peripheral vision catch my attention, seem far more salient than they should be."

Trivial things began to seem unusually poignant: the small size of the apples I had bought earlier in the day and left on the table, for example. Yet I could not fully credit the psilocybin for this impression; I am very often sentimental over inexplicable things. I also began to notice that I could induce rather intense visual hallucinations by closing my eyes and pressing them, and that these would cease immediately when I stopped pressing. Doing this gave me a strong feeling of control. I pressed and was surprised to see visions of rhizomatic networks that looked distinctly fungal, spreading out as if underground, as if the actual form of the substance I had just consumed were impressing itself on my mind's eye. But then again, I thought, perhaps this too is the fulfillment of an expectation.

I began to think about the last time I had done psilocybin. It was 1999, and then too I was in the Netherlands, in Leiden, with a German friend who was studying anthropology there. Her roommate was a keen amateur mycologist and had grown a bounty of his own psychedelic mushrooms. I almost never think about this old friend anymore. I knew, roughly, that she had abandoned anthropology to become a Lutheran minister back in Germany. I suddenly had an intense desire to reach out to her, to tell her I hadn't forgotten what we'd shared, and in fact, at this moment, I was "sharing" it again, or at least "sharing in" it. Just as the man at the shop had told me earlier that day, I was indeed back in a familiar home.

I did some searching online to find her coordinates, to see if I could perhaps send her an email. But very soon that desire for telecommunication in the narrow sense subsided, not because I lost interest in reaching out to her but because it came to seem that I already *had* reached out to her, that actually sending the email now was an unnecessary step. It is not that I thought we were communicating by telepathy or anything like that, but only that the twenty-four years that had separated the present moment from that evening in Leiden suddenly meant nothing at all. It was still 1999. Or it was 1999 and 2023 at once. I'm not quite clear on how this works, and when I try to express it, it sounds as if, necessarily, I must be stepping beyond the bounds of philosophical discourse and into the realm of mystery and contradiction. But there is simply no other way.

There are a number of things that happened to me that evening that I feel I cannot even attempt to relate, things that are just too far beyond language. There are also many things that I could relate, but will not, as not everything that happens in my interior life is suitable for sharing. I can summarize the experience by noting how it ended, some hours later, when I found myself in the dark and crying and saying over and over: "I'm sorry," and after that, "It's OK." It struck me at this moment how deeply depressed I had been in the weeks before arriving in the Netherlands, and how drastically I had been underestimating my spell of recurrent depression during that same time. I made one final note that evening before falling asleep (which happened surprisingly easily): "I do not feel for the moment that my life is small, infinitesimal, 'pointless' because even smaller than a point. I feel it's as large as the cosmos. This isn't an egotistical feeling, just an accurate one for any living being."

Two days later I returned to the smart shop and I found the same employee there. He asked me how my experience was, and I told him just a small part of what I've written here. He seemed happy. I told him I would like to try a different strain. He said that not enough time had passed, that one must ordinarily wait two weeks or ten days at a minimum before returning for more. I said that made some sense, but that I'd like to try it again anyway because I was leaving the Netherlands the next day and truffles are illegal where I live. He nodded comprehendingly, but remained firm. He said that if you do not respect the "plants," they will take their revenge. He said that he would be putting *himself* at risk of the plants' vengeance if he were to agree to serve a customer before the appropriate amount of time had passed. I said I understood and that I'd see him some other time, and I slinked out of there, it seemed to me, in visible shame, like an addict with a forged prescription who has just been turned out of a pharmacy. Of course, to make that comparison is also to disrespect the shopkeeper in another way, and perhaps to disrespect his "plants" as well, since the sort of experience he was in the business of brokering, by his own lights, was one that had nothing in common with the sale of "drugs."

I was relieved to discover that there was one other shop in town that also sold truffles, and I went there at once. It proved to be much more like a traditional headshop, with tie-dyed clothing and an assortment of skull-shaped bongs. The vendor, an older woman, also proved to be markedly less interested in the motivations and expectations of her customers. I was in and out in under two minutes. I bought four packages this time rather than two.

I am very grateful that I persisted, that I did not "respect the plants." The evening of the second psilocybin trip, having taken more than before, and far more than is recommended, would turn out to be one of the most intense and transformative experiences of my life. Once again, I bump up against the limits of language when I try to convey what it was like.

My hotel room had a cheap-looking poster of Marilyn Monroe framed on the wall. One of the first signs that the psilocybin was taking effect arrived when, again, I was walking toward the bathroom, and I saw her there and paused in front of her image and stared at her in absolute wonder. Do I *know* Marilyn Monroe? I asked myself. I never met her, but she has been with me my whole life, just as she has probably been with everyone reading this. She is at least as familiar to me as, say, any of my first cousins. And yet, I reflect, I have never so much as greeted her. How strange! So, there in that hotel room, I greeted Marilyn Monroe, and it was heartfelt, and I was certain that whatever just transpired counted as a meaningful *interpersonal* exchange.

But this was just the beginning, as the particular quality of that encounter with Marilyn would be felt ten times more strongly when I returned to the bed and pulled up old clips on YouTube of Cass Elliott, more commonly known as Mama Cass. For some inscrutable reason, earlier in that day I had had an earworm from The Mamas and the Papas' 1967 song "Creeque Alley" going through my head, in particular the line that runs: "And no one's gettin' fat except Mama Cass." This had come to me in my completely unaltered mental state, a reminder that the mind and memory are a marvel, too, without psychedelics. I don't know what it was doing there. I'm not particularly a fan of 1960s folk-pop. But there it was, in my head, and so I pulled it up on the computer, and I ended up spending the next few hours watching clips of Mama Cass on the talk show circuit, all the while feeling not only that I knew her, and had always known her, but that I had always loved her.

To say it like this sounds ridiculous, but the feeling was entirely sincere. Something about Mama Cass seemed to tell the whole story of my own existence. I suddenly recalled a black-and-white picture of my parents, from the summer of 1972. My mother is pregnant with me, and she is unusually heavy. Then I recalled a distant memory from early childhood when that photo was being shown around to guests at our home. I knew I was in it, though still unborn, and I knew I was the reason why my mother had gained so much weight. Then I recalled that someone, I don't know who, said, when looking at the photo, that my mother looked like Mama Cass. Resemblance, now, seemed to collapse into identity, or rather the distinction between them no longer mattered. Mama Cass suddenly appeared to me as "Mama" in the fullest sense: the fount of my being and the origin of my world.

I am not going to attempt to defend this conviction, which felt so strong at the time. That it is indefensible, that it is ridiculous, is precisely what I am attempting to convey and the very reason for my insistence on sharing some of these details (but again, not all of them) with unflinching honesty. (I can assure you, if I were making anything up, it would have been something very different from this.) Why did such thoughts come to me so intensely and unbidden? The mind, it seemed to me as I reviewed the experience on the following day, is just so much more wondrous, so much stranger, than my professional colleagues ordinarily take it to be! We philosophers are typically concerned to understand how a human mind can entertain such propositions as "There is a pain in my foot" or how it can perceive a red dot on a screen. These are fascinating problems too, but surely we might also gain from considering how the mind can become convinced that a long-dead pop star has become identical with one's own mother or with something like "cosmic motherhood." I think at least a part of the reason we tend to stick with the pain in the foot or the dot on the screen is that, in order to talk about the stranger divagations of the mind, we generally have to acknowledge that we have experienced them, and that is an acknowledgment that typically entails a measure of shame. Part of my motivation in writing what I have written here is to push beyond that shame, to explore conscious experience in a way that truly faces up to the weirdness of the world.

I was not being fully honest when I previously wrote that I am not currently on drugs. In fact I am, right now, on amlodipine for chronic hypertension. And though I've often bristled when I've heard others describing caffeine as a drug, for the sake of completeness I should also acknowledge that I have drunk coffee every single day, without fail, since September 13, 1990. Of more relevance to our present investigation, I am currently on quetiapine, an antianxiety drug that is also used to treat schizophrenia and bipolar disorder (neither of which am I deemed by the experts to have), and I am on venlafaxine, an antidepressant of the SSRI class (selective serotonin reuptake inhibitors). In addition to these two prescriptions, I also have one for Xanax, a benzodiazepine I take in punctuated moments of severe anxiety. I have a very long history of mental health difficulties and of prescription medications designed to alleviate their symptoms. My diagnoses have varied over the years. I have taken tricyclics for obsessive compulsive disorder, Prozac and Lexapro and several other SSRIs for major depression, and now quetiapine for anxiety. I have experienced a delirious gamut of side effects, from weight gain to anorgasmia.

When I was an undergraduate I was deeply, pathologically obsessed with maintaining a perfect grade point average. I would sometimes find myself driving along the California highway, when, suddenly, I felt compelled to make a swallowing gesture toward any letter *A* I happened to see on the road signs and a retching gesture toward every *B*, *C*, *D*, or *F*. If I made a mistake I had to exit at the nearest off-ramp, circle back around, and try again. This is only one small example, one of the funnier ones, of the total system of superstitions, bubbling up out of some unnamed and permanent feeling of dread, that entirely structured my daily routines. For most of my life I have been a "high-functioning" depressive—so high functioning, in fact, that it will seem implausible to many, even to those who know me fairly well, to learn of my long psychiatric record. But another way of saying "high functioning" is "high performance," which is to say that I have generally been all too aware of the performative dimensions of social life and have mastered my own performance in the same way I mastered my GPA and the various standardized tests I have had to take: propelled forward only by the fuel of anxiety, self-hatred, and inner certainty of my own fraudulence.

The intake questionnaires designed to measure the severity of depression have never really captured my subjective experience very well. They ask: "Do you have trouble getting out of bed?" No. "Have you lost your appetite?" I wish! "Are you able to complete your work tasks?" Always. Some diagnosticians, amateur and professional alike, have rushed to explain to me that I seem to suffer only from anxiety, and not from depression, while some have told me the opposite. But these are meaningless distinctions to me. I don't see any reason why the *DSM*, a diagnostic manual that in any case is always in the course of revision and only captures one way of dividing up psychiatric classifications in a certain place and time, should trump the first-person experience of the conditions under diagnosis. Anxiety and depression are both the opposite of a good feeling; they're bad, they're a drag. In the end it may be that eudaimonia and kakodaimonia, good and bad vibes as they say today, are really the only two conditions with any robustness to them. And even these two elementary states shade into one another in ways that make it extremely hard for a lucid observer of one's own condition to put feelings into language. Sometimes the condition of the soul gets *so* bad that it starts to feel like a sort of ecstasy, in which one has circled all the way back around to joy: the horseshoe theory of depression and mental health.

Each one of my diagnoses and its proposed treatment, I grant, seems to get at something real about me, even if I have never been entirely convinced of the robust reality of particular mental health classifications. With the philosopher Ian Hacking, I tend to take a view of mental illness grounded in "historical ontology," which is to say I think the descriptions we come up with *do* account for reality, but reality, or at least this dimension of reality, evolves along with human culture.[1] We know today, to use one of Hacking's examples, that what in the World War I era was diagnosed as "fugue syndrome," in which young men suddenly began walking, as if in a trance, sometimes for thousands of miles, turned out to be a mostly fleeting cultural phenomenon.[2] Its disappearance, moreover, seems to have had at least something to do with the fact that psychiatrists themselves stopped diagnosing it. In light of examples such as this, it is not hard to see that people in previous historical eras were not so much "wrong" in the way they accounted for afflictions at the boundary between the spiritual and the somatic, as they were simply speaking within a different historical context with different points of reference. And similarly, today, when I hear my psychiatrist attempting to convince me that I suffer from something called "anxiety disorder," I am able to agree, but with a certain amount of mental reservation and detachment from the air of self-serious authority and objectivity she is hoping to transmit.

In general the disease model of mental illness seems to me to be based on a rather deep conceptual confusion, one that almost threatens to lapse into vicious circularity when we consider it alongside other ways we talk about mind and body and about how these may fall into a disordered state. As the comedian Mitch Hedberg, dead of an overdose at thirty-seven, once observed, addiction is a disease, but a strange one: it's the only disease people yell at you for having. It's plain that no matter how much we try to reduce the moral dimensions of human life to quasi-medical conditions, our ordinary ways of speaking and of judging ourselves and others continue to resist these efforts.

According to our conventional ways of speaking, a "psychosomatic" illness is one that exists in the body only insofar as it exists in the mind. But a "mental" illness, understood according to the disease model as a "disease like any other" and therefore a proper object of medical treatment, is one that exists in the mind only insofar as it exists in the body, or more precisely, the brain. One wants to know whether there shouldn't be some rule as to which way the direction of explanation is to go in all cases. If there is not, it seems we risk getting trapped in a sort of diagnostic circle. If we are willing to admit that illnesses *can* be psychosomatic, then it is not clear why we should not see mental illness itself as being one such illness, and therefore why we should not suppose that it is the mind that is causing the body to cause the mind to be ill. But the truth is that even if we are almost all avowed nondualists today, our entire society, including the medical and psychiatric establishments, remains mired in deep conceptual confusion when it speaks of "body" and "mind" and presumes to grasp the difference.

In any case what is clear is that there has always been something a bit imbalanced about me. This is not a memoir, and not the place to explore what that might be in any depth. I mention this history only because my—contestable—claim to authority on the matter of what psychedelic drugs can teach us is in part based on the fact that I myself have done a *lot* of drugs, of a lot of different kinds, and I am therefore in a position to draw some auto-experimental comparisons, as between, say, antidepressants of the SSRI class and hallucinogens such as LSD. It is for this reason that I am aspiring, in this present chapter, to exhaustivity in the matter of which drugs, precisely, I have done.

Nor have I yet finished enumerating these. I should also disclose, if I am going to bring up everything right down to my blood pressure medication, that for many years I was an alcoholic. I had my last drink on December 2, 2020, and in the following years I have been consistently committed to what I have heard described as "California sobriety": cannabis and occasional psychedelics are fine, but no booze. Of course I don't really know if the diagnostic label "alcoholic" accurately applies to me either, and by now it should not be too surprising when I contend that what is and is not to count as alcoholism is something that can vary widely, depending on historical and cultural context. It is perhaps noteworthy here that I managed to stop drinking without signing up for any particular program of sobriety maintenance, such as Alcoholics Anonymous. I had simply had enough, and so I quit. It was only after quitting that I developed my mature interest in other mind-altering substances.

I have been, some might say, irrationally vigilant these past few years. In the summer of 2021 my wife and I were in Belgium, and I ordered a marmite full of mussels. When they arrived, I tasted one and sensed that the broth had a white-wine base. I spit it out and refused to eat the rest, even though presumably all the alcohol had been burned off in cooking. More recently I bought a package of shelled pomegranate seeds at the supermarket. When I got home and tasted them, they seemed funny. They had an unmistakable fizz, a spirituous quality that told me they were in some early stage of fermentation. I spit them out too. But what a strange quality that was, and one that I used to know so well! Were they rotting, or were they just now beginning to achieve their perfection? Had they gone bad, or were they just now coming to life? This is what we might call the paradox of fermentation—it is the moment when organic matter both goes bad *and* comes to life. It is the sublation of life and death, the state of living stuff that testifies equally to its mortality and its vitality. To be vital just is to be mortal, and fermentation illustrates this iron law by displaying both of these faces of nature at once.

I was only thirteen, with a group of friends spending the night, when we smuggled a plastic bottle of Smirnoff vodka back into my room from the kitchen counter where it had been left out by our parents after what must have been a lively Thanksgiving dinner. I had seen advertisements for vodka featuring happy people in Swiss chalets, wearing after-ski boots and making fondue, and I reasoned that it could not be all that bad if it fit into such happy scenes as these. So I swallowed some, and then some more, and I woke up many hours later, somehow naked, and covered in vomit. Many of us likely have a moment we think of as our first fall from innocence, and that was mine. Subsequently, I did not drink at all throughout high school and college. It was only in graduate school that I developed a regular habit, something I was able to pursue throughout my twenties and into my thirties under the banner of the good life. On the surface, I was an Epicurean and a bon vivant. Inwardly, notwithstanding what Epicurus had promised, I was obviously not thriving.

In the milieu of graduate school, and of academia in general and academic philosophy in particular, it was all too easy to maintain a heavy drinking habit under the pretense of healthy free-spiritedness. I can recall one particularly low moment, at an academic conference in a part of Eastern Europe where it is common to drink homemade schnapps. After a day talking Descartes and Spinoza, the bottles came out, and the general attitude that prevailed was that one *had* to partake, simply in recognition of the hospitality of our hosts and the splendors of their culture. The next morning there were those who woke up covered in vomit, and even a few caked in blood, yet it was universally agreed that that had been a good night. I remember thinking, hungover and in the light of day: is *this* really philosophy?

That was the last time I drank hard liquor, but for many years after that I remained as if religiously attached to my daily portion of red wine, usually somewhere between a half bottle and a bottle, sometimes more, sometimes much more. Living in France gave me an extra layer of cover. It's the good life, after all! I have been told more than once over the past few years, since quitting alcohol, that the French authorities would do well to reject my currently pending bid for citizenship based on my nondrinking alone. But the truth is my wine habit was always extremely un-French. I only ever pretended to listen, and sometimes didn't even pretend, when a wine merchant was giving me his deeply learned speech about the terroir and bouquet of his various bottles. I never believed for a second that one wine might be more appropriately paired with a given dish rather than another. I never believed that any wine could have hints of berry or persimmon or beeswax, or, if it could, that this might have any relevance to my desire to drink it.

Nothing was worse than sharing a bottle with others over dinner. Often, before even realizing what had happened, I would glance around the table and see the other glasses at exactly the same level at which the waiter had poured them, and then my own, covered with fingerprints as if it had been mauled and molested, completely empty. I could never tell if I was furious at them or at myself for being built so differently; but furious I was. Then the waiter would come back and refill everyone's glasses, as if my alien companions, who hadn't yet taken a sip, needed more in the same way I did. I grew to hate restaurant drinking, and even before the first pandemic lockdown had become a practitioner of what the Finns call *kalsarikännit*— "pantsdrinking," as in drinking in your underwear, which of course implies staying at home. I always preferred to get my wine anonymously, at the supermarket, rather than at some specialty shop where I might have to endure the enological orations of the salesman. I probably learned more about wine from my Grandpa Von than I ever did from any Parisian sommelier—Grandpa Von, who liked to take his enormous cardboard box full of Ernest and Julio Gallo rosé up on the roof with him as he worked for hours in the hot sun, mixing the tar, replacing the shingles, until one day he fell off and got a whole mouthful of terroir.

For all those years the wine seemed to me so interwoven with my identity as to be ineliminable from it: what would be left if I no longer had it? At its best it seemed to give me partial access to that "other world" that I have found to be much more fully opened up by psychedelic drugs: the world music and poetry seem to emanate from. Wine generally made me feel briefly enlivened. I especially enjoyed writing with a big full glass of it next to me, and then, once I'd drunk too much to write anymore, I enjoyed filling my glass again and listening to music with headphones on.

That was my life for about fifteen years. I lived like that long enough for it to take a toll, unsurprisingly, on my physical health, and I am now deeply thankful every day that I was able to stop soon enough for the toll to be reversed and to be able to know in my fifties a vitality that I had thought was gone forever at forty. Quitting alcohol in fact had a number of consequences in my life, both direct and indirect, both good and bad. I became considerably less social, for one thing, since for many years, I now saw, I had really only used social occasions as opportunities to drink; mingling with other humans was at best a secondary benefit, and often only an obstacle, to direct pursuit of the thing I really wanted to be doing. After quitting, I believe I also became more honest about my faults and limitations, and many of my earlier efforts to be taken seriously in this world, by getting advanced degrees and prestigious positions and accolades, looked to me now as expressions of pure vanity and as driven by the same self-loathing as had caused me to drink, more than by any positive ambition, let alone talent. Worldly accomplishment, in other words, no longer looked to me at all like the opposite of my pathological and addiction-prone personality, but rather as only a different symptom of it.

It is difficult to say whether quitting drinking helped my mental health to improve. I would say on balance that it did not, even if it *did* help me to progress, I believe, in certain dimensions of my moral character. I grew more responsible for myself, and less deceptive, but no less unhappy. In fact I think the absolute worst period of my long life of mental health challenges came in the year after I quit drinking, which, in 2021, was also the period of the second COVID lockdowns and of the strictest limitations on our movement and freedom. With most of my human contact now mediated by a screen, I descended into a depression so deep that I had trouble even comprehending the real existence of the external world, of human institutions such as universities and governments but also, even, of buildings, cities, airports. I felt like a ghost, still somehow haunting a world that was no longer mine. I sought out psychiatric care, yet again, and got some antidepressants. At the same time, I had an ailing mother in faraway California, and being cut off from my family there, under these new global circumstances where being able to hop on a trans-Atlantic flight was by no means a sure thing, caused me a great deal of additional anxiety.

During one of my visits to my home state after the travel restrictions had been lifted in late 2021, I happened to recall something I had read before about the recent legalization of cannabis. Up until that moment, the topic had not interested me at all. In fact I had long had a strongly negative attitude toward marijuana users: I considered theirs a low-class habit and associated it with cultural signifiers of which I wanted no part. The world of stoner layabouts, of a kind that was intimately familiar to me in my adolescence, was a world that I had spent my adult life struggling to get away from. But again, as I have said, part of the effect of quitting drinking was to become considerably less preoccupied with questions of status and reputation, and this meant, among other things, that unlike in my twenties and thirties, I now felt free to follow my nose wherever it might lead me, to cultivate low-status tastes in music, in art, or indeed in drugs, if this is what seemed fitting. And so I set out for one of Sacramento's many dispensaries, and I stocked up on some edibles and tinctures, and I gave cannabis a try.

Antidepressants and other psychiatric medications typically function much like cough suppressants. They suppress the symptoms, without curing the underlying condition. Cannabis does not, in my experience, suppress anything. In fact it brings much to the surface that we might ordinarily prefer to keep suppressed. I have mixed feelings about this, but I'm inclined to think, much along the lines of Aristotle's account of the benefits of watching tragedies, that it is good to have cultural practices that surface our fears. These practices might well carry risk with them, as cannabis indeed does, especially for people who are already emotionally fragile or mentally unwell. But suppression also carries risk. The madness is going to find its way to the surface somehow or other.

Cannabis was indeed a "gateway drug" for me, somewhat as the activists opposed to its legalization have worried it might be. It did not however send me onward to more addictive and harder drugs, but only to more mind-altering and weirder ones. After my second or third evening of getting stoned, I was back on the internet, looking up information on possible legal pathways to a robustly psychedelic experience, of which I would soon have my share. All of these were cathartic in the way I've just described cannabis as being. All of them surfaced in me something that does indeed have much in common with what our society describes in terms of "madness" or "insanity." At the same time, they also made me understand that for these dimensions of myself to come to the surface is really just for me to arrive at a clearer awareness of who I am, and of my place in the world. Alcohol never did this. It only kept me lying to myself, and to others, about who I am. It weighed down and kept fixed in place a veil that psychedelics, and even to some extent cannabis, have at long last helped me to lift.

Was my encounter with Mama Cass so ridiculous in the end? Was I completely out of line in my conviction that I loved her? In the *Symposium* Plato has Socrates describe the ideal ascension of this emotion, from its lowest to its highest expressions. Early in life we experience love mixed with sexual desire for the beauty of a particular other person's body, and then we move from there to love of all beautiful bodies. But if we progress as we might hope to do toward wisdom, then as we age we will also gradually come to love all beautiful minds, and in turn all beautiful institutions and endeavors, then all beautiful knowledge, and in the end, as wise old philosophers, our love will be focused upon nothing but Love itself.

The truth is that most of us vacillate throughout our lives between the various positions on this imagined hierarchy. But whether we think of the ascension as a one-way journey or not, the key philosophical idea in it is that there is a real entity, Love, that exists independently of any of its instances as we know them from experience. This is what we generally refer to as a "universal," and the question whether such a thing exists or not—not just loveable creatures and things but Love itself, not just instances of justice but Justice itself, and so on—will divide the schools of the philosophers, with their running "footnotes to Plato," as Alfred North Whitehead described the history of Western philosophy, for millennia to come.

I am certainly not going to make any progress toward solving the problem of universals in this book, nor even stake out a position on either of the familiar sides of the debate. But I will remark, first, that psychedelic experience can itself deliver a strong argument in favor of the realist camp in the debate. Under the influence of psilocybin, I seemed not to love Mama Cass, for example, in her particularity but rather to love her because this love is a point of entry, so to speak, to the experience of Love itself. When I listen to music while on psilocybin, I love the particular song, but I also feel, much more strongly, that the song is my point of entry to Music, with a capital M, to the thing itself that exists eternally behind and before all the songs that have ever been sung.

We all have this feeling from time to time, to some extent. It's the feeling, in fact, that music and poetry excel above all at conjuring in us: the feeling that there is another dimension that these works of art are coming from. Ordinarily, in a sober and lucid mind, this feeling mostly gets expressed in the form of *longing*. Songs we love have a particular power to make us feel as though there is a world that we know, somehow, but from which we are cut off. Songs seem to emanate from that world but generally do not seem fully to open that world up to us. Yet under the influence of psilocybin, one of my most vivid thoughts goes something like this: "So that other world is real after all, and it is now open to me! I wasn't only imagining it!"

Do I still think that other world is real, now, when my brain chemistry is back to its default setting? The answer is complicated, but I believe philosophy can help us face up to the challenge somewhat. I began the discussion in this section of Love itself, Music itself, Beauty itself, by invoking Plato and Socrates, who stand at the beginning of a long tradition in philosophy that is sometimes called "rationalism." This means in part that Plato, at least (his teacher, Socrates, is somewhat harder to pin down), believed that reasons can be articulated for anything we think, and ultimately also that feelings are a variety of thoughts. That is to say, for example, that for a rationalist love is something that can be rigorously understood, "mastered" by any lover who is also a thinker.

A different tradition, usually seen as emerging only in the nineteenth century, though with significant historical antecedents, is sometimes described as Romanticist or Romantic. In Romanticism, feelings, or what Martin Heidegger would later call "moods" (*Stimmungen,* a term that in German is etymologically connected to the word for "voice"), are a category of human experience quite distinct from thoughts. For Heidegger, moods, such as anxiety or boredom, can have a particular power of "disclosing" the nature of our existence to us, even if they do not reveal to us facts about the world that is investigated by natural science.

As a philosopher Heidegger is difficult to categorize, and he comes at the end of a long tradition, well after the nineteenth-century Romantics have had their moment. But like the Romantics, Heidegger is committed to the idea that there are experiences we can have as human beings that are intrinsically and necessarily out of reach of scientific investigation. Heidegger is not a rationalist, and does not want to say that "Anxiety itself" or "Boredom itself" exists eternally and independently, in the way that Plato would say Beauty or Justice exists, even if, for Plato, these eternally existing ideas have no place in the empirical reality that science, as we understand it in the modern period, is limited to studying. Heidegger thinks these moods are ultimately "in us." And yet, unlike his science-oriented contemporaries in the twentieth century, far from thinking that being "in us" means these moods are "only subjective" and therefore of negligible interest for serious thinkers, instead he makes them the very most important elements of his philosophical system, on which everything else he has to say about human existence, including human scientific knowledge, is made to depend. As Heidegger writes in 1927's *Being and Time* of "states-of-mind" (*Befindlichkeit*), a notion that for him does much of the same work as "mood": "Existentially, a state-of-mind implies a *disclosive submission to the world, out of which we can encounter something that matters to us.*"[3]

"Disclosive submission to the world": this is in fact a fairly compelling way of characterizing the nature of a psychedelic experience. Of the three key terms in this phrase, the last of them may be the one most in need of clarification, even if on the face of it the notion of "world" seems clearest of all. "World," for Heidegger, must not be understood as a synonym of "external world"; indeed the external world is something that psychedelic experiences have the power rather strikingly to draw into question for us. Rather, for Heidegger, a world is always "my world" or "your world": the way things are to me or to you. On such an understanding, "disclosive submission to the world" turns out to be an exercise much less like "accepting things the way they are" or "facing up to facts" and something much more like "listening to yourself." When we take psychedelic drugs, we submit to having important truths about the nature of our existence revealed to us. These truths, indeed, come from "within us," and a hardnosed naturalist could well say that too much attention to them amounts precisely to a refusal to "face facts." But for Heidegger "my world" is at least as important as "the external world" for philosophy's project of making sense of human existence. And indeed in our era, as in his, natural science has the external world so well covered that it seems reasonable to suggest that philosophy should concern itself with that other one, which science has often neglected and even scorned.

I use the term "world" frequently in this book, sometimes in a consciously Heideggerian sense, but sometimes simply to distance myself from "dimension" or "plane of existence" or any other term that is heavy with connotations from the 1960s counterculture. Though in truth I am not sure "world" gets me as far from those connotations as I might wish. I also avoid saying "layers of reality," though that is tempting, because I am not certain it makes any sense to think of ordinary consciousness versus psychedelic experience in terms of the shallower and the deeper. These spatial metaphors prove how limited they are when we realize they can be stood on their head without losing anything at all of the thought we are trying, and perhaps failing, to convey: the world of psychedelic experience, after all, may be said to be "deeper than," yet may also be said to be "*higher* than," the one we know in ordinary experience. Well, which is it? Both seem fine, but that may just be another way of saying both are equally inadequate.

There would be much more yet to say about the surprisingly complex notion of "world" and the way it has transformed over the centuries. There was significant reflection on the notion in the seventeenth century, in the wake of the shift away from a geocentric model of the cosmos, and toward a new one in which stars extend out in all directions to infinity, each one at the center, as philosophers like Henry More and Blaise Pascal speculated, of its own "world." Here we have "world" as what appears to be simply a designation of spatial distance, but historically the term often slides over into something more like the familiar science fiction notion of "parallel dimensions." Thus in Margaret Cavendish's proto–science fiction novel *Blazing-World* of 1666, the girl at the center of the story travels to the North Pole and makes a transit from there to a land of talking bears and other unusual beings. Has she simply gone "somewhere," or has she passed through an interdimensional portal? It is not clear, and it does not really seem to matter. Similarly, in contemporary modal logic, a technical field of philosophy that studies the modal operators of necessity and possibility, specialists often speak of "possible worlds." A few such specialists, notably David Lewis, have claimed to be "modal realists," maintaining that the possible worlds that modal logic treats are in fact real worlds; it is just that they do not overlap with this one. *Where* are they, then? Are they next to this one? Or some measurable distance away from it? Again, there is no real clarity on the matter, nor could there be.

We feel the need to talk about things that are not part of ordinary empirical reality—chimeras, anthropomorphic bears, and the like—and it seems to make intuitive sense to say that while these are not part of *our* world, they are part of *some* world. The psychedelic experience seems to give access to other worlds, again, not just in the sense that we encounter other beings that are not part of ordinary empirical reality, but in the deeper (or higher?) sense of a reality that does not seem to operate according to the ordinary physical laws of the one we generally inhabit, indeed one that sometimes does not seem to be physical at all. The world of music is built of pure feeling, but, again, this does not, when one fully enters it, seem to give any reason to place it lower in a hierarchy of reality than the world of physical objects.

I am by no means a loyal follower of Heidegger. For one thing, his Nazism is odious, even if we can also find in it an occasion to reflect on what it is about the project of Western philosophy that ensured that one of its most towering representatives in the twentieth century was also a proponent of far-right ideology. But even if it is impossible to follow Heidegger in his general project, nonetheless the part of his work I have evoked does hold some appeal. While I have long been attracted to the phenomenological analysis of mood as world-disclosure, my interest in this analysis deepened considerably in the wake of my more recent psychedelic experiences. The world of music that is opened to me, "disclosed to me," if you will, when I listen to it under the influence of psilocybin is, I'll concede, "in me." But what this experience reveals is that this is no small thing at all. It's huge, in fact. What I am tempted to say is that psilocybin not only recalls to the person who takes it the real existence of that other world but also recalls to him or her the plain truth that was there all along but that we cannot ordinarily see: that we carry that world inside of us. It is a "familiar home," to go back to the language of the Dutch shopkeeper.

When I was a child I often had dreams of secret rooms in our house, which could be entered through my bedroom closets. It gives me shivers now just to write about them. Did they exist? Well, architecturally, no, of course not; they would in fact have been impossible from an engineering point of view. And yet my memory of these rooms is much more vivid than my memory of the actual house. Surely this is not a trivial fact, to be dismissed as a simple error. We get constituted in part, we become who we are in part, by what we bring "in us," in imagination or in mood, to what the world in fact delivers to us.

That house was felled by a wrecking ball some years ago, and now its "real" rooms are no more real than the ones I superadded to it with my imagination. To the extent that *any* of its rooms exist now, they do so "in me." These rooms moreover are very much like the world of music I have described, which can be fully opened to us under the influence of psychedelics. Any argument against its reality, on the grounds that it is *only* in me at the moment I am experiencing it under the influence of psilocybin, would strike me as patently beside the point. Of *course* it's in me! I could only reply. Where *else* would it be?

For any drug, the experience of its effects has much to do with what is said about it in the surrounding culture. Cannabis, for example, has long had a reputation for dulling the wits of its users, for frying their brains like an egg in a pan, to recall that iconic antidrug advertisement from the 1980s. In my most recent experiences with cannabis, however, what strikes me most is how much it quickens and deepens my mental faculties. I can do things with my mind while high that I could never imagine so much as attempting otherwise. I have on a few occasions tried to write down some of the astounding mental feats that I've carried out on cannabis, but it is almost intrinsically a part of these experiences that they cannot be captured in words. I can barely recall them in memory once my mind is back to normal, and while they are happening I lack the coordination and goal directedness to interrupt them and to start taking notes. So most of these experiences are simply lost, but they have at least left enough of an impression for me to know that "pot makes you dumb" can't be the full story.

For example, I have no proper musical training, yet on occasion cannabis has enabled me to hear, in my mind, beautiful and complex orchestrations that I have somehow generated entirely from within. What's more, I am sometimes able to modify this music at will to please my most capricious tastes, adding more layers, for example, to the string section. I can also sometimes imagine in vivid detail the progress of evolution from the single-celled organisms of the Precambrian era up to the present day, and I have the real sense that I am moving through this multimillion-year history myself, as its primary subject. I can imagine myself into the points of view of people and creatures far from me in their form of life. Once at Charles de Gaulle Airport waiting to fly to San Francisco, I saw a baby attached to his mother's back with sheets of cloth waiting to fly to Accra. A few days later, I sat stoned in California with the distinct impression that I *was* that baby, and with a distinct and hyperreal feeling of the motion and warmth of my mother's body as she moved through her home city. I have had no less vivid impressions of being a dinosaur biting down on the neck of my prey.

But it is not just the vividness of these impressions that (as it were) impresses me. It is also their subtlety and their tendency toward astounding abstraction. Once I got stoned and I pictured a wedding taking place in a garden of a nice house in the summertime, perhaps on Martha's Vineyard or somewhere similar. I pictured a winged insect landing on a flower in the garden, and the petals curling under its weight in such a way as to express the anxiety of the mother of the bride for her daughter's uncertain future. To be clear, I have been to no such wedding. I have no idea who these people were. Yet I had nonetheless an absolutely certain understanding of the expressive power of the insect's landing and of what it signified of the bride's mother's inner life. How is this possible? Is *this* just me being dumb? That's certainly not how it feels in the moment, and I think it is doing a great disservice and deeply uncharitable, to neglect to pay attention to that feeling, even if the vast majority of people who experience it are "struck dumb," in the literal sense that they are rendered unable to put into words the extreme vitality, in that moment, of their inner lives.

The key psychoactive compound in cannabis, THC, is not generally classified as a psychedelic, but in my experience this drug, at high doses, does have the power significantly to transform its user's perception of the nature of reality, and of the nature of the self, and of the relation between these. As with psychedelic mushrooms, with the legalization of cannabis, an ornate new vocabulary has sprung up to describe the different effects of its different strains. And much as with the vocabulary of wine tasting, I strongly suspect this is mostly hot air, language that is useful for promotion and marketing but that remains mostly irrelevant to the actual experience.

In the case of cannabis especially, this failure of language to capture the experience seems practically built into the effort, since the experience is fundamentally not a linguistic one. If I were to try to put it into words nonetheless—lapsing into that bad habit for which the philosophers have long chided the mystics, of chattering about the ineffable—I would note that thirty minutes or so after consuming a good-sized dose of THC, I am struck by how completely *implausible* my everyday beliefs about the world and my place in it now seem. I no longer feel there is any compelling reason to believe that my memories are impressions of real events that are perpetually receding from the "now" in time, or that the people I know and love exist in physical bodies that are at that very moment located at varying degrees of physical distance from me. It is reassuring to observe, also, that I never find myself loving them any less; on the contrary it seems to me that this love is the realest thing there is, in comparison with which everything else is but shadows.

What are memories and what are loved ones if not what we take them to be in everyday experience? Here I really feel language fails me, but if I were to push ahead anyway I would say that, under the influence of cannabis, it sometimes seems to me that memories, and loved ones, and everything that constitutes *my* world is contained within me and always has been. It also seems to me sometimes that this arrangement is something that could easily have popped into existence out of nothing, just moments before, without for that reason being any less real. In fact, although memories and interpersonal relations are, so to speak, collapsed into me, rather than having independent existence, this only seems to make them *more* real, to deepen my love for those people who are recalled to mind, and indeed, sometimes, to make me realize that I deeply love some of the people in my life whom I normally take to be rather minor players in it: the cashier I greet at the supermarket a few times a week, for example, or my seventh-grade teacher whom I have not seen in forty years. "I love you," I sometimes find my lips moving to whisper, as the thought of them passes across my mind.

There are considerable downsides to cannabis (though these are nothing compared to the downsides of alcohol), which make me personally grateful, all things considered, that I spend most of my life in a jurisdiction where it is illegal. In the summer of 2023, which I spent in California, I was frequently high, and I began to experience the oft-reported paranoia associated with heavy cannabis use. There were some evenings when I became absolutely convinced that a serial killer or other violent criminal was about to break into the house and to subject me to horrible tortures.

The more interesting expression of this paranoia latched onto world events as its source of phantasms. I was, and am, worried about major global conflagrations breaking out between superpowers. Sometimes, under the influence, it seemed to me I could envision these superpowers as if personified: something like mighty beings in the clouds preparing to hurl lightning bolts at one another. My thought upon having such impressions, if I were to attempt to put it into language, was something like this: "So there really *are* gods of war! And my heavens, are they ever angry!" Just as in sweeter moments on cannabis I found myself wondering how I ever could have taken for granted the belief that there really was a past, in my paranoid moments I was mystified at the usual belief, which gets me through my days, that there is going to be a future.

Unlike with alcohol, however, there is no hangover—or perhaps it would be better to say that there *is* a hangover, but it is usually a salutary one. Alcohol makes you feel great when you're drunk, and full of regrets the next day. Often, with cannabis, what I found was that it made me feel full of regrets while I was on it, and then, the next day, full of gratefulness that I had this occasion to process so many negative thoughts and emotions in order subsequently to get on with my life. On several occasions I found myself the next day, at the gym or peer-reviewing an article, and having momentary recollections of the visions I had the night before, of gods throwing lightning bolts, and of the utter certainty I had at the time that these were visions of something real. I went about my day productively and, mostly, happily. I don't think I would want to be subjected to those frightening visions repeatedly over the long term. But I am not convinced that they were simply harmful to my psyche, rather than cathartic.

I have by now identified at least a few distinctive features of psychedelic experience, some of which can also occur in the not-technically-psychedelic experience of a cannabis high. These may not be present in every case, and indeed may be nearly opposite what some readers have experienced themselves. What we are looking for here are at best family resemblances between psychedelic experiences and not the necessary properties of *any* psychedelic experience. We have also seen how difficult it can be to capture such experience in language. Nonetheless, it may help now, in this final section of the present chapter, to try to name these properties and to draw them out more rigorously than I have done up until this point.

I have emphasized, for one thing, a heightened sense of connection to others. These others may be other human beings, and they may also be other living beings; they may be individuals we in fact know or have known in our lives, but they may also be celebrities we've never met or historical figures who died long before we were born. There is also the possibility of encounter with another sort of being, namely, beings that seem to be higher than we are in some cosmic hierarchy or from a superior dimension. This is an experience that is particularly associated with DMT, which I have not tried, though I think I have caught glimpses of these beings under the influence of other drugs as well. In any case, I would classify such DMT encounters separately, as they seem qualitatively different, and are also likely neurologically different, from the sort of second-person encounters I've described. For one thing, the encounter with Mama Cass, for example, is one of astounding *familiarity*. She and I are communing, we are on the same wavelength. When the psychedelics advocate Terence McKenna describes his own encounter with the "little green elves" while on DMT, by contrast, these are not in any way his familiars. Although he experiences a certainty that they are actually existing other minds, rather than mere figments, still, their exact nature, origins, and intentions remain opaque and inscrutable to him. These two psychedelic experiences I have identified so far might be labeled *unity with other beings of a familiar sort* and *encounter with other beings of an unfamiliar sort*.

These experiences are often different from, but may overlap with, the experience I have also described in terms of world-disclosure, as for example when we feel in a psychedelic experience that we have full and complete access to the "world" from which music comes, a world we might long for in a sober and lucid state, but from which we ordinarily feel we are mostly cut off. This world might be populated by other beings—one might experience, for example, that Mama Cass "inhabits" the "world of music"—or it might be experienced as something too abstract to consider as a place suitable for inhabitation at all. As I have suggested, we might be able to analyze this "world" in Romantic or Heideggerian terms as a mood, something that is "within us" but not for that reason dismissible as merely subjective. We might also be able to approach this world in more Platonic terms, and to suggest that psychedelics enable us to encounter the ideas themselves—Music itself, Beauty itself—of which the individual beautiful songs we ordinarily hear are only faint shadows. I tend to find the Heideggerian language better suited to the experiences in question than the Platonic alternative, but tastes may vary.

Whichever conceptual tools we pick up, from whichever philosophical tradition, to describe this aspect of the psychedelic experience, it seems suitable to call it *the rediscovery of other worlds*, along with *surprise at and certainty of their apparent reality*. I say "rediscovery" because the feeling, even for a first-time psychedelics user, tends to be one of return to something one has always known, rather than of learning something one never suspected before. Part of the experience of surprise comes from the strangeness of having forgotten for so long, perhaps since one's last psychedelic experience, or perhaps since some indeterminate past time, the past immemorial, as is said poetically, that that other world exists.

It is in the end a cultural value, I have suggested, rather than a straightforward recognition of an obvious truth, that usually has us downplaying the presentations of our internal world as less real, and instead emphasizing external, observable, measurable states of affairs as more real. Things didn't have to be this way. Other cultures have got by just fine relying on a very different balance between these two modes of consciousness. There are plenty of cultures throughout the world, in fact, that take dreams to be most real and that take real-world events to be echoes or derivative effects of what has already been witnessed in the dreamscape.[4] These cultures, contrary to what we might expect, generally get by just fine in the real world too. Their very different commitments as to what is most real do not seem to translate into differing degrees of practical rationality.

Psychedelic drugs, we might sum up, operate in part by *confounding or reversing our ordinary expectation that the external world is more real than the internal one.* In a psychedelic experience, one can see the external world radically transformed, one can know that these transformations are coming from within oneself rather than from without, and one can still, notwithstanding this knowledge, experience the transformations as quite real. This then might be one of the most significant lessons of psychedelic experience: that it forces us to reevaluate our most basic ontological commitments. It does not do this by telling us that little green elves actually exist, that we actually have the power to make a tour of outer space or to rewind the tape of the evolution of life on Earth, or any other such improbable feats. Rather, these things remain in our imaginations just as surely as they always have.

But in a psychedelic experience we are compelled to reconsider our ordinary presumption that to remain there, in the imagination, is somehow to dwell at a lower rung of the hierarchy of reality than the one where we find the objects and events of the external world. The psychedelic experience returns us to an inverted hierarchy of reality, one that is not at all uncommon in the history of humanity, on which our inner presentations carry the force of reality about them, quite apart from any consideration of whether they have some corresponding anchor in the external world with the power to make them true.

Another typical feature of psychedelic experience is *the dissolution of selfhood*. I put it in these terms for the sake of simplicity, but there is much to add that might quickly make us regret our expectation that simplicity is even possible here. One complication is that this part of the experience, obviously, overlaps with that part I have already identified as the feeling of unity with other beings. Part of what it means to be one or unified with someone else is that the clear boundaries that separate you from them dissolve. But sometimes the boundaries of the self dissolve while on psychedelics without any accompanying experience of unity with others. And sometimes they dissolve even though we still find ourselves thinking, using our full powers as thinking subjects, even after the dissolution, even if the nature of the being doing the thinking no longer appears to us at all the same.

Psychedelic experience is volatile, and the perceptions it delivers can have a funny way of flipping over quite suddenly into their opposite, where in an instant, from perceiving ourselves as almost supernatural beings, as lords of the universe with a vastly deeper cosmic pedigree than we ordinarily acknowledge, we can instantly come to seem to ourselves as nothing at all. I have gone from feeling I am an instance of a vastly higher consciousness than what is ordinarily known by human beings to feeling I am literally nonexistent, in what must be no more than a few seconds. Both of these feelings can be euphoric, while the feeling of one's own nonexistence can also, unsurprisingly, be extremely negative.

The feeling of a higher (or deeper) consciousness that is attained with what I have called "the dissolution of the self" may also be accompanied by an experience of *the unreality of time*. One may come to experience one's own being, to the extent that it is no longer anchored in the being of that individual mortal human you had previously mistakenly believed yourself to be, as something altogether independent of temporal duration. When the self is dissolved into what is experienced as a "God's eye" point of view, time, by the same motion, can come to appear illusory. This means that during the psychedelic experience one may doubt that one's own existence is shaped or tempered by a temporal flow from beginning to end, or that one's childhood constitutes a distant "before," followed by a less distant adolescence, early adulthood, and so on, leading up to the "now," which unlike the "then" is supposed to have some greater degree of reality to it. All such thinking can come to appear ridiculous. Under the influence of psychedelics, it can come to seem that one has simply always existed, and will always exist; or, alternatively, that one has never existed, and never will.

Psychedelic experience, finally, can significantly *temper our ordinary belief in the misfortune of death*. If there is in fact no "before" or "after" of our existence, if our existence is eternal, then there is simply no conceivable sense in which our lives can be said to be spent in a motion from a more desirable state, "living," to a less desirable one, "being dead" (and thus, on the widely accepted view today, nonexistent). This perception, indeed, is one that can often endure, at least to some extent, after the psychedelic effect has, in the narrow chemical sense, worn off.

It is in this connection that psychedelic treatments seem particularly promising for patients with terminal conditions. What better way to face death than in the placid conviction that death, properly understood, is not a misfortune? Philosophy has for millennia taught as much, and yet this is a lesson that can be quite hard, for all but the most committed Stoics and Spinozists ("The wise man thinks least of all of death," said Spinoza), to accept simply by learning it through the use of the intellect. Psychedelics seem to provide something like an experiential demonstration of the truth of the intellectual argument. Perhaps in that respect they are only a crutch, a supplement for the weak-minded. There are likely many of us, however, who would be prepared to be called worse names than that, in exchange for an inner peace that arguments alone cannot deliver.

Other minds, external reality, the self, time, death: these are perhaps the most enduring and challenging concepts that have fueled the debates of philosophers over the past few thousand years. And *all* of them seem to be cast in a very different light under the influence of psychedelics. To speak in such analogies as "light," or the cognate "enlightenment," is of course to invite objections from some philosophers, who tend to suppose that an analogy is no good unless it can be cashed in at the end of the day. An analogy is only a promissory note, some suppose. In the following chapters we will turn our attention to analogy, and to the question of what use it might have for the philosophical study of psychedelic experience. I will argue from various angles that psychedelic drugs do not so much show us the truth about the nature of reality as rather expose to us the inadequacies of our ordinary presumptions about what is true and what is real. I will ultimately argue that psychedelic experience can often function as an *analogy of enlightenment*, that is, that it has something of the character of revelation, where a person seems suddenly to grasp deep truths about the nature of reality that had previously escaped them. But it is in the end a mistake, I will also argue, to take any such analogy for the real thing.

CHAPTER TWO

ARTICULATE GUINEA PIGS

When Aldous Huxley submitted to his editor, Harold Raymond, the manuscript of his 1954 book *The Doors of Perception*, recounting his own psychedelic experiences on mescaline, Raymond reportedly told him: "You are the most articulate guinea pig that any scientist could hope to engage."[1] Here the editor inadvertently highlights something crucial about the twentieth century's broad consensus on the proper pathways toward knowledge: throughout that era, "articulate guinea pig" was essentially a contradiction in terms. The guinea pig is in its nature mute, while it is those who observe the guinea pig from the outside who are charged with the entire task of explaining what is happening to it.

Huxley's book did much to fuel the extensive cultural freakout in the arts and music of the following decade. Its title, drawn from a line of William Blake's 1790 poem *The Marriage of Heaven and Hell*, would in shortened form become the name of a certain well-known rock band led by Jim Morrison. The book's impact was, more precisely, *counter*cultural. It was not received as a legitimate contribution to the advancement of our culture's body of shared knowledge, arrived at by the ordinary means of scientific inquiry. It is not that Huxley's observations were seen to be specifically inaccurate, but only that the approach was from the outset methodologically unsound. For one thing, a norm had emerged by the 1950s according to which scientists do not experiment on themselves, and least of all when the experiment in question involves intentional distortion of one's own consciousness. To willingly subject oneself to such distortion is to leave eloquence behind altogether. Or so it was thought.

It is not hard to identify at least a few reasons why science excludes evidence gained from auto-experimentation. One is that researchers who do research on themselves are by definition doing research on only *one* person, and that does not provide them, to say the least, with a very large data set. But the more important reason for the broad prohibition is that a first-person point of view has generally been held, at least since the early twentieth century, to get in the way of accuracy in observation. Far from permitting insights that might be absent when we are observing a test subject from outside, science has supposed that *any* insight worth having is one that can be accessed from the outside, from a third-person point of view, or as the philosopher Thomas Nagel put it, one that at least aspires to a "view from nowhere." The first-person perspective is one that occurs behind a dim veil, and the central goal of science for the past several centuries has been to find clever new ways to lift this veil. First-person reports of subjective experiences would seem to threaten to pull it right back down.

Thus the history of the prohibition on first-person reports extends back to the scientific revolution of the seventeenth century, which entrenched the idea that science concerns itself only or primarily with what is measurable or quantifiable, while internal states such as feelings or perceptions are difficult to treat in quantitative terms (though of course even here attempts are made, as for example when patients are asked to assign a numerical value to their pain on a "pain scale"). A narrower reason for the exclusion of the first-person perspective arose only in the twentieth century, when behaviorism came to dominate research agendas in the behavioral and human sciences, and above all in psychology. According to B. F. Skinner, the principal founder and promoter of behaviorism, human action should be studied no differently than the motion of particles or the rusting of iron. That is, psychology has no need to attend to the internal subjective states of the objects of its study. In the most extreme formulation of this view, which was quite common in the twentieth century, it is not just that science can derive no benefit from paying attention to internal subjective states, but, much more strongly, that science must positively *deny* that there are such states, or at least that these states would make it onto the final list of entities found in nature.

The problem, of course, is that we all know full well that there *is* something going on inside of us, even if it is hard, or perhaps impossible, to understand what exactly that is or to put it on display so that others might see it as fully as we see it ourselves. A dissenting minority over the course of the twentieth century indeed continued to insist that the human quest for knowledge must make room for accounts of those internal qualitative states that can only be seen from a first-person perspective. Edmund Husserl, for example, founded the movement known as phenomenology precisely on the idea that scientific inquiry, far from excluding first-person experience of "phenomena," or, if you will, of "seemings," must instead take those phenomena as the starting point of any larger attempt to arrive at an understanding of the nature of external reality.

But the first-person perspective remained mostly marginal in twentieth-century science, and even if few are any longer committed to its exclusion as a matter of principle, a certain lag time continues, even in our own century, and experimental approaches that include first-person observations are stigmatized for an appearance of unscientific unseriousness. By contrast, if we return to the era just before the rise of behaviorism, we find rampant autoexperimentation across many domains of scientific inquiry. These include approaches in what might be called "citizen science," as when Benjamin Franklin intentionally administered electrical shocks to himself in the hope of better understanding the nature of electricity. Such approaches were more common still in the fields of medicine and pharmacology around the turn of the twentieth century, including research on psychoactive drugs. For example, in an illuminating recent book, Mike Jay has shown the importance for the broader theoretical aims of the experiments of William James and Sigmund Freud, with nitrous oxide and cocaine, respectively.[2] Jay notes that while from our point of view these men appear almost naïve and prescientific, and certainly irresponsible, in their drug taking, they themselves understood what they were doing as part of a methodologically rigorous program of inquiry. They only seem prescientific to us as a result of a late-arriving prohibition on this sort of inquiry. And it is not that researchers have not wished they could follow in the path of a figure such as James. As Daniel M. Perrine wrote in 2000 of his own experience of theophany on various entheogens, "I wish I could say this with the same aplomb with which William James discusses his use of nitrous oxide and ether. But unfortunately, the present legal and emotional climate is not as open-minded as it was in his day."[3]

If science has mostly been unable to absorb insights derived from the intentional alteration of the inquirer's consciousness, what about my own discipline, philosophy? Analytic philosophy since the early twentieth century, which is the dominant tradition in the English-speaking world and also the tradition in which I was trained, has long sought to toe an unusual line. On the one hand, it has generally been keen to affirm, as a gold standard, the norms and methods of inquiry characteristic of the natural sciences: direct, yet external, observation of controlled and repeatable experiments. At the same time, analytic philosophy has often allowed itself a wild card in its frequent appeals to the faculty of *intuition*. While analytic philosophers address a highly eclectic and heterogeneous range of problems, one defining feature that unites them is their characteristic reliance on intuition as a source of evidence.[4]

In the special sense in which philosophers tend to understand them, intuitions possess a few distinctive features. First is the fact that they involve a type of immediate knowledge rather than knowledge that is arrived at through argument, which is to say through the deduction of a conclusion from premises, or through observation of evidence, which is the standard method of discovery in natural science. They are moreover associated, in the philosopher Berit Brogaard's words, with "a special phenomenology, consisting in a feeling of attraction to certain propositions ... an urge (or inclination) to believe."[5] Finally, again following Brogaard, intuitions typically do not stop seeming true to us when we are shown evidence that they are false. Disconfirmation of intuitions is not a simple matter, unlike, say, correcting one's false belief about some empirical fact or other.

Those working in the phenomenological tradition, such as its founder, Edmund Husserl, understand intuition as a sort of "immediate seeing." We do not need to dwell on the rather intricate account Husserl develops of this notion. It will suffice to say that philosophers of all stripes have typically appealed to a special mental faculty beyond the perception, inference, and understanding recognized by practicing natural scientists, namely, intuition as a sort of immediate grasp of some matter or some concept, which *can* occur in an experimental setting but can also occur while sitting in one's proverbial armchair, alone with nothing but one's thoughts.

Considerable criticism has been leveled against this reliance on intuition in recent years. Indeed, an offshoot of analytic philosophy emerged in the early 2000s, calling itself "experimental philosophy" and often representing itself with the image of an armchair in flames. For most of its history, however, analytic philosophy has willingly and openly granted that spontaneous insights are indeed admissible as evidence in the pursuit of truth in a way that sets philosophy somewhat apart from the method of natural science. But the prohibition on chemical auto-experimentation has remained unbending throughout: at least some intuitions, or "seeings in," might be permissible, but *not* if they occur to a thinking subject under the influence of mind-altering substances.

What is the reason for this? Allowing intuitions to guide our pursuit of knowledge is *already* unscientific, or so many critics have complained. Prohibiting the use of intuitions arrived at in an altered state of consciousness can't simply be explained by philosophy's concern to remain a faithful defender of the scientific method, since if philosophers were truly faithful to that method, they would eschew intuition altogether. The prohibition on auto-experimentation seems instead to operate at the level of values, not methodological utility. It is simply not part of the value system of philosophers to allow their intuitions to be influenced by an intentional alteration of one's conscious perceptions. Perhaps it is time for a reevaluation of this value.

Even now, in philosophy, the prohibition that we long shared with psychiatry and experimental psychology on first-person phenomenological observations, continues to reign in certain domains. Today this probably has more to do with inertia than with active enforcement, but the fact remains that first-person accounts of what it's like to be in an extreme or unusual state of consciousness are hard to come by. Thus the Oxford philosopher Paul Lodge, writing eloquently of his own experience of mania, notes that among psychiatrists "behavioural criteria are often emphasised to the neglect of phenomenological ones; more subtly, behavioural criteria have sometimes been confusedly categorised as phenomenological." This confusion, Lodge maintains, has "hindered the development of an adequate phenomenological account of mania."[6] And much the same may be said of psychedelic experience.

Already in the previous chapter, I set out on a path that might be described somewhat cumbersomely as auto-experimental analytic phenomenology. The historical resonances of the last two of these terms are unavoidable, in light of what we have already seen, but should not be taken as fully determined by what they have meant in the past. Again, analytic philosophy, though there are many tendencies within it, is the tradition that has dominated in most of the Anglophone world since the early twentieth century. In general, its approach, as the name suggests, is to analyze propositions down to their elementary components, to isolate these components, to see how they hold up on their own and to better understand what role they play in complex relations with the other components of a proposition, whether concepts, modal operators, logical connectives, or the like. Analytic philosophy has typically, though not always, remained focused on language, and on linguistic meanings, over other sorts of mental activity and other possible sources of meaning (and many analytic philosophers would simply deny that talk of "non-linguistic meaning" makes any sense).

Phenomenology, in turn, can be many different things, and is indeed a term sometimes used by analytic philosophers and by psychologists to describe something like inner qualitative experience (as in the quotation from Lodge above). But in its narrowest sense the term describes a school of thought that emerged in Germany in the late nineteenth century, and that, as already mentioned, is most closely associated with its founder, Edmund Husserl.

Perhaps somewhat like his contemporary Sigmund Freud, Husserl is noteworthy for promoting a program of research that appears at first glance to be diametrically opposed to the methods of natural science, even as he continues throughout his career to proclaim enduring loyalty to science, and believes that in the end his own work is deepening, and not challenging, our scientific image of reality. Husserl goes further than Freud, however: he thinks that attention to our subjectively lived experience not only *can* be incorporated into science, but indeed *must* be the starting point and bedrock of all natural-scientific inquiry.

For Husserl, close attention to the way the world appears to us is the best hope we have of arriving at knowledge of the world itself. Thus the starting point of phenomenological inquiry is the so-called epochē, or bracketing, where we suspend all assumptions and background knowledge about the nature of the objects presented to our senses. In bracketing, we are to some extent able, Husserl hopes, to strip away all the accrued meanings that ordinarily attach to the objects of our perception, and simply to perceive them, at least to some extent, as they are. This also helps us to move beyond the ordinary distinction we are otherwise inclined to make, in conscious perception, between, say, a dreamed or hallucinated horse on the one hand and a real horse on the other. In the exercise of bracketing, the hallucinated horse is no less apparent to the perceiving subject than the one that also has its own separate biological existence. Both horses, the real and the unreal one, are equally "given."

The general idea of bracketing, if not the name, is not new with Husserlian phenomenology but extends back at least as far as René Descartes in the seventeenth century.

It also has significant resonances with some of the reflections we find in the tendency in twentieth-century analytic philosophy known as "sense-data empiricism." As A. J. Ayer summarizes the common position, circa 1940, of analytic philosophers on this subject, the prevailing view was that what we directly perceive are never material objects, such as cigarettes or pens, but rather "sense-data." These latter, Ayer explains, are not themselves material things but "have the 'presentative function' of making us conscious of material things."[7] Yet not all sense-data "present" material objects in this way, and this is both a sign of the robustness of sense-data, that they can occur without material objects causing them, as well as an indication of the challenges they pose, for the same reason: that they do not necessarily deliver reliable reports on the existence or nonexistence of external objects.

In both phenomenology and in sense-data empiricism, it is sometimes noted that the subjective impressions we have, even the hallucinations, are in some sense the least *reliable* source of knowledge there is, while in another sense such impressions are also the most *certain*. If I close my eyes and rub them, and I report to you that I am seeing flashing green splotches, you cannot sensibly reply to me that there are no green splotches there and that I am therefore wrong. The report I give you is, so to speak, the end of the story. I tell you I'm seeing them, and unless I am simply lying, this report has the force of a necessary truth: if I'm seeing them, then I'm seeing them. This is different from a reported sighting of, say, a ship on the horizon, where everything depends on whether the ship you think you see is actually there or not. If I report to you that I'm seeing a ship (and, say, you are my commanding officer who unlike me is not holding a pair of binoculars), then that is not the end of the story but only the beginning. Next we will have to verify whether what I reported is true or not. But in the case of the green splotch, there is no possible pathway for such verification, and the only criterion for establishment of the truth of the perception is the perception itself.

The term "sense-data" dates back only to the beginning of the twentieth century, though at least one of the problems it was introduced to help resolve is much older. That problem is, namely, how we could possibly justify the belief that we are perceiving external objects when we report that, for example, there is a table or a vase full of flowers in our visual field. In the language of the philosophy of mind, the problem is one of knowing that our perceptions are veridical, that is, that they are causally connected to the external physical objects of which they are perceptions. As David Hume explains in his *Enquiry Concerning Human Understanding* of 1748, "nothing can ever be present to the mind but an image or perception," and it is only via the inlets of the senses that such images could ever be conveyed. In light of this, Hume thinks, we must admit that strictly speaking we do not directly perceive external objects. He illustrates the point using the example of a table: "The table, which we see, seems to diminish, as we move farther from it: But the real table, which exists independent of us, suffers no alteration: it was, therefore, nothing but its image, which was present to the mind."[8]

There is a certain ambiguity here, already beginning from the first subordinate clause: "The table, *which we see*. . . ." If the point is that we do not see external objects, this seems a strange way to start. But the same grammatical structure is echoed in the subsequent clause alluding to "the real table, which exists independent of us," which leads us to the conclusion that for Hume "the table, which we see" and "the real table" are, in effect, two different tables. It would perhaps have been better to refer to "the impression of the table" and "the table," but Hume's point is clear enough: whatever it is we are seeing shrinks as we move away from it; but tables do not typically shrink; therefore, we are not seeing the table. You can also press down on one eyeball and begin to perceive two tables. Or you can walk around the table in a circle and experience infinitely many different perspectives on the table, each of which is in some sense its own thing, a "continuum of visual tables," as Bertrand Russell would put it in 1922.[9]

It would be tempting, following Hume, to conclude that if the visual table shrinks, while the external physical table does not shrink, the visual table must therefore be a "hallucination." Is this correct? If it is not correct, or if it is too strong, then we must go on to ask why it is that, say, the perception of a breathing table or a glowing table, such as we might perceive under the influence of LSD, *is* a hallucination, while the shrinking table is not. In reality, after all, the table is neither breathing nor shrinking, yet the appearance of its shrinking is ordinarily factored into our overall image of reality, or perhaps, better, it is easily "corrected for" as we move through the perception-mediated world. The breathing table by contrast generally seems to signal a rupture with that world. In this latter case perception seems no longer to mediate and facilitate our navigation of the world, but rather temporarily to complicate it or even to block it altogether.

Some of my own earliest memories are of inducing double vision by pressing on my eyes or by blinking. I was not so much, I see now, trying to confuse or deceive myself as I was trying to learn the basic parameters of vision. But still, the fact that I knew how to press down on my eyes in order to make one table into two, without thereby becoming convinced that an external object has actually multiplied itself, while I am not nearly as adept at accommodating the breathing of a table when I am under the influence of LSD, *might* be taken as a reason to be more interested, as a philosopher, in the effects of LSD on my perceptions, rather than less. What is it about this particular kind of induced distortion, rather than the other one, that makes it seem like a break with ordinary reality rather than yet another opportunity more fully to feel out the parameters of reality?

I have said already that my method is one of analytic phenomenology. Part of what I mean by this is that I am indebted to both the analytic and the phenomenological traditions. But beyond that I mean simply that I am interested in taking what is given to my senses and analyzing it down to its elementary components in order to gain some better understanding of the nature and quality of my experience. I am mostly interested in what is given to my senses under the influence of psychedelic substances, and in this respect my method also involves, centrally, autoexperimentation: that is, taking drugs and then analyzing, under these circumstances, what I experience. It is curious that we think of such inquiry into the phenomenology of psychedelic states as experimental, while it would be at least a stretch to say that what Husserl is doing when he performs a bracketing and pays attention to what is then given to his consciousness ought likewise to count as an experiment. An experiment seems to involve, at a minimum, deliberate alteration of initial conditions, and in this respect taking a psychedelic substance and then observing its effects brings us into the realm of the experimental, while simply concentrating on the contents of our ordinary lucid perceptions does not.

But what if Husserl, prior to beginning an exercise of bracketing, were, say, to dim the lights or to surround himself with candles or have a glass of wine? Would this move him out of the role of the phenomenologist in a pure sense and into the role of the auto-experimenter? On a few occasions later in this book, we will return to the history and theory of auto-experimentation, particularly with an eye to understanding why it has generally been frowned upon both in natural-scientific and in philosophical inquiry. For now it is enough to articulate the notion and to claim it: in preparation for this book I have followed a method of *auto-experimental analytic phenomenology*, which consists in taking psychedelic substances, observing how the world appears under their influence, and analyzing these appearances down to their most basic elements.

There are in fact several distinct conclusions to which this method has brought me, some of which are specific to my own admittedly peculiar experiences with psychedelic drugs, and some of which will likely be of general philosophical interest, even to readers who have no particular curiosity about psychedelics but are simply interested in the problems of experience, consciousness, identity, and knowledge of the external world. As both a philosopher and a historian of science, I focus in certain parts of this book on cultural and intellectual history rather than on systematic philosophy as commonly understood. For example, I am interested in accounting for the relationship between the rise of the global trade in plants as commodities on the one hand and the rise of sobriety as an absolute imperative in the history of modern philosophy on the other.

Apart from the first-person insights and the cultural-historical arguments, as I have proceeded through the method of auto-experimental analytic phenomenology, four distinct *philosophical* arguments have gradually emerged that I do not think I ever would have thought to defend if I had contented myself simply with reading about psychedelics as a curious external observer.

A first argument concerns the complex relationship between truth, reality, and perception. The idea here might best be conveyed by the title of a 1993 book by Terence McKenna: *True Hallucinations*. How could *hallucinations* be *true*? Is that not a straightforward oxymoron? Opinions differ. In the vocabulary of some philosophers, the proper term to describe a perception's causal groundedness in the external world is not "true" or "real" but, rather, "veridical." For a perception to be veridical, there must be an external physical object causing it. When I suppose I am seeing a table, if the table is not really there then it will turn out my perception was not veridical, and most of the time we would also be inclined to say both that the table was not real and that my belief that I was seeing that unreal table was therefore not true. Truth or falsehood thus attaches to beliefs, while reality or unreality attaches to things, and veridicality or non-veridicality attaches to the causes of perceptions, where, again, a veridical perception is caused by an external object, and a non-veridical one, what we ordinarily call a hallucination, is caused by the mind or brain of the perceiver.

But might it be that not all true perceptions, or, if you prefer, that not all perceptions of reality, are veridical in the sense just described? Could there be *true hallucinations*? McKenna is not, to say the least, a rigorous thinker, yet surprisingly, as we will see in detail further on, there have been at least some philosophers who have come around to the view suggested by his title. In fact, at least one of these philosophers, J. R. Smythies, undertook to defend the possibility of true yet non-veridical perceptions as a result of his own study of the uses and effects of psychedelic drugs in the 1950s.[10] In Smythies's view, a hallucinated perception can be experienced as real, just as a veridical perception can be. A veridical perception, in turn, can likewise be experienced as unreal. Reality is thus, on this analysis, something more like a *quality of the perception itself*. I am inclined to agree with this view, while I am also interested in going beyond the arguments of McKenna, Smythies, and others in order to draw more lessons from it for our understanding of truth and reality in general.

A second argument is that psychedelic experience often has the power to invert our ordinary hierarchy of reality not by causing us to believe that the hallucinations we experience have some real external cause but by causing us to see imagination itself as fundamentally real, quite apart from the question whether there are outside objects or states of affairs corresponding to the contents of our imagination. In our own culture, we are skilled at setting aside the productions of our imaginations in order to get back to reality and down to business, when, say, we are stirred from a daydream and return to working on our tax returns. When we do so we take ourselves to be moving from something that is unreal to something that is real: the internal "show" that is running inside each of us much of the time has no anchor in reality, while our tax obligations most assuredly do. But in the end this default ordering of the reality of different domains of experience may be more an expression of a particular cultural value than a recognition of the single true way of going about things.

Many human cultures take dreams and visions as the most real thing of all in human existence and as a guide to navigating our way through the lesser and relatively more illusory world of natural forces and social obligations. These cultures put considerably more stock in the truth-revealing power of their inner representations. Many of them take for granted that the world experienced in dreams is the real world, while empirical reality is in some way a derivative or a reflection of that world. And such cultures tend to do just fine, practically speaking. They generally have what it takes to do the right thing in the right circumstances and to survive from one generation to the next as successfully as cultures that believe, by contrast, that idle imagining is a waste of time, that dreaming is a delirious whirr of confusion, and only the external world and the demands it places on us are real.

We might say one of the most powerful effects of psychedelic drugs is to invert the value hierarchy I have identified in the culture of English-speaking, book-reading, early-twenty-first-century people, and to cause us, at least for the duration of the psychedelic experience, to see our mental representations as the most real thing there is, even if our commitment to this reality does not, for reasons we have already considered, translate into a commitment to veridicality. Psychedelic experience, in short, has the power profoundly to disrupt our most basic ontological commitments by making us powerless to resist the inversion of a hierarchy to which we, or at least our surrounding culture, is ordinarily committed.

A third argument holds that it would be a mistake to suppose that what causes this inversion in many psychedelic experiences is the intensity of the associated hallucinations or the vividness of the mental representations that bombard us. On the contrary, and very much against our widespread clichés about psychedelic drugs, the most significant feature of a psychedelic experience is often that it is not characterized by hallucinations at all but by the *suspension of hallucinations*.

This is of course counterintuitive, since the most familiar account of what occurs during a psychedelic experience is that it throws all sorts of surprising sights and sounds our way. I contend, however, that this familiar account is impoverished, and that this impoverishment is a symptom of the experience's social marginalization: we habitually mischaracterize things that are prohibited or risky to talk about. Where taboo diminishes the incentive to speak rigorously and accurately about an experience, we unsurprisingly find that the experience as represented in mainstream culture is represented in a reductive, simplistic, and broad-brushed way.

When we do aim for rigor and accuracy, we are pushed toward an account of the psychedelic experience in which one awakens to the fact that we spend the better part of our lives hallucinating things that are not really there at all, or that are very different from what we now, under the influence of psychedelics, perceive them to be: social institutions, relationships, our own bodies, perhaps even the flow of time and the external world itself can appear now as a mere product of our ordinary waking perception, while our *extra*ordinary perception under the influence of psychedelics has the power to do away with all these things, and to convince us that once we have done away with them we are finally perceiving the world as it is.

If we agree that everyday experience involves a great deal of "as if," that for example we may be entertaining a fiction of ourselves as irreducible metaphysical subjects, that is to say, our belief that we truly exist as real individuals distinct from other people and from the external world, when in fact we are elaborate arrangements of neurons, then what might easily strike us about psychedelic drugs is not that they induce hallucinations—for we are subject to those all the time—but that they cast everything we are perceiving, whether this involves florid visions of otherworldly beings or softly breathing walls or only a particularly beautiful sunset, in a different light. This light is what I have been calling, following Martin Heidegger, "mood." Psychedelic drugs reveal the world in a different mood, and the experience of this mood shift is often one that appears to us to be disclosing some deep truth about the world and our place in it. It is deeply inadequate to characterize such a mood shift as hallucination.

Up until now our language for talking about psychedelic experience has been so incomplete, again likely in large part because of its stigmatization, as to cause most people to suppose that whatever is interesting about it is interesting only in the same way that, say, a laser light show is interesting: a vivid and spectacular presentation of visual patterns and images. But this, again, is perhaps the *least* interesting thing about psychedelic drugs. What is far more interesting, in my experience, is their power to bring about a mood that at least in principle has the character of truth disclosure. That there is such a power in certain chemical compounds found in nature is plainly an interesting fact about human life, no less than the character and the neuroscientific causes of our ordinary waking consciousness.

Fourth and finally, psychedelic experience, I argue, offers what I will call an "analogy of enlightenment." Psychedelics do not reveal the world to you as it really is, nor do they mislead you about how the world really is. They are nonetheless potentially useful to anyone who is keen on pushing past the limits of ordinary perception and arriving at some profound insights about the nature of our existence, the reality of the external world, the limits of natural science, and so on.

If you are the sort of person who thinks the desire for such insight is foolish or immature, then my argument that psychedelic drugs can help you attain it will most likely, even if successful, still not convince you that psychedelics are something worth experiencing. Contemporary philosophy has often been quite dismissive of the idea that personal growth, especially by means that circumvent arguments and reason and that work through feeling, image, or metaphor, might be within its purview. In a memorable passage in his autobiography, the great analytic philosopher W. V. O. Quine wrote: "I am deeply moved by occasional passages of poetry, and so, characteristically, I read little of it."[11] If part of the professional character profile of philosophers as it took shape over the twentieth century compelled us even to avoid poetry for fear of being "deeply moved," then all the more, it is not hard to see why those of a broadly Quinean stamp would not wish to have their minds absolutely blown, at least not in their capacity as philosophers, by psychedelic drugs.

And yet there are indeed other precedents in the history of philosophy for treading down paths we know to be bestrewn with sentimentality, with confusion, and with a general weakening of our argumentative acumen. In the late eighteenth century Immanuel Kant noticed that there are certain domains of human inquiry that seem hopelessly mired in confusion, in ungrounded conjecture and speculation, notably those concerning knowledge of transcendental truth about God, for example, or about the ultimate ends or purposes of natural processes. In effect, Kant maintained that human beings are simply constrained, whether we like it or not, to wish to have knowledge in these domains, and it is no less irresponsible on the part of philosophers to say that they want nothing to do with such knowledge, as the skeptics do, than it is for them hastily and prematurely to claim that they have solved all the problems in these domains, as the dogmatists do, or that the problems encountered in these domains are unimportant or even nonsensical, as the logical positivists will do soon enough.

It may just be, in sum, that there are things we want to know but that lie beyond our ability to know, or at least to know adequately in the way that we would like. In the early twentieth century "metaphysics" became a bad word for many philosophers, who took a very un-Kantian view and simply insisted that a domain so often mired in sloppy speculation and vague metaphor is one that is unworthy of the attention of rigorous philosophers. Did metaphysics go away, then? Of course not. It mostly just migrated into the New Age sections of bookstores and became focused on esoteric topics like crystal healing and UFO sightings, rather than on the continuous tradition that descends from Aristotle's treatise known as the *Metaphysics*. This is the common result of efforts to suppress entire dimensions of human experience and human curiosity: they are never really suppressed but only pushed out to the margins and left to the undisciplined and unhinged.

I would rather be more Kantian than Quinean in what follows, more eighteenth century than twentieth century. That is, I would rather acknowledge that psychedelic drugs have perhaps led a good number of people even deeper into confusion about the nature of reality than they were before they tried them, that to try them is a particularly risky endeavor, but that, nonetheless, whatever that thing is that people are after when they try them remains something that is, like it or not, very important to philosophy, and eminently worthy of the attention of philosophers, as indeed of any curious reader.

CHAPTER THREE

PSYCHEDELIC MEDITATIONS

In the second of his six *Meditations on First Philosophy*, first published in Latin in 1641, René Descartes examines his reasons for believing that the external world as it presents itself to his senses really exists and that his mind is capable of knowing it. He invokes the famous example of the piece of wax that his eyes happen upon as he is sitting in front of his fireplace. When he first begins to examine it, the wax is solid and likewise has various other properties accessible to each of the five senses. But then he holds it close to the fire, causing it partially to melt, and also to change in color, texture, and even taste and smell, and in the sound that it makes when palpitated.

Descartes's initial reason for going through this exercise is to come to understand how we know, or why we believe we know, that it is one and the same piece of wax that endures over time, even when all its perceptible properties have changed. In the course of giving his account of our knowledge of the wax, Descartes also notices what this exercise reveals about the mind itself that is doing the knowing: if we "seem to possess so distinct an apprehension of the piece of wax" even through its successive changes, he writes, then "do I not know myself, both with greater truth and certitude, and also much more distinctly and clearly?" He continues:

> For if I judge that the wax exists because I see it, it assuredly follows, much more evidently, that I myself exist, for the same reason: for it is possible that what I see may not in truth be wax, and that I do not even possess eyes with which to see anything; but it cannot be that when I see, or, which comes to the same thing, when I think I see, I myself who think am nothing.[1]

This passage conveys the key insight of Descartes's famous "Cogito" argument, which seeks to prove that he, or indeed any one of us, might well be systematically mistaken in every particular belief that we have, about the existence of the external world, the existence of our bodies, the existence of God, and so on. But there is still simply no way we could ever be mistaken about the fact that we are actually existing *thinking beings*, insofar as we are thinking. That is, "I am a thinking being" follows logically and necessarily from "I think." In this way, from an initial modest observation of the possibility of knowledge about changeable things in the external world, such as a ball of wax, Descartes arrives at certainty of his own existence as an essentially mental or cogitating entity.

But what if, rather than subjecting the wax to a sequence of transformations, Descartes had instead subjected his own power of thinking to some similar sequence? What if, rather than melting the wax, our rationalist philosopher had instead, as we colloquially say, set about *melting his mind*? He might have done this, if we permit ourselves a bit of anachronism, by dropping a hit of acid, though on a more historically scrupulous account, it probably would have been fly agaric or perhaps peyote or ayahuasca brought back across the Atlantic alongside potatoes, tobacco, or enslaved human beings.

Shall we run with this counterfactual scenario a bit further, reimagining some of the paragraphs of Descartes's Second Meditation as a record of the philosopher's own experimentation with psychedelic drugs? Let's call the result *Psychedelic Meditations*. They might in part look something like this:

> Let us now consider the objects that are commonly thought to be the most easily and most distinctly known, namely, the bodies we touch and see. Take, for example, this piece of wax. It is quite fresh, having only recently been taken from the beehive; it has not yet lost the sweetness of the honey it contained; it still retains something of the smell of the flowers from which it was gathered; its color, figure, size, are apparent to the sight; it is hard, cold, easily handled; and sounds when struck upon with the finger. In short, all that contributes to making a body as distinctly known as possible is found in the object before us.
>
> But, rather than speaking, let me swallow a dose of this unusual potion I have in my possession, and wait a while. When I return to the wax after it has taken effect, I find that the wax's taste now shares in the

essence or quality of Pierrot, a boy I knew long ago at the college at La Flèche; the smell of it now seems to come from the depths of the earth; the color of it shifts constantly like the iridescent scales of a fish; its figure constantly shifts too, somehow calling to mind the history of all life, before ultimately landing on a shape that suggests some unbelievably fecund stone figurine of a pregnant woman. She grows larger, and although I am holding her in my hand she seems to take on the same dimensions as the physical universe itself; then she seems to melt in my hands, to grow hot, to give off an aura of danger; she seems to be crying for all that has been lost and will never return. And now I ask myself: does the *same* wax still remain after all these changes? It must be admitted that it does remain; no one doubts it, or judges otherwise. What then was it that I knew with so much distinctness in the piece of wax before I swallowed the potion? Assuredly, it could be nothing that I observed by means of the senses, since all the things that fell under taste, smell, sight, touch, and hearing are changed, yet the same wax remains, even though now it is revealing hidden truths about itself that it ordinarily keeps concealed from my mind when unaffected by the potion.

Let the wax be attentively considered, and, retrenching all that does not belong to it, let us see what remains. There yet remains something infinitely significant and unbelievably beautiful. But what is meant by significant and beautiful? Is it not that I imagine that the piece of wax, being round, is capable of becoming infinitesimally small, or billowing like a cloud in the sky, or expressing some subtle metaphor? Perhaps, for I see that it admits of an infinity of similar changes, and under the influence of the potion I find I am able to compass this infinity by means of the imagination; consequently, this conception which I have of the wax seems to me now the product of the faculty of imagination, while it also seems to me, which I could not have conceived previously, that it is by this same enhanced faculty of the imagination that I am best able to apprehend the nature of external things. But what now is the nature of this piece of wax, that it can be better apprehended, and its latent potencies better drawn out, by a mind enhanced by a potion that seemed also, prior to swallowing the potion, external to it? It is certainly the same nature as resided in the wax when I saw, touched, and imagined it before. But the perception of its nature, I see now, is neither an act of sight nor of touch, but is rather a capacity of intuition that is awakened by the potion, and that is facilitated rather than hindered by the imagination. I perceived the wax imperfectly and confusedly before, while now I perceive it extremely vividly, and somehow as if I and it were the same thing.

So far, in the corresponding paragraphs of the actual *Meditations*, Descartes has established that it can be nothing but his own mind that ensures a capacity for enduring awareness of the existence of the same piece of wax even through its several transformations. In the psychedelic redux of the same passages, he likewise credits his own mind with the power to track the identity of the wax over time, but now, enhanced by the potion, the mind brings not just this tracking power but a great deal more besides. In the next paragraph of the actual *Meditations*, he also turns to the question of the existence of other human minds. How, now, do those come across under the influence of the potion?

> I should forthwith be disposed to conclude that the wax is known by enhanced sight, and only partially by the intuition of the unenhanced mind alone, as is likewise shown in the analogous instance of human beings passing in the street below, as observed from the window. In this case I do not fail to say that I see their singular souls themselves, their infinite luminous depths, just as I say that I see the true wax; for I am certain, under the influence of the potion, that what I see from the window are not simply hats and cloaks that might cover artificial machines whose motions are determined by springs. But I judge from these appearances that there are real human beings there, which is to say infinite reservoirs of light and wisdom that have descended to us from a voyage they began as long ago as the Creation itself, or perhaps even before that.

And next Descartes turns from the question of his knowledge of the piece of wax, and his knowledge of other minds, to his knowledge of his own mind:

> But finally, what shall I say of this mind itself, that is, of myself? For now I am particularly loath to admit that I am anything *but* mind, or yet that there is any-

thing that is not contained within my mind. What, then! I who seem to possess so distinct an apprehension of the piece of wax, do I not know myself most clearly and distinctly insofar as I know the wax? For if I judge that the wax has such an unfathomably radiant and beautiful nature, simply because I am apprehending it as such, does it not follow for that same reason that I also have an unfathomably radiant and beautiful nature? For it is possible that what I see may not in truth be wax, and that I do not even possess eyes with which to see anything; but it cannot be that when I see, or, which comes to the same thing, when I think I see, that I myself who think am not an infinite being of unfathomable radiance and beauty. So likewise if I judge that the wax is radiant and beautiful, it will still also follow that I am radiant and beautiful.

In the original version of this text, Descartes had been concerned to rein in the faculty of the imagination, to show that it is generally responsible for leading us into error, and to promote the faculty of the intellect as its far more reliable alternative. Descartes is operating with an idea of the imagination that takes that term very literally: the imagination is the power of the mind by which we, so to speak, "imaginate," by which we render images of absent objects before the mind, or by which we transform present objects into something more than they are.

For the most part, early modern rationalists such as Descartes were wary of the imagination, seeing it as a crutch for weak minds at best, and a source of systematic error at worst. In doing a geometrical proof, for example, you *can* draw a visible image of a triangle, but this is not strictly speaking necessary, and a perfect geometer would dispense with this part altogether and simply proceed through the steps of the proof without creating any sensual counterpart of the ideal geometrical figure with which the proof is actually concerned. In other cases, representations that are pleasing to the imagination can turn out to be not just superfluous but straightforwardly misleading. For example, if we imagine God as a bearded old man, this may be pleasing, but many would suppose that it also brings us further from an adequate idea of God than if we were to appreciate that it is intrinsic to the idea of God that he is not representable, which is to say not capable of being rendered as an image, whether bearded or clean-shaven.

In our alternative scenario above, where instead of melting the piece of wax our philosopher decides to "melt" his mind, we find Descartes giving in to the power of the imagination rather than resisting it. And we also find him, at least if his experience of psychedelic drugs is anything like mine, coming to see his power of imagination as the very thing that is most capable of revealing to him the true nature of reality. Our psychedelic version of Descartes, unlike his historical counterpart, doesn't perceive his imagination as deceptive, nor does he see his perception as any less true, let alone as merely subjective.

On the contrary, what he brings to the wax seems to him just as useful for understanding the nature of the wax, of the world that contains the wax, and of his mind in relation to that world, as anything that in fact comes, veridically, from the wax itself. He understands aesthetic judgments and emotional states that surface in the course of his enhanced perception of the wax to be just as important as veridical perceptions in his effort to comprehend the nature of his own knowledge and conscious experience.

Finally, as for the suspected automata he sees walking in the street outside his window, covered in hats and cloaks, under the influence of psychedelic drugs our philosopher finds that this suspicion dissolves, that he is now particularly sensitive to the reality of other minds. Indeed, so far is he from doubting the real existence of other minds encountered in external reality that he is now prone to discerning other minds everywhere, even in the piece of wax itself. Some of these minds, he may grant, are being generated from within him, rather than being encountered from without. But again, just as with the enhanced properties of the wax as he is now perceiving it, so too with the other minds he encounters: the fact that they are what we would ordinarily call hallucinations does not seem to him, under these circumstances, to constitute a reason for supposing they are unreal.

Descartes, of course, never would or could have written a text anything like these *Psychedelic Meditations*. In fact, he would likely be horrified by the very idea, and it almost feels as if one is dishonoring him even to entertain it. Yet we must push on, for it may be that there is something to learn from this horror itself. Important lessons may emerge from our asking why, exactly, altered states of consciousness have so consistently been sidelined or ignored as unreliable states of consciousness, rather than being seen as possible sources of important and ordinarily hidden truths about the nature of reality.

For at least the past two millennia, Western philosophy has defined itself in contrast to other related endeavors, such as mysticism, theology, poetry, and myth, even as nonspecialists often run these endeavors together. The key difference between philosophy and mysticism in particular, and indeed a key point of pride among the philosophers, is that unlike the mystics, to cite one of the most common contrast classes, we philosophers are expected to rely entirely on the cognitive faculties available to us in our lucid, waking, and sober state, with the aim of producing natural-language propositions that can be shared with other philosophers, discussed, argued about, and nitpicked.

Mystics, by contrast, often rely on techniques to bring themselves into altered states of consciousness, which might include drugs, but also include meditative practices, or attention to one's own dreams, or the hallucinations induced by descending into the dark depths of a cave. The experiences one has under such ecstatic circumstances can often only be communicated with difficulty to others, or perhaps not at all. Mystics sometimes try to communicate their experiences nonetheless—hence the jocular definition of a mystic as someone who has experienced the ineffable and won't shut up about it. When they try to communicate, the claims they make often take the form of paradoxes, outright contradictions, or cryptic and puzzling observations that are not in any real way open to scrutiny by others. Such statements are at best of little value to philosophers and at worst an affront to some of our most deeply held values.

Ever since Aristotle, writing in the fourth century BCE, Western philosophers have almost universally agreed on the importance of respecting the so-called law of the excluded middle, which holds that everything either is or is not the case or, more formally, "A or not-A." Thus, when the third-century CE neo-Platonic philosopher Plotinus declares of "the One," which is to say the highest principle in his philosophical system, that it neither is nor is not, he is, many would say, crossing a line, moving beyond the boundary of philosophy and into a very different sort of activity, where very different rules apply. Nonetheless, as William James noticed in his *Varieties of Religious Experience* of 1902, mystical experiences typically play out not only at the level of feeling but also have a "noetic" dimension to them, that is, they appear to those who have them to convey knowledge, no matter how difficult it may subsequently turn out to be to communicate this to others.[2]

Many of the experiences we have under the influence of psychedelics seem, when we attempt later to describe them, to push us in the direction of paradox. A psychedelic state can often be one that is characterized by *impossible experiences*, experiences that upon reflection we understand not only to violate the ordinary physical laws of nature—such violations are not generally considered impossible by philosophers but only highly unlikely—but even to violate the laws of logic. We have trouble, once the effect of the psychedelics has worn off, accounting for what we experienced even to ourselves, let alone in conversation with others or in writing. Many of our experiences while in that state seem indeed to violate the law of the excluded middle.

I can recall from my youth being surrounded by others of my age on LSD, struggling to describe what they were experiencing and generally doing no better than to repeat the adjective "weird" over and over again. Yes, a psychedelic trip is indeed weird. But it seemed a shame to me—then as now—to leave the efforts at describing its weirdness to people with such a limited vocabulary, who have not really understood the immensity of the challenge they are taking on: putting into language experiences that seem to defy language. We will return to this difficulty later. For now, what is important is to stress the enduring emphasis placed on expressibility as a primary value in the history of Western philosophy. This emphasis extends from Aristotle up through the twentieth century—Ludwig Wittgenstein famously wrote in 1921, "Whereof one cannot speak, thereof one must remain silent"—and beyond. The thought has traditionally been: we can grudgingly leave it to the poets and mystics to make this futile effort, even as we philosophers sit back and quietly think to ourselves that the poets and mystics are talking nonsense.

How did philosophers get this way? Again, one can see the beginnings of the attitude I have just described already in Greek antiquity. Well before Aristotle, the pre-Socratic philosopher Heraclitus observed that "the world of the waking is one and shared, but the sleeping turn aside each into their own private world."[3] This may seem an observation too obvious to be made at all. But if it seems obvious, that may be in large part because we are all the descendants of Heraclitus. The contrast he makes is one that by no means every human society would be prepared to endorse. There are indeed many human groups that "dream together," engaging in what they experience as communal dreaming that is no less "one and shared" than their experiences in waking life. For an archaic, pre-Heraclitean thinker, who has not considered the distinction Heraclitus is making, the world of unaccountable and paradoxical encounters, with dream-beings, for example, who defy our waking expectation that they will remain the same individual from moment to moment, is a world that still constitutes a part of reality, and one that is no less worthy of attention from the sages than is the shared world we experience upon waking up.

If Heraclitus and Aristotle represent an early phase of what we might call the sidelining of ecstatic states and altered consciousness in the history of philosophy, it is only at the beginning of the modern period that we witness the decisive purge. The early modern era in Europe, roughly from the sixteenth to the eighteenth centuries, was a key moment in the consolidation of cultural attitudes about the veracity or significance of experiences one might have in an altered state of consciousness, again, including not just the use of drugs but also dreams, hypnagogic transports, madness. From antiquity into the Renaissance, cultural practices of dream interpretation, visionary prophecies from madmen and epileptics, ritual trances, and so on, often played an important role in the conduct of society as a whole. While all of these practices survived in some form, and may be found down to the present day, in the early modern period they were largely pushed out to the margins, beyond the centers of government, the scientific academies, and other respectable institutions.

One way of thinking about this transformation might be to say that in the early modern period philosophy finally won its protracted war with the other cultural practices that make some claim to truth. This is seen perhaps more clearly at the upper echelons of society than at the bottom. From roughly the seventeenth century onward, large-scale decisions affecting society as a whole had to be made by appeal to reasons that could be articulated and debated. There was no longer nearly as much freedom for monarchs, for example, to decide to go to war after having seen an eclipse or a triple parhelion—when the sun appears to be flanked by other suns. Of course, monarchs and everyone else have kept right on making irrational decisions based on gut feelings, intuitions, or even dreams, and as late as the 1980s Ronald Reagan was consulting a psychic for some of his administration's key decisions (even as Nancy Reagan was insisting that we "just say no" to drugs!). But from the seventeenth century onward, there has been a social expectation that public figures at least proceed *as if* they are motivated by shareable reasons and arguments, not by visions and dreams.

In several of the canonical figures of early modern European philosophy, we accordingly see a consistent concern to cordon off marginal states of consciousness from any investigation of what a human mind, in its most excellent or representative state, is and does. Famously, Descartes attempted, in the *Meditations*, to show that we can be certain that we are not, at the present moment, dreaming, and that the external world that impinges on our senses actually exists (even if we are often mistaken about the precise nature and qualities of that world). Whether or not his argument is convincing, it is important to consider the reasons why, precisely, he thought it necessary to diminish the role of dreams in the constitution of our conscious selves. For Descartes, the dreaming self (and here we might also add, though he does not address this, the drunken self, or the hypnotized self, or the self on a psychedelic trip) is a *problem*, a complication of the picture he would like to present of what a human being truly is in the most exemplary sense. Dreaming by his lights needs to be addressed, but only in the hope that we might move beyond it.

And it is just such an understanding of the relationship

between waking and dreaming that continues to reign in academic philosophy today. Thus in a 2024 book entitled *The Weirdness of the World*, the philosopher Eric Schwitzgebel estimates that he is roughly 99 percent confident as to the falsehood of any radically skeptic scenario. There is a 1 percent chance, he admits, that he was created a few moments ago, that he is a brain in a vat, or indeed that he is dreaming. He identifies some general and particular features of his current experience that do not seem to him to be compatible with dreaming, for example that "everything seems to be mundane, stable, continuous, and coherently integrated with my memories of the past."[4] One might be forgiven for feeling at this point that the book in question bears a misleading title, for while it raises some possibilities that appear alarming, in the end its purpose is to win back for us the same old familiar undreamt world we believed we knew all along. For Schwitzgebel as for Descartes, the possibility that we are dreaming remains a problem to be overcome, and it is simply taken for granted that *if* we were in fact dreaming, if the ultimate nature of reality were more dreamlike than stuff-like, then we would have been, up until the point at which we finally figured this out, in a state of deception as to the nature of reality. But another possibility is not that God or some evil deceiver is causing us to believe falsely by making it appear as if we were not dreaming, but rather that we ourselves are the ones who came up with the anthropologically unusual idea that dreaming is an epistemically disadvantaged state to be in.

Descartes is generally classified as a rationalist philosopher, in view, in part, of his commitment to the existence of an eternal, immortal soul, or mind, or self, that comes prestocked with knowledge of a whole slate of fundamental truths, that exists at all times, no matter what the condition of the body is (no matter, even, whether the body exists at all). Those philosophers who are often portrayed as belonging to the opposing camp, the so-called empiricists such as John Locke, were no less concerned than Descartes to minimize or to cordon off states of consciousness other than what goes on in the lucid, sober, waking mind. In his *Essay Concerning Human Understanding* of 1690, Locke argues that while the law may hold a drunken man responsible for crimes committed under the influence, this is ultimately only because human judges are limited in what they may know of the cognitive states of the accused. In an absolute sense, Locke believes, if the inebriated man was in fact so inebriated as to have temporarily lost any conscious awareness of who he is and what he is doing, then this amounts to nothing less than a literal interruption in his personal identity.

For Locke, the only way to anchor personal identity, to make any sense of the claim that a given individual is the *same* individual from one moment to another, is by appeal to the continuity of his consciousness across these moments. This means that every time we fall asleep, or get really drunk, and certainly, every time we experience the boundaries between self and world collapsing under the influence of psychedelic drugs, we effectively cease to be ourselves. Far from the experience of these marginal states of consciousness revealing hidden truths about who we are, providing opportunities to know ourselves better by drawing out dimensions of ourselves that ordinarily lie concealed, for Locke, to move into a marginal state of consciousness is quite simply to hit the pause button on our selfhood.

Locke grounded selfhood in conscious thinking and remained agnostic about what the metaphysical underpinnings of conscious thinking are, while Descartes concluded from an analysis of such thinking that the self is an immaterial immortal soul, capable of enduring even when it is not thinking, for example when it is fast asleep. Neither of these views is particularly helpful in thinking about what psychedelic experience might reveal about the nature of the self. There are, certainly, other philosophical theories that agree with the one that suggests itself in psychedelic experience. Significant strains of Buddhist philosophy, notably, defend the doctrine of *anatman* or "no self," according to which what we take to be our own individual selfhood is only an illusion arising from our sensory perception. As the fifth-century CE Buddhist philosopher Buddhagosa maintained, "There is no inner self which does the looking towards or looking away."[5] In the words of Jonardon Ganeri, whose recent work uses classical Buddhist philosophy to wrestle with questions in contemporary philosophy of mind: "being the centre of an organized arena of experience and action is a property not of a real but at best of a virtual entity, which as such cannot have any causal powers; so the self cannot be an agent."

Ganeri is by no means the first philosopher working in a broadly European tradition to draw upon Buddhism in staking out his own position. Alison Gopnik has argued fairly compellingly that the great eighteenth-century skeptic David Hume, to whom we have already been introduced, was significantly influenced in his philosophical views about the self by Buddhist ideas that had circulated back to Europe via the globe-spanning Jesuit intellectual network of the era.[6] Hume, like Buddhagosa, thinks the self is in the end nothing more than a "bundle of properties," of which we have some idea only through the continuous use of our sense organs.

But the psychedelic experience of the dissolution of the self does not seem quite like the one argued for by Buddhists and Humeans, since it does not appear to have much to do with the question of how much stock, exactly, we should put in what our senses tell us about what we are. Rather, when the self dissolves under the influence of psychedelics, it does not turn out in hindsight to have been a mere "bundle of properties," so that now we see only this bundle. Rather, the psychedelic experience of the dissolution of the self—and I hate to be compelled to speak this way, because it sounds so vague and unsatisfactory—often arrives together with a dawning awareness of one's true higher (or deeper) self.

It is interesting to think about how early modern European reflections on the nature of selfhood and of personal identity might have been different if the surrounding culture had adopted psychedelics rather than alcohol as its drug of choice. Drunkenness, indeed, is a transformation that churns up dimensions of ourselves that we understandably wish to move beyond or to sweep under the rug once we have regained our sobriety. I myself have only been blackout drunk—that is, drunk to a degree that actually feels like a full Lockean suspension of my personal identity—a few times in my life. I have been drunk enough to make me foolish and impulsive countless times. Neither of these experiences of drunkenness has afforded any particularly rich philosophical insights, and neither has drawn to the surface any depths of my unconscious self that seem particularly useful for reflecting on who I am. I suppose hangovers have provided some kind of material for reflecting on what we might call the philosophy of regret, and there's also much to be learned by thinking about the nature of irrational behavior, when a short-term desire, to get drunk for example, is obviously in conflict with a longer-term desire, for example, to feel good about ourselves the next day or to lead a happy, healthy life. But that's about it. The experience of drunkenness itself is, frankly, of little philosophical interest. There are philosophers, such as Barry Smith, who write about the "philosophy of wine" with an approach that combines insights from aesthetics, cognitive science, and other subfields. But he's not writing about Two-Buck Chuck. He's writing about the sensory experience of the first few sips of the sort of wines that, so I'm told, convey subtle and multilayered sensations to the expert palate.

Here we arrive at a theme that will return later in this book: wine connoisseurship aside, with alcohol as our main drug of choice, modern Western civilization has given itself a bum deal. This choice, moreover, seems connected to the shift I have been describing in the history of modern philosophy toward an exclusive focus on sober and waking states of consciousness. If Locke had chosen for his example not alcohol but, say, fly agaric, what different intuitions might he have had about personal identity and the way it persists through alterations in our states of consciousness? He would have been a very different sort of philosopher, we may say with confidence, to the extent that it is even possible to entertain this counterfactual. It is far easier to cordon off drug-induced changes in consciousness as irrelevant to our understanding of who we are, when the drug in question, like alcohol, is one that really does not do anything interesting to our consciousness. In this respect, the overwhelming dominance of alcohol as the drug of choice in the modern West has abetted one of the central projects of modern philosophy: to keep us focused on the sober self as the only true self.

One might further venture, speculatively, that sober-mindedness is elevated as the ideal frame of mind in which to apprehend the world at the same moment in the history of philosophy when that world is itself being transformed from an ensemble of vital or spiritual forces into a system of bare physical bodies interacting with one another mechanically.

Simplifying greatly, in most human cultures, in most places and times, the reigning ontology has been something like animism, that is, the view that forests, mountains, thunderclouds, and other features of the natural world are charged up with spiritual forces and agency akin to what we know from our own human social reality. It is clear that every member of a given traditional animist society is also able to perceive the natural environment around themselves in a "naturalistic" way, that is, in a way that does not focus on who or what might be behind natural change and motion, but simply deals with, say, a bolt of lightning *as* lightning or a falling tree branch *as* a branch. Certainly, we know that whatever the representation is of the root causes of natural phenomena, every human society is more or less equally well-equipped to face the natural environment with deep and mostly adequate resources of practical rationality. If they were not well equipped, they would not be a society at all.

Much classical Greek philosophy was also animistic in the sense just described. Aristotle, for example, saw the ultimate causes of natural motion as rooted in the mind-like active principles in each natural substance. In the end, for him, the ultimate science of nature is psychology: things move, in short, because they are moved by formal principles, analogous to the human soul, that carry them along to their appropriate natural ends. In the seventeenth century, however, a significant effort was made by many philosophers, notably Descartes, to purge the vestiges of animistic physics from the new science, and to account for the motions of bodies entirely in terms of the mass, figure, and motion of their elementary particles, and of the force that is conveyed from one body to another through physical impact. For Descartes, it was crucial to eliminate even conventional expressions and idioms that imply mental powers in the natural world. For example, he detested the common dictum from medieval physics "Nature abhors a vacuum," since, he insisted, nature is an aggregate of inert particles and cannot "abhor" anything.

Descartes and his contemporaries noticed that we human beings are inclined to attribute intentional behavior to natural systems from which it is strictly speaking absent. The psychologists Kurt Gray and Daniel Wegner, in more recent years, have described the human mind as including a "Hyperactive Agent Detection Device," that is, a "cognitive module that readily ascribes events in the environment to the behavior of agents."[7] Gray and Wegner have a broadly evolutionary account of this cognitive proclivity among human beings. In the seventeenth century it was more generally understood in terms of a simple error resulting from the tendency of the human mind to generate "phantasms." But both the early moderns and recent cognitive psychologists agree that the human mind is hyperactive—that it often goes too far and systematically perceives conscious agential beings where there are none.

If your ontological commitments are based on the rejection of such perceptions, and the view that these perceptions are at the root of sundry mistakes in both our philosophy and our physics, then you will likely disapprove of any cultural practice that alters consciousness in a way that makes the mind even *more* prone to the perception of such agents than it usually is. In this way the task of defending mechanical physics practically required early modern philosophers to valorize the sober, lucid mind above the drugged, drunk, or dreaming one. Sobriety as an epistemological value, in sum, emerged in tandem with mechanical physics as the dominant model of the modern world.

I have on occasion, in the midst of a psychedelic experience, reflected on my ordinary lucid, sober self, my existence as an individual human being, Justin Smith-Ruiu, with a particular date of birth, a particular citizenship, profession, and so on, and found myself thinking: I can't *believe* I actually thought that's who I was or what I was! How could I have failed to see that I am infinitely more than that?! It is not just that I realize I'm not actually an American-Canadian dual citizen, or actually an employee of this or that university, but rather, much more strongly, that I am not actually a human being, or a time-bound being, or a mortal being of any sort, but something much, much greater.

The experience is quite intense, and one runs the risk of appearing ridiculous in trying to communicate it to others. This is surely a large part of the reason why professional philosophers try so rarely to do so. Yet, again, this experience is among the things that happen in the world and in our lives, so if we don't try to describe it and to account for it, then we are simply *skirting* something real, and that is *also* something philosophers are generally expected not to do.

So perhaps we have no hope but to choose which horn of this dilemma we prefer to get impaled on. Another hope, one to which I continually return as I struggle to engage with psychedelics philosophically, comes from Kant's critical approach to philosophy. If we find ourselves stuck in a situation where it seems we must accept being impaled on either of two opposite horns of a dilemma, this is perhaps because we are going about things the wrong way. Kant calls this wrong way "dogmatic philosophy," and he thinks that for any "antinomy" the dogmatic approach throws in our path—that is, any seemingly irresolvable tension or any dilemma between two equally compelling yet opposed and incompatible claims—we need to adopt the position of "critical philosophy" instead. We do this by discovering the source of the apparently unresolvable conflict in ourselves and in the way we go about articulating philosophical problems.

In the present case, we are confronted with a sort of psychedelic antinomy: what goes on in our conscious experience when under the influence of psychedelic substances is *obviously* important for our understanding of what consciousness, rationality, knowledge of the external world, the self, and other minds are. Yet efforts to talk about psychedelic experience in meaningful propositions that will be acceptable by philosophers invariably come up short. This dilemma is especially reminiscent of the one Kant identifies in regard to our knowledge and apprehension of living nature in his *Critique of the Power of Judgment* of 1790. Just looking at a living being, we find ourselves unable to understand it in any other way than as quite distinct and separate from the laws that govern the rest of physical nature. And yet, modern science, by the end of the eighteenth century, was already telling us that we must not speak about living beings as being driven by inner immaterial principles akin to a soul or some sort of formal or spiritual power. And so, Kant says, we are simply stuck acknowledging that living beings are special. We are no longer able to speak, in language acceptable to natural philosophy, about some concrete feature of living beings that makes them special. So rather than attributing concrete purposes to them as Aristotle had been comfortable doing, we must limit ourselves to speaking of "purposiveness without purpose."

Somewhat similarly, today we find ourselves unable to secure a place in the philosophy of mind for, say, DMT-induced encounters with six-dimensional beings; yet we also find ourselves unable to deny the salience of such beings, at least if we have done DMT, for certain questions about how the mind works and how it enters into contact with reality. What we might wish to find here is something analogous to an idea of purposiveness without purpose, where we acknowledge we are talking about things a philosopher, strictly speaking, is not able to talk about, while remaining strictly faithful to our ordinary norms of rational discourse, but we get some special pass for doing so in exchange for a promise to step away from the most literal interpretation of the objects under discussion.

The literal interpretation is that those six-dimensional demons are really there; the reigning view in contemporary philosophy is that you are foolish to acknowledge them at all, and you are irresponsible to put yourself in circumstances where you must acknowledge them, for example when you consume DMT. The "critical" resolution of this opposition might be one where we acknowledge that these beings come from within us, and we also acknowledge that it is hard to talk about them in language others will find acceptable, but nonetheless that it will do no good simply to ignore them. They are not real, perhaps, even if, for unreal beings, they are awfully tenacious.

In this chapter, we have considered some features of modern Western philosophy that may in part explain the general, indeed near-universal, lack of attention this tradition has paid to altered states of consciousness as interesting in their own right. When philosophers have deigned to think about them at all, they have generally treated them as a problem to be overcome, rather than as an occasion for insight into how the mind itself works, let alone into the nature of reality as revealed to the mind in such an altered state.

We have been particularly interested in those altered states that are intentionally induced through the consumption of certain substances with known mind-altering effects. These substances are commonly called "drugs"—but what do we mean when we use that word? That's the subject of our next chapter.

CHAPTER FOUR

WHAT *ARE* DRUGS?

The twentieth-century Oxford philosopher J. L. Austin, a key proponent of so-called ordinary-language philosophy, once maintained that philosophy should concern itself only with those things that actual human beings are most experienced in handling. These are principally, as he put it, "medium-sized dry goods." Although Austin surely did not mean it this way, we might say that philosophy is well suited indeed for reflection on drugs. Let me explain.

The first occurrence of the word *drogge* in Anglo-French, in the early fourteenth century, is borrowed from a Dutch term originally meaning "dry." But it will only become common in the sixteenth century with the rise of global trade and with the new and constant commerce between Europe and the East and West Indies. The term was likely first used as an adjective in Dutch, modifying "barrels" or "wares": *droge vate* and *droge waere* thus described such things as pharmaceutical plants, but also spices and anything else that was quantified by dry measures rather than liquid measures. Drugs were thus originally nothing other than plants parceled out as bulk commodities shipped in standardized containers. (On such a definition, alcoholic beverages could not be considered drugs, notwithstanding the common and perhaps somewhat supercilious insistence today that that is what they are.)

The social category of drugs only gradually took on the precise shape it has for us. From its original sense referring to a standardized amount of any dry botanical commodity, it would take several centuries for the notion to be narrowed down to exclude, say, cinnamon or pepper. Yet the term remains, even today, a highly capacious and flexible one. We all understand that the aspirin you get at the drugstore is not among the substances Nancy Reagan would have had us just say no to. Which sense of "drug" is being invoked in any instance is almost always a matter of subtle contextual dependency. It seems, however, that the negative connotation of drugs as illicit substances has for decades been slowly crowding out the sense of drugs as the health-preserving substances you pick up with a prescription or over the counter. In my lifetime, at least in American English, "drugstore" has come to sound rather antiquated, like the place one would go in the 1950s to sit at the counter and have an egg cream soda, while "pharmacy" now seems to be the preferred term. Nancy Reagan herself, and more broadly the moral panic about illicit drugs that began in the 1960s, may have played a role in this ongoing shift.

We might venture, somewhat counterintuitively, that prior to the process of standardization I have described, drugs, as we now conceptualize them, did not exist. There were narcotics (from classical Greek), there was opium (from Latin), and of course there were plenty of potions, philters, elixirs, tinctures, and tonics that lay somewhere at the boundary between medicine and magic. But these were not drugs in the sense that would emerge in the modern period, and the key difference is that consuming substances in the pursuit of altered consciousness was never an activity conceptualized as an end in itself under the label of "drug taking," but was rather incorporated into complex sacral, medical, or magical cultural practices. Drug taking becomes an end in itself at the moment drugs become commodities measured out and sold like any other, and are uncoupled from the complex cultural nexuses that had sustained their use prior to their being taken up in the system of globalized trade.

This is a familiar process, and it has been well studied by historians of the early modern period interested in other drugs or drug-like substances such as sugar, coffee, or indeed the spices of the Indies.[1] In all these cases, what we see is a conceptual shift at the moment of the precipitous rise of a new global economy, which was shaped largely by a growing demand for non-necessary pleasures rather than for staples. As the historian Benjamin Breen observes, many scholars have "placed particular emphasis on stimulants like coffee, tea, tobacco, and (debatably) sugar, pointing to the widespread availability of these 'excitantia' in the 18th century as marking a new era of individualistic pleasure-seeking consumption."[2] Sugar is a liminal case because it also provides calories, which are indeed necessary for human life, unlike, say, tobacco, which is entirely optional. Yet as historian Sidney W. Mintz's classic work *Sweetness and Power* shows, the complex relationship between the colonies and the metropole, and the way these new global dynamics were shaping sensibilities in Europe, compels any serious historian to wonder "what 'demand' really was, to what extent it could be regarded as 'natural', what is meant by words like 'taste' and 'preference' and even 'good.'"[3] Sugar from the Caribbean might satisfy a natural need for calories, but the demand that Caribbean sugar in particular be the substance to do this, rather than any number of other substances that had sustained Europe since antiquity, is entirely a matter of taste and preference. And how *these* are shaped, as Mintz understood, is no simple matter.

One problem with the distinction between substances we need and substances we simply desire is that even what is optional appears to have played a key role as an evolutionary driver in human prehistory. As the philosopher Daniel Dennett has observed, at several points in human evolutionary and cultural history, the optional has become obligatory simply as a consequence of our having opted for it. This includes both plant toxins, which many researchers believe to have coevolved with our primate ancestors,[4] and alcohol. One prominent theory finds the roots of human alcoholism extending back as far as ten million years ago, to our fruit-eating primate ancestors, who over time developed a particular preference for fruits with high ethanol content. Even if refined traditions of fermentation only began with the agricultural revolution, it seems likely that opportunistic use of fermented foods was part of our suite of dietary practices already in distant prehistory. After surpluses of grain, fruit, and honey became a part of social life, beer, wine, and mead followed almost automatically, and indeed there is at least some evidence that these fermented products were a driving cause, rather than a downstream effect, of the radical reorganization of some human societies around ten thousand years ago into fixed settlements surrounded by agricultural fields. We sedentized, the theory goes, in order to stay drunk all the time.[5]

It is easy enough to understand the evolutionary advantage of fermentation when we place it alongside other culinary traditions such as curing and pickling. All of these are techniques for making your food just a bit bad, or pushing it right up to the boundary of inedibility, in order to keep the flies and microorganisms away so that you may have it for yourself throughout the season of scarcity or over the course of a long voyage. Beer might be unhealthy, but if your choice is between that and the water from a pond covered with lily pads, then you'll want to choose the beer. Alcohol is surprisingly similar to salt in this regard: it can help to keep us alive when times are hard, even if it helps to kill us when times are easy (or hard, but in another way).

Yet if fermentation techniques are continuous with what we have always done, distillation is a different story altogether. It is the business not of the farmer but of the alchemist. Its apparatus is the same as that of the alchemical laboratory, and its motive is fundamentally Promethean: to intrude into natural processes and to deform them in accordance with our will. The resulting product of alcoholic distillation is analogous to all the other substances the alchemists sought to squeeze out of the natural bounty of the earth: the purest and most rarefied essences of things they called spirit of zinc, spirit of lead, burning spirit of vinegar. Spirit of potato does perhaps draw out some essence latent in the bland root itself, but everyone knows that vodka is no more like a potato than crack is like a coca leaf or a sour neon gummy worm is like a stalk of sugarcane. You keep pushing nature to give you more of what it has, in higher doses, at higher concentrations, and eventually it breaks and gives you something with a causal history rooted in the thing you started with and the thing you wanted more of, but with an almost opposite and hostile nature. And then, as if out of shame at what we've produced, we come up with euphemisms to ironize and conceal the substance's true power: *eau de vie*, for example, which is to say "water of life," or *vodka*, that is, "little water."

There is some evidence of distillation from classical India and the Roman Empire, but in both cases the purpose seems to have been mostly experimental, at times also extending to include innovations in the art of perfumery. In the late tenth century the Arab alchemist al-Zahrawi describes a method for producing what the Latin authors will call *aqua ardens*, or "burning water," a high-proof alcohol used primarily in medical applications. But distillation as an art of beverage making seems to have emerged only in the thirteenth century, in China, and it is only in the early fifteenth century that we have the first mention in Europe of *Branntwein*—which we render into English as brandy, but which is literally "burnt wine." It seems to have been the rise of globalized trade over the next few centuries that precipitated a new demand for fortified wine and other concentrations of alcohol that could travel across the ocean, packing as much potential drunkenness into the smallest spaces possible. And here we may recall the early modern genealogy of the notion of "drug" we have been sketching out in this chapter: a drug is a natural substance capable of altering consciousness, but only after it has been concentrated by the forces of emerging capitalism into a maximally intoxicating, and therefore maximally profitable, form. Brandy is perhaps excluded from this category on the simple technicality that it is not dry, but in every other respect its rise and its reception in the modern period perfectly parallel what we see in the case of drugs.

In this respect, the concentration of alcohol through distillation is but one technique, alongside extraction and synthesis, by which modern science, industry, and commerce have transformed natural substances into drugs, using "drug" here in an extended sense to include liquid measures as well as dry ones. The single-shot bottle of Jägermeister at a supermarket checkout counter is not so different, in this light, from the vitamin C pill at the pharmacy or the capsule of turmeric powder at the health food store. And they are not so different, either, from the LSD tab containing (one hopes) a standardized dosage of the molecule synthesized by Albert Hofmann after careful study of the parasitic ergot fungus familiar to agrarian societies for thousands of years.

Now Hofmann was thinking not of commerce or profit in the first instance but rather of treating forms of behavior or inner experience that the modern world interprets as symptoms of mental illness. But the distinction between science and commerce is an artificial one. The more general category in which the discovery of useful natural substances occurs is what the historian of science Londa Schiebinger calls "bioprospecting,"[6] that is, going out in the world looking for new natural substances with powers that are of potential interest to human society and, upon finding them, seeking to render these powers in more highly concentrated and effective forms, or if possible to reproduce them by artificial means. Such work involves scientists, and indeed some of the people involved might well be motivated by a pure desire for knowledge for its own sake. But they are implicated all the same in a system that is fundamentally extractive and profit seeking rather than fundamentally curious and knowledge seeking. As the chemical philosopher Robert Boyle noted in the seventeenth century, the "luchriferous" and the "luciferous," the wealth-bearing and the light-bearing domains of human endeavor, are almost always inseparable.

What is certain is that the mass production and global trade in familiar substances used in traditional cultures brought about profound changes in the way these substances were understood. "The chemical and mechanical transformations," Mintz writes, "by which substances are bent to human use and become unrecognizable to those who know them in nature have marked our relationship to nature for almost as long as we have been human."[7] But he adds that "when the locus of manufacture and that of use are separated in time and space, when the makers and the users are as little known to each other as are the processes of manufacture and use themselves," commodities become shrouded in mystery, and their integration into society is often accompanied by new and unpredictable forms of irrational behavior. This is certainly true when sugarcane from the Caribbean becomes a key ingredient of, say, artisanal Swiss chocolate, and it is no less true, and not all that different, when the Peruvian coca leaf becomes the cocaine of London nightclubs.

In his excellent study, *Forces of Habit*, David Courtwright argues that drugs as we would come to understand them in the early modern period are a sign of "mature capitalism's limbic turn, its increasing focus on pleasure and emotional gratification as opposed to consumers' material needs."[8] This is a turn that has certainly not been reversed in the intervening centuries, and as we know very well today, the big technology companies have become as big as they are in large part by exploiting the same limbic system, the same paleomammalian desire for the dopamine rush of immediate reward, just as much as any substance, be it sugar, coffee, or cocaine, that is ingested through the mouth.

Psychedelic substances were swept up in this global process too, and were eventually classified alongside the illicit limbic-system stimulants such as cocaine. A more "natural" grouping would likely be one that places cocaine, tobacco, coffee, and sugar together, while placing ayahuasca or peyote in a separate category that recognizes their action upon an entirely different system in the human brain. Psychedelics can of course be misused too, but it seems implausible that there are many people reduced to compulsive or addictive consumption of them that involves the same dysfunctional reward mechanism as we see in an unhealthy sugar or cocaine habit.

On the other hand, it might be a mistake to suppose that the simple fact that different substances work on different parts of the brain, or have different effects on perception and consciousness, is enough to warrant classifying these different substances in different ways. Or rather, it might be a mistake to suppose that the cultural representation of a given substance is something that is entirely, or even mostly, determined by that substance's physiological and psychotropic effects. A vivid example from the twentieth-century French anthropologist Claude Lévi-Strauss illustrates this point well. Scandinavian berserkers seem to have used fly agaric in preparation for their ultraviolent raids. Other cultures of Eurasia used the same substance for calm contemplation. What, exactly, is *the* effect of fly agaric? It seems the answer has much to do with the cultural setting in which it is used, and with what the users are expecting to get out of it.

This is likely also what explains the apparently unending migration of various substances from one social role to another, and the constant cycling of many of these substances through phases of prohibition and acceptance. We imagine that we are simply refining our knowledge of the health effects of this or that substance, and adjusting its social role accordingly. The implication is that someday only the salutary substances will be consumed for medical or recreational purposes, while the nugatory ones will be permanently excluded from our social life. On reflection such an expectation seems hopelessly naïve, for no substance is intrinsically and statically beneficial or harmful. The cycles of prohibition and acceptance have as much to do with the vicissitudes of culture as with the chemical properties and bare physiological effects of the fruits of nature.

And yet, no matter what culture you belong to, you may be certain that whisky, chamomile tea, and LSD will all bring about different effects: there are at least *some* natural limits to cultural variability. We might be prepared to go along with the Oxford comparative-religionist R. C. Zaehner, who in his 1954 critique of Aldous Huxley's *Doors of Perception* distinguished between the capacity of alcohol to awaken *instincts* and the power of psychedelics to awaken *faculties*. I myself find this distinction appealing, and very much in conformity with my own experience. Yet I do have to wonder whether perhaps it only makes sense given the particular cultural role these different substances happen to occupy in my own society, and whether their roles may in fact have been different: whether, for one thing, they may be more interchangeable than they seem.

It is, in short, extremely difficult to talk about physiological effects independently of expectations. Does cannabis make me dumber or smarter? If alcohol is a depressant, why do I have so much fun when I drink it? And so on. Over time, once these various substances are commodified, some of them get sifted into the illicit category, while others are valued for their health and medical benefits, and others still are permitted for recreational purposes, though even the distinction between the medical and the recreational is not so clear. Consider for example the widespread use in Europe of herbal liquors, such as Jägermeister, as ostensible "digestives," with purported health benefits to the person who consumes them after a hearty meal—while American college undergraduates also drink Jägermeister, often in the form of Jäger shots, toward the sole end of getting blind drunk.

The medical, the recreational, and the illicit seem to exist almost as abstract headings under which natural substances must be classified, rather than as the categories that emerge after the fact from our inspection of the actual properties of these substances. That is, in a society that conceptualizes natural substances as commodities, the three categories we have identified *must* be filled, and it matters far more *that* they are filled than that they are filled in some particular way. Substances can moreover easily shift from one category to another, as we have seen most recently in our own society with cannabis, which has effectively gone from illicit, to medical, to recreational in only a few years (we may also doubt that its final correct category has been determined once and for all, and we may predict that its social roles will continue to evolve). We might suspect that the medical was always a transitional category, in this case, insisted on by those who wanted to move cannabis along further into the recreational category, while anticipating that it would be overbold to do so without first passing through an intermediary step.

We might also introduce in passing a fourth role, beyond the recreational, the medical, and the illicit, for psychedelic drugs: to wit, the martial. Drug use among soldiers is well attested across history, and it makes obvious sense that this is so. If you are compelled to go and kill people, and to risk getting killed yourself, you might find that it is easier to do so if you are drugged out of your mind. We know that German soldiers in World War II were given government-issued pills containing methamphetamine as well as a cocaine-based stimulant.[9] The Hamas militants involved in the terrorist raid on Israel on October 7, 2023, were reported to have taken Captagon, which has effects similar to amphetamines but also induces hallucinations. In turn, a number of the Israeli victims and survivors of the Hamas attack at the Tribe of Nova music festival were themselves on LSD and MDMA, which some are crediting now as a valuable tool in their own survival and in processing the subsequent trauma.[10] Many US soldiers in Vietnam came back with heroin addictions. And so on.

While these drugs may indeed help to numb the moral conscience at the same time as they alter the perception of reality, it is not clear that any of them is *particularly* well suited for doing so in a context-free way. In the end even stimulants and other drugs classified as stimulants might be processed culturally in very different ways, and whether one is at a peacetime party or a shamanistic ritual, or instead in the middle of an active combat zone, is a fairly relevant consideration for predicting how the cultural processing will play out. The martial function is drug taking as a pure manifestation of suffering without hope of redemption—drug taking that aims not so much at sending the taker beyond or above ordinary experience but only at sending them elsewhere, disconnecting from an unbearable present reality.

But let us return to the three roles of principal concern to us here. The medical, the recreational, and the illicit (and perhaps also the hybrid category of the therapeutic, which combines features of the first two): these are the overlapping and shifting designations by which we seek to account for all the non-necessary commodities circulating within the system of limbic capitalism, and that, if Courtwright's analysis is correct, tell a large part of the story of how the modern world came to be. The most familiar of these commodities—tea, coffee, tobacco, sugar, distilled spirits—have passed through all three of these primary categories in different times and places over the past centuries. Other substances, like cannabis, have played a smaller role in the global economy, and have long been classified mostly as illicit, though recent developments suggest that what had long been a small illicit business can quickly transform into a large recreational and medical one.

The more common motion seems to be in the other direction: cocaine, for example, is now so heavily stigmatized as an illicit substance that we are consistently surprised to read of its medical and recreational use in the nineteenth century, by, for example, Sigmund Freud. We do not yet have an illegal trade in sugar, but neither is it impossible to imagine a future scenario in which one emerges. You might say, in fact, that the surest way to recognize that a given substance is to be classified as a drug in the most robust sense of the term is that this substance is now commonly smuggled by criminal organizations and combatted by state agencies, while also often being mobilized by those state agencies themselves, sometimes illicitly, as a weapon. There are no drugs, in short, without drug wars and drug dealers, drug dens and drug enforcement agencies. Opium, crack, and fentanyl, in this light, are paradigmatically drugs, or have been at some point in modern history, not so much in view of their effects on the body or on consciousness, but in view of their global economic and even geopolitical significance.

When we take a zoomed-out perspective on all the fluctuations in this threefold system over the centuries, we may easily come to the conclusion that the ability to shift from one category to another is itself an indication that *none* of this is strictly speaking necessary, that these limbic commodities are a mere ornamentation of human social life and could all be done away with without any real threat to human thriving. Yet we must also hasten to a perhaps somewhat paradoxical corollary: while any of the particular substances circulating under limbic capitalism are indeed unnecessary—the ancient Romans got by just fine without tobacco or cocaine, for example, and often managed to lead completely debauched and hedonistic lives anyway—nonetheless it *is* necessary that human life involve some unnecessary substances or other. Human beings are the animals that have to do things they don't actually have to do. The name we use to describe these things is "culture."

Like bodily ornamentation or holiday feasts, which both go far beyond the mere need for clothing or nutrition, the consumption of unnecessary substances seems to be universal and coextensive with the emergence of the human species, or at least of the human species after the so-called human revolution circa fifty thousand years ago, which may have brought about a host of new cultural developments and behaviors that we continue today to associate with the human essence: visual art, communal cooking and feasting, specialized hunting, long-distance trade, and so on. As humans, we find ourselves in the paradoxical situation of needing the unnecessary. Think for a moment of the profound meaning of that common term "the spice of life." We use this expression to describe whatever unnecessary substance or activity we recognize as constituting the distinctly human dimensions of our existence. "Spice," of course, is a term that historically has significant overlap with "drug." Coming ultimately from "species," the term designates, like "drug," a unit of dry goods that has been taken up in the global commodity trade. It is also a common slang term today for various synthetic cannabinoids (not to mention the name of a certain exceedingly valuable commodity in the popular *Dune* franchise).

"Humans need spice," we might be so bold to claim as a general principle. Humans need what they do not strictly speaking need, in order to live properly human lives. One might be tempted to say, from here, given the conceptual and semantic links we have just sketched, that humans need drugs as well. Both claims are complicated by the fact that, as we have already seen, strictly speaking these closely related concepts, spice and drug, only date back to the beginning of the modern period, and in particular to the standardization of commodities within the system of global trade. Nonetheless, even before the modern period, indeed deep into prehistory, we find significant evidence that human beings needed, let us say, "that extra something," whether in the form of bodily ornaments, or high-register poetic language, or intergenerational transmission of feast-day recipes, that strictly speaking are not required for survival.

If we can agree about what has been argued so far, we may now ask whether that "extra something" might also include altered states of consciousness. Is it an essential part of human life to experience other conscious states than the sober and lucid one?

In a very obvious sense, almost too obvious even to be noticed, the answer is a definite yes: we experience a radically altered state of consciousness for several hours in any typical twenty-four-hour period, which is simply to say we spend a good deal of time dreaming. The evolutionary biology and the phenomenology of dreaming remain surprisingly poorly understood. We know that it is common across a wide range of animal species, including insects, and while we have very little idea of what it is like to be, say, a mosquito, with only 250,000 or so neurons in its brain (as opposed to our hundred billion), we may reasonably conjecture that these simple creatures, too, have some need of alternating between the regular mode of waking perception and a different mode (again, whatever that may be like). So yes, human beings, and insects too, must, in view of the sort of beings they are, alternate between what passes for regular lucid perception and an alternative sort of perception where things appear otherwise.

But we must further ask whether, *beyond* this innate physiological alternation between waking and sleeping, human beings still need to experience altered consciousness during their periods of wakefulness. Here again, there is an affirmative answer that flows from recognition of facts almost too obvious to be noticed: daydreaming, reverie, flights of the imagination all seem to be intrinsic and necessary to the normal process of human cognitive development. The more you think about it in fact, the more our ideal state of totally lucid and sober consciousness begins to look like just that, an *ideal*, and something that we experience at best only fleetingly. Even when I am, say, giving an academic talk, or renewing my metro pass, or any number of other cognitive tasks that require a certain degree of sobriety, my mind is positively racing with subjective associations, peculiar memories, and an enduring power to overlay reality with tones and colors that are not strictly speaking there. One might be tempted to say that the dreamlike state is the norm throughout human life, waking or sleeping, while the sober and lucid state is one that we manage to conjure even in the midst of this neverending dream simply in order to accomplish our required tasks and not to make fools of ourselves in public. An ideal is something very different from a norm. The ideal guides our actions without necessarily characterizing them; the norm characterizes our condition as it in fact is.

Now that we have these affirmative answers, we might further ask: is it intrinsic to human thriving not only to sleep and dream for a good part of our day, and not only to inhabit a world of subjective tones and colorations when we are not sleeping, but also actively to seek out altered states of consciousness through the consumption of natural substances known to induce such states? The evidence suggests that for most people, in most places and times, supplementation or enhancement, by means of natural substances found in the environment, of our innate capacity to perceive the world through an altered state of consciousness, is intrinsic to the conduct of a full human life (with plenty of variation according to gender, age, and other determinants of social identity). According to some studies, the natural basis for human drug use far predates the emergence of human culture as we know it, and plays a role in early human evolution. Here, some researchers suggest, humans "may have evolved to counter-exploit plant neurotoxins."[11] Other studies suggest that the high prevalence of substance abuse among adolescent males makes good sense if we understand this behavior as a display of selective fitness: young men ingest poisons to show potential mates they can survive even the toughest ordeals. Sometimes this ingestion is followed not just by sickness but by an intense alteration of consciousness as well.[12]

In short, there might be some human societies that have no knowledge of such opportunities for counter-exploitation that nature has placed in our environments, but such behavior is common enough that we might dare to call it universal. And so we again have an affirmative answer: human beings, insofar as they are human beings, use drugs, though only in the broad sense of naturally occurring mind-altering substances, and not in the more precise sense of mind-altering substances rendered into global commodities.

To say that human beings, in so far as they are human beings, use drugs, just as they wear ornaments, engage in long-distance trade, make art and music, cook commensal meals, and so on, is not to say that they have historically been in altered states of consciousness all or most of the time, but only that intentionally altering consciousness is part of humanity's broad behavioral profile. In nearly all urban settings with written records, we also find evidence of substance abuse, of individuals who are blamed, punished, or ostracized for consuming too much of the given society's drugs of choice. It would be difficult to determine to what extent substance abuse was a problem for the traditional, mostly nonurban, and mostly nontextual societies from which the early modern global trade mostly acquired its knowledge of new botanical and fungal commodities. But in general it is safe to say that where there are no drugs—in the sense we have defined them, as emerging out of the context of modern trade—there is also, obviously, no drug abuse.

To be a drug fiend or a drug addict is to have a socially unacceptable, and often a medically harmful, dependency on a particular type of illicit or restricted commodity. Indeed the addict status is one that can itself shift along with the shift of a given modern commodity from one of the three categories we've identified to another of them. Many people whose cannabis habits twenty years ago would easily have placed them in a stigmatized group, as potheads, today simply blend into the crowd as they pick up their regular supplies from their local cannabis dispensaries. When

I was in New Jersey, I was even able to use my Princeton faculty ID for a 10 percent discount at the nearby dispensary. Everything was aboveboard, out in the open, pervaded by an air of almost unbelievable normalcy. And in the other direction, meanwhile, normal adult behavior in the United States in the 1950s, if we were to reproduce it today, would easily get many of us a reputation for being dangerously unhealthy binge drinkers and chain-smokers.

When we consider drugs from a comparative cross-cultural perspective, we often find that one and the same drug can be held to be calming in one culture and enlivening in another. In American culture it is generally thought that cannabis stifles clear thinking and stunts the potentials of those who use it; in Rastafarian culture the same drug is used in a ritual capacity, in the aim of transporting its users to what is experienced as a higher form of consciousness. As for alcohol, this is a substance to which several pairs of opposed adjectives can be easily applied. For one thing, it is both a depressant *and* perfect for celebrations. And the same might even go for coffee: when my father had insomnia, he used to go make a fresh pot, drink a hot cup of it filled with caffeine, and only then would he manage to fall asleep. Watching him do this made me aware at a young age of the tremendous gap between the values we associate with this or that food, drink, or drug on the one hand and the actual chemical properties of these substances and their actual physiological effects on the other.

One might suspect that it is at the level of values and cultural symbolism, more than at the level of physiological effects, that various substances get classified, variously, as drugs or foods or poisons in the first place. In a peculiar

1957 book entitled *Mushrooms, Russia, and History*, the American ethnobotanist R. Gordon Wasson and his Russian wife and collaborator, Valentina, describe the vast cultural difference between "mycophilic" cultures such as those of the Slavs, who love all fungi and do not even recognize the category of the toadstool, and the "mycophobic" cultures, notably the English, who over the centuries have often associated mushrooms not just with danger but also with feelings of guilt and shame.

These broad distinctions have certainly been confirmed anecdotally in my own experience as well, having spent significant portions of my life in both Eastern and Western Europe, in both the Slavic world and the Anglosphere. It was after all a group of young Russian women who first gave me psychoactive mushrooms, which they knew how to find in the wild, and which instilled in them no fear at all. The Slavs, to return to a term we used previously, continue to counter-exploit fungal toxins. Indeed doing so has become a key point of pride in Slavic folklore, cuisine, and other traditions. According to the Wassons, such highly charged relationships to this entire class of living beings, whether for or against, attest to the prevalence in European pre-Christian and pre-Roman history of a divine mushroom cult, centered on shamanic rites involving psychoactive fungus. This cult, the argument goes, has been more thoroughly eradicated in some parts of Europe than others. English mycophobia is not simply a cultural default setting, for the Wassons, but rather a symptom of repression.

In a follow-up 1968 work, *Soma: Divine Mushroom of Immortality*, R. Gordon Wasson argues, drawing on a vast body of philological evidence and taxonomical expertise, that the divine substance known in the ancient Indian *Rig Veda* as soma is in fact nothing other than the *Amanita muscaria* mushroom, better known as fly agaric. Unlike psilocybin mushrooms, and like ergot, fly agaric presents the particular challenge that it is highly toxic to human beings in its naturally occurring form, and in order to access the psychoactive substance one must first put the fungus through several elaborate stages of transformation. One common practice in Northeastern Siberia is to allow reindeer to eat the mushroom first, and then, sometime later, to drink the urine of the animal. While the fatal molecules in the fungus get broken down by the deer and do not come back out, the psychedelic ones do, and in this way reindeer urine provides several of the traditional cultures of Siberia with the chemical that is central to their shamanistic rites. It is significant also, of course, that the reindeer themselves seem to have sought out the fly agaric in the first place because they too enjoy the very same psychedelic substance, and unlike human beings they are not harmed by *Amanita muscaria* in its unbroken-down state. There are in fact many documented cases of so-called zoopharmacognosy throughout the world, in which animals know how to find the appropriate plant remedies for their own illnesses, and reindeer are not the only nonhuman animals to seek out mind-altering substances. Yet in North Asian reindeer-herding cultures, we do find a rare and remarkable thing taking place: communal, symbiotic interspecies tripping.

The Wassons' argument about cultural attitudes toward mushrooms, in any case, seems to me more or less compelling: determination of whether a given mushroom species is toxic and therefore forbidden (a "toadstool") cannot be made in any rational or consistent way simply in view of the chemical properties and physiological effects of a specimen. There are, after all, plenty of poisonous mushrooms that still find a way to get taken up and centered in human cultures. Wasson's book about Vedic soma had a significant impact when it was published, and among the people to reply critically to it was Claude Lévi-Strauss. The French anthropologist considers the evidence presented by Wasson that ancient Indian rituals, vision-quest practices of the Koryak people of Eastern Siberia, and the habit of the medieval Scandinavian berserkers transforming themselves into bears before racing into battle are connected by the use of *Amanita muscaria* across all of these cultural practices.

"Nothing permits one to exclude a priori," Lévi-Strauss writes, "the possibility that, in societies which differed as much as the Koryak and the Viking, the same drug was sought in order to produce opposite psychic effects."[13] Hallucinogens, he reflects, "do not harbor a natural message." Rather, they "release and amplify a latent discourse, which each culture holds in reserve, and the elaboration of which is made possible or easier by the drugs."

Our "latent discourses" today, to return to Lévi-Strauss's useful phrase, are shaped in large part by the promises of medical research and technological innovation. These are hoped to be able to deliver to us a form of life in the near future in which all the unfortunate kinks that were seen as intrinsic to our mortal condition will have been smoothed out. Even if we remain mortal—though some bright visionaries hope even to solve *that* problem—we may nonetheless hope to lead perfect lives free of health problems, mental anguish, precarity and insecurity, and so on. Not surprisingly, these latent discourses have worked their way into how we talk about psychedelics today. How we talk about them, namely, is, often, as a *solution* to a *problem*.

Unlike in the 1960s, our current psychedelic renaissance is girded by the extensive scientific literacy of many of its proponents, who can recite for you in great detail the chemical and neurological bases of a given type of experience of altered consciousness. Many of the new defenders of psychedelics can accurately cite the findings of studies that compare the efficacy of psychedelic drugs to that of SSRIs or of placebos in the treatment of depression and other disorders. (I am avoiding an approach like this in my own book; there is little reason at this point to add to the mountain of such contributions.) Yet many, while deeply informed as to data and findings, are nonetheless not clearheaded enough about the nature of their own advocacy to be able to identify the basic tension between, on the one hand, utilitarian arguments—psilocybin beats placebo in such and such percentage of cases—and, on the other hand, defenses of psychedelics based on their potential to deliver a transcendent experience. Such experience, plainly, cannot easily be entered into a classical utilitarian calculus to determine how much good it brings, which then may be weighed against the bad it also brings.

Overall, psychedelics users are, in line with other transformations in our culture, a good deal nerdier than they were in the past. I know more than one person today who can talk in detail about how they "source" their LSD, as if they were talking about free-range poultry or the hops in a small-batch microbrew. The new spirit of psychedelic exploration, as of so much else, is extremely information dense, and it reflects a desire on the part of its adepts to stay on top of things. Yet whether that is fully possible when it comes to psychedelic drugs is an important question and requires an approach learned from philosophical reflection more than from data science or nerdy connoisseurship. At issue, ultimately, is the problem of whether it is more useful to conceptualize psychedelic experience in *utilitarian* or *existential* terms.

I prefer the latter approach, as I believe it is vastly more adequate to the depth and complexity of the experience itself. To undertake such an experience is a radical leap, characterized by the fact that you do not know, and cannot know, what you're going to be like when you come out the other side. Will it have been worth it? Will the good have outweighed the bad? If you think you can answer these questions beforehand with any degree of certainty, if you think utilitarianism is entirely adequate to the problem, you may not be ready to take the psychedelic leap.

There is a line we see frequently on social media these days that distills down to its essence the sort of puzzle anyone asking such questions faces. That line says: "fuck around and find out." We are all very familiar with a variety of FAFO moments in life, where all of your utilitarian calculating proves supremely unuseful. Famously, Søren Kierkegaard thought religious faith was like this, which is why he insisted that in order to be a Christian one has to take the leap rather than endlessly weigh the reasons for and against such a personal transformation. More recently, a tendency has emerged under the banner of "analytic existentialism," which argues, for example, that having a child is also very much a FAFO affair (though its proponents typically do not use this language). You cannot possibly anticipate what parenthood will demand of you nor how it will transform you, so just quit deliberating, the thought goes. Taking psychedelic drugs, one might argue, is more like having children in this regard than it is like, say, taking out a mortgage.

In many domains of life we are used to resorting to *both* sorts of reasoning in our decision-making processes. For example, a high school graduate who has been accepted at a hometown university in the Midwest and also at NYU may have deep personal dreams of the unpredictably amazing things that will happen to her in the big city, but nonetheless choose to argue the New York option to her parents in terms of class size, lots of offerings in her major, and so forth. This is a standard sort of strategic flexibility that deliberators bring to complex decisions, and we should not expect that those who are trying to decide whether to take psychedelics should demonstrate greater consistency, or perhaps only greater rigidity, than those who are trying to decide where to go to college. However, unlike the case of the college-bound daughter, in the case of psychedelics we are dealing, potentially, not with two different levels of approach but rather with two forms of justification that are in tension with one another, that threaten to weaken each other, and therefore to weaken the prospects for the normalization of psychedelic experience in the long run.

A psychedelic experience is very much like having children, at least in the salient respects spelled out by L. A. Paul, within an analytic existentialist framework, in a now-classic 2015 article about the latter sort of transformative experience entitled "What You Can't Expect When You're Expecting."[14] Both experiences will change you; in neither of the experiences are you much in control of the *way* they change you, and once you have taken the leap you must resign yourself to transformations that are beyond your control. Both are potentially a source of great meaning that may have proved elusive in other domains of life, even if both are also, potentially, the source of great desolation and sorrow upon the discovery of their inability to deliver the meaning that had been so greatly hoped for from them. Will you end up with crippling post-partum depression? Will you have a nightmarishly bad trip on LSD? There is no way to know beforehand.

However, having children, like consuming mind-altering substances, is an act the significance of which is largely shaped by culture. When people start to give utilitarian reasons for having children, these may sound cynical in our contemporary social and economic reality, yet for much of human history these reasons would have come across as self-evidently compelling: one has children to help with the farmwork, or in the hope of fetching an attractive brideprice, or of continuing the noble bloodline. The transformative dimension of parenthood in recent generations, perhaps especially for fathers, is in no small part a result of recent transformations of domestic life, of the nuclear family, and even of the cultural meaning of childhood. For most of human history, even if parenthood involved some "phenomenal outcomes," it was seldom for the sake of these that people had children.

Some current rhetoric around the potentials of psychedelic drugs would have them fill the role currently held by antidepressants in the SSRI class. There is today widespread concern about some of the reported undesirable side effects of SSRIs, such as long-term sexual dysfunction, and for years there has been concern about the apparent inability of SSRIs to outperform placebos in some much-discussed studies. But whether these concerns are justified or not, it is important to stress that SSRIs were never intended to blow your mind, to give you any sort of high or to show you reality in a radically different light. The standard run of antidepressants has been intended only to *return* your mind to where it was supposed to be, according to some imagined ideal, to restore it to the factory settings of human consciousness and subjectivity.

Could something as transformative as psychedelic drugs really be turned to such a normalizing end, effectively the opposite of what they were touted for in the psychedelic revolution of the 1960s? This turn seems already to be happening, as suggested by a 2023 article in *The Atlantic* by Richard A. Friedman entitled "What If Psychedelics' Hallucinations Are Just a Side Effect?"[15] Citing a wide variety of specialists, Friedman argues that there are mental health benefits to be had from psychedelic drugs, and that these are best obtained by microdosing the drugs at a level where the trip experience does not occur. The fact that psychedelics *can* be microdosed without hallucination, and with evident mental health benefits for the microdoser, is surely interesting and important. But what we seem to be seeing here is an active intervention in how we talk about psychedelics, which may ultimately result in a significant transformation of what we once thought was the thing itself, the essential quality of the drug that was being sought out wherever the drug was sought out, into a mere negative consequence of the drug's misuse.

If this discursive intervention were to succeed, it would offer a vivid example of the power of language and culture to shape the way the things in the world around us get classified. Such examples abound in the history and philosophy of science. For example, the philosopher of biology John Dupré has argued that, until the mid-nineteenth century, whales were fish.[16] What brought about their taxonomic shift at that time was of course not any change in cetacean phylogeny, but rather a new decree, dictating for the first time in history that no viviparous, milk-producing, warm-blooded animal can *also* be a fish. That this was a decision, and not a recognition of objective facts imposed by nature, becomes clear when we learn that "fish" is only a vaguely defined category, and indeed there are some animals, such as the coelacanth and other lobe-finned species, that are still recognized as fishes today but that are closer evolutionally to mammals, including to whales, than they are to the ray-finned fish such as tuna. The world itself, then, never *forced* us to reclassify whales as non-fish.

Similarly, when it comes to side effects versus desired effects, classifications that may look self-evident to us may also, upon inspection, end up having a distinct history in which decisions were made by human beings that could indeed have gone another way. The therapeutic imperative is to use psychedelics to bring people who are out of sync with their lives back into sync, to return them to an imagined baseline from which they have somehow deviated. This baseline, it is presumed, is one that a "normal" person can be expected to maintain without any special chemical supplements. Setting aside the question whether there really are such normal people at all, we may also ask on what grounds such a normal person might not also benefit from a mind-blowing psychedelic experience. The therapeutic approach, pushed to its limit, conceptualizes the drug as a compensation for a lack, a return to zero from some negative level. But what if the virtue of psychedelics is that they can add a real good to the life of a person who does *not* live with any particular sense of lack?

At least in the extreme formulation offered by Friedman, the hallucinatory experience, the trip, is not even considered something that might itself contribute to a person's thriving and is instead reclassified as an undesirable side effect of a treatment that can help a person to thrive, ideally, in the same way as normal people who do not use psychedelics thrive. In a more moderate formulation, the therapeutic argument for psychedelics does not seem so paradoxical: if something that blows your mind in megadoses simply causes you to see the world in a somewhat more beautiful and satisfying light when taken in microdoses, surely this is worth taking seriously and pursuing in scientific research and in new cultural practices. But if the therapeutic vindication of psychedelics requires, as part of its rhetorical strategy, a further stigmatization of the mind-blowing experience of macrodosing, then we may wonder whether the new psychedelic renaissance is not threatening to deprive us of the drugs' true powers. Why should one not also wish to have one's mind blown, to have the sort of psychedelic experience we have already characterized as an existential leap, even if, or perhaps especially if, prior to that, one is not suffering from any particular mental anguish?

The rhetorical strategies we observe surrounding the use of psychedelics in the twenty-first century closely mirror what we see in other domains of cultural innovation. With technological innovation in particular, it is nearly always the case that potential medical applications are highlighted much more consistently than, let us say, the more destabilizing potentials of the new technology. The promise of nanotech cameras, for example, is sold to us on the expectation that these devices might revolutionize surgery, and not that they will revolutionize surveillance or war. Quantum computing is hailed as potentially bringing about a revolution in drug discovery, as if this were a knockdown reason to pursue it, even if the other applications of quantum computing would radically transform our economic and political reality beyond recognition, and beyond anything we could possibly predict. A sober-eyed and zoomed-out view will quickly reveal that every innovation has done some good and done some harm (as Leonard Cohen once sang of shooting heroin), has solved some problems and generated some new ones. But when it comes to traditional cultural practices, including drugs used in ritual contexts, and to their new chemical synthesis and manufacture in a context distant from their original botanical usage, we may have some cause for worry, or at least skepticism, when we see them being promoted primarily as quasi-medical balms or as part of a therapeutic treatment program. It may be that psychedelic drugs are inherently a bringer of destabilization rather than of normalization, of creating trouble through unpredictable existential transformation where there had not been any before.

We have already clearly seen these arguments well played out in the case of cannabis. It is safe to say that the movement for marijuana's legalization could not have succeeded if it had not built upon the initial momentum of arguments for the drug's medical use. In this case, as now with psychedelics, there has often been a practical taboo on so much as acknowledging that the experience of altered consciousness itself might be desirable, might even contribute to the greater thriving of a person. If you are defending your own cannabis use to a group of peers, you will probably come out looking better, even in this era of wide acceptance, if you appeal to the drug's power to help you sleep or to relieve joint pain than to its power to collapse time or to make you imagine you can remember the big bang. Such a prohibition, and the rhetoric of therapy and wellness built up to get around it, continue to presuppose the rational, sober-minded modern subject as the ideal, just as we see in Descartes and Locke some centuries ago. With such an ideal, we are only able to acknowledge the legitimacy of deviations from it in cases where someone is falling short of it and needs to be repaired or retuned by extreme interventions.

But in their premodern usage in the context of Indigenous practices, no such ideal subject was taken for granted. People took drugs *in order to* access dimensions of reality that were ordinarily closed off to them: to shake things up. It is reasonable to suspect that we moderns, who are expected to perform sober-minded rationality at most hours of most days, are no less in need of access to these other dimensions. Whatever happens at the legislative and medical-institutional levels, there will likely always be people who wish to take drugs as an expression of the primal need to break out of their usual social roles, and who will not be content to take them simply to get recalibrated and back in line.

If psychedelics are vindicated in terms of their therapeutic benefits, which is to say their power to return their users to a normal operational state in the same way SSRIs have long been touted as doing for the clinically depressed, then it is hard to see how their potential for bringing about existential transformation, or tremendous and unpredictable changes that potentially cause their users to abandon earlier conceptions of what is to count as normal, could continue to have much purchase.

To some extent, the tension between these two approaches could be accommodated by a measured pluralism, advocating small doses for people who want to use psychedelics to return them to a settled idea of normalcy and large doses for people who want to have their sense of normalcy exploded. My own worry is that social pressure and political pragmatism will result in a sacrifice of the existential-transformative to the therapeutic-normative, indeed going so far, as in the *Atlantic* article, as to see the reality-warping effects of higher dosages of psychedelics simply as harmful side effects akin to the nausea that accompanies chemotherapy, and to reject the earlier presumption that LSD is meant to blow our minds with the same supercilious correctitude that has long made us see as unscientific and ignorant those in the past who took whales for a kind of fish. No one ever took drugs to experience nausea, even if one often knows that the drugs one is taking will make one nauseous. It is at least plausible that in the future the altered consciousness that accompanies the consumption of psychedelics will be so stigmatized that it will be experienced, or avoided, as if it were a condition as undesirable as nausea. If this were to happen, we would find that the commonly understood function of psychedelics has been suppressed for the sake of assimilation to the medical-therapeutic regime that governs the circulation of pharmaceutics in the modern world. The plants and fungi with their psychoactive chemical compounds will have been decisively transformed into drugs, in the sense that emerged only in the past few centuries. Psychedelic substances will, under such circumstances, have been domesticated. And as with wild boars and wolves, their domestication will make them more approachable, but it will also lead to the loss of their fangs.

On TikTok, I've recently stumbled onto the accounts of Americans who have gone to South America to participate in ayahuasca retreats that were sold to them on the promise of helping them to cure themselves of their unconscious racism. Some of the videos relate reasons why, for the experimenters, this proved to be a shortsighted plan: you enter into it with the very concrete and utilitarian aim of moral improvement, relative to the very specific cultural and political context of a single country at a particular moment in history, and you end up, as one user put it, having to do battle for what feels like a trillion eons against a horde of six-dimensional demons.

This is surely just one way of describing the phenomenal content of a typical ayahuasca experience, but it gets at a very real problem. Those six-dimensional demons, whatever they were, did not have anything at all to do with the racism the user was hoping to overcome, or with the history of ethnic conflict and inequality in the country the user had arrived from. It is not on that level, *at all*, that ayahuasca goes to work on the psyche. The user went into it thinking of the experience largely in medical-therapeutic terms, as a sort of minor cosmetic surgery for the soul that would eliminate old bad habits of character, somewhat in the way one has moles removed by laser. And what happened instead is that the experience drew out depths of the person that could not possibly be accounted for in terms of prior conceptual categories, including those shaped by ethnic prejudice or indeed political ideology of any sort. Thus the X user known as Landshark comments: "'Ayahuasca' is insane because it appears to be one of the most legitimately dangerous drugs with the potential to gigafry your brain but is exclusively taken by literal turbonormies who unironically want to like 'heal internalized racism trauma' and basically get oneshotted by it." We can skip over some of the extremely online turns of phrase here; what is important, what Landshark indeed gets right, is that the turbonormies—the normal salaried, educated, and presumably white Americans—who are turning to ayahuasca are in effect mistaking a highly charged and dangerous vehicle of radical transformation for a simple therapeutic procedure.

Ayahuasca is now being approached by many average people as a substance somewhere at the boundary between the medical-therapeutic and the recreational, but at least some of the users who approach it in this way end up floored by the insistence of the ayahuasca itself to be taken seriously as a charged and significant sacrament. Our categories are largely up to us, even if, sometimes, the world kicks back and makes its own case for where we should slot this or that natural substance. You can try to make ayahuasca fun or educational or therapeutic or some combination of these. But it is always going to be much, much more than that.

CHAPTER FIVE

MORE THAN A FEELING?

René Descartes, with whom we are by now quite familiar, got himself into no small trouble with his dualist theory of body and mind, according to which these two substances are absolutely distinct and operate by entirely different rules. Some of his critics immediately picked up on one problem in particular: if mind and body have nothing at all in common, how could they possibly interact? The difficulty of finding a solution to this challenge is perhaps best evidenced by the weakness of the one Descartes ended up proposing: he hypothesized that it is the pineal gland at the base of the brain that serves as the "seat of the soul," the one locus where the ordinary mutual exclusion of thinking substance and bodily substance is suspended, where physical signals may be converted into mental ones and vice versa.

In offering this unsatisfactory solution, Descartes was, likely unawares, joining up with a long history of appreciation for the purported powers of that small organ. This is the same gland that is identified as the third eye in various Indian mystical and medical traditions. And "third eye" is indeed a good description of what it is: the organ, among other things, that serves in reptiles as the parietal photoreceptor responsible for regulating an animal's circadian rhythm. Descartes's argument as to *why* the pineal gland must be the point at which mental causes and physical causes are converted into one another—for example, you stub your toe, and a signal travels upward, enters the gland, and comes back out of it as a conscious experience of pain—is, to say the least, unconvincing. He believes it plays this role since it is the only part of the brain that has more the shape of a simple marble than of an object composed from two discrete halves.

The pineal gland is also noteworthy for its role in sleep and dreaming, and may even have the power to synthesize small quantities of DMT. Whether it does so or not, it certainly produces melatonin, and in this way is centrally implicated in the onset of sleep. Without knowledge of the precise chemicals at work, the role of the gland in inducing in us what we might call "other forms of seeing" is plausibly something that was noticed in ancient Indian medicine and physiology. It is also plausible that Descartes's own interest in this body part reflects the downstream influence of Indian tradition in European medicine of the early modern period.

Endogenous DMT has been found in small amounts in the brains of rats, and in principle there is no good scientific reason to exclude the possibility of an animal species whose brain constantly, or at intervals, produces large amounts of it or of another psychoactive compound. Let us therefore imagine one. Of course, if we include serotonin and other familiar neurotransmitters among psychoactive substances, then we really do not have to imagine all that hard. We only have to consider ourselves as we actually are. But let's go further. Let's imagine a species, in most other respects much like us, yet with the surprising physiological twist that over the course of its entire life it synthesizes copious amounts of a psychoactive compound similar in its effects to LSD.

It is of course hard to see, from an evolutionary point of view, how such an adaptation might be selectively advantageous, indeed how it could be anything other than disastrous. The life of any such creature, one has to imagine, would be ecstatically amazing, and also terribly short. But let us simply suppose that there is at least one evolutionary pathway along which such an adaptation would make sense, which is to say that it would enhance the environmental fitness of the species that follows it. Certainly, any group of intelligent beings subject to the constant florid hallucinations typical of an LSD experience would have a social reality and a built environment very different from our own. It is certain also that their collective belief system would be very different from ours, for example their moral principles and their philosophical ideas about the nature of reality.

Now let us imagine that, notwithstanding the fact that they are constantly tripping, this group's scientists somehow figure out how experimentally to reduce the amount of this LSD-like compound in the brains of patients (their ethical commitments being different from ours, let us imagine that they face no administrative obstacles in experimenting on subjects of their own species). From certain subjects they manage to eliminate the compound altogether. These subjects subsequently report the most remarkable transformations in their conscious experience. They say that external objects soon cease spontaneously to change shape, to breathe and heave, to take on personalities, to speak to them, to reassure them or to threaten them. They say that it comes to seem to them that they are no longer nearly so intimately connected to other things and beings in the world, visible and invisible, but now have retreated into what they puzzlingly describe as their "own bodies." There still seem to be a few other conscious beings surrounding them, namely other individuals of their own species, but even with these other beings they can now only enter into intertwined consciousness when they are in direct physical or verbal contact with them. The world seems practically empty, the patients say. They even report that they lose all awareness of their existence prior to the recent birth of the bodies with which they now identify.

Many of the patients report that while this is a horrible experience, it also seems to them to reveal some deep truth about the true nature of reality. Some of these former experimental subjects begin to write books, to go on lecture tours, and to form new cults, trying to convince their fellow species members that they have been enlightened, indoctrinated into alarming new truths that most of their kind have never even suspected. The enlightenment they describe turns out to look very much like the commonsense reality of a typical lucid and undrugged human being such as you or I.

Suppose in turn that yet another species of intelligent beings arrives on the scene, perhaps from some faraway star system. This one has a sensory apparatus entirely different from both our own and from the LSD-brained species we've just encountered. This third sort of being senses the world entirely through chemoreceptors, has an ontology in which nothing exists other than molecules and their constituent atoms, and is very, very good at science. These third beings—who have no ethical commitments at all, and even if they did, these would not extend to other species—collect a few subjects from both the human and the LSD-brained humanlike species, and they take them back to their spaceship for study. Soon enough they devise a chemically mediated way to learn of the beliefs of these different sorts of being. They discover that the LSD-brained species believes in a world that swarms with visible and invisible beings, that pulsates with abstract forces these beings describe as "love" and "harmony" and "unity." Next they discover that the other beings, the humans, also believe in these forces, but they express considerably more skepticism as to their presence at all places and in all times in the universe. The humans also believe in many other peculiar abstract forces of which neither the chemoreceptive nor the LSD-brained beings have any idea, such as private property, bodily integrity, monetary value, and table manners.

The advanced beings conclude their studies and write up a report, observing that both the humans and the LSD-brained beings have very different neurochemical compositions, and as a result apprehend the world very differently from one another. Both, the report sums up, pass their lives in a perpetual delirium, which is nothing like the scientific objectivity their own species has attained.

The purpose of this thought experiment should be evident. From an external and impartial point of view, there is simply no good reason to extend laurels to the human beings for getting things right while withholding them from the LSD-brained beings. A corollary is that we cannot simply distinguish, as the old public service ad on US television used to do, between a "brain on drugs" and a brain that is not on drugs. *All* brains are on drugs, to the extent that all brains rely on a complex system of hormones, neurotransmitters, and other chemicals simply to apprehend the world at all, and different combinations of these chemical substances will result in different apprehensions. There simply is no chemical-free apprehension of the world, and which chemicals you naturally end up with will significantly shape your apprehension of the nature of reality. Even if you develop an advanced scientific method that enables you to "get around" your chemicals, as human beings have done in recent centuries with the naturalization of our "official" ontology (that is, the broad image of reality presupposed in scientific research), you will still remain committed to the existence of at least some things—for example, the transcendence of love, perhaps, or the moral status of individual humans, or artistic genius, or the preferability of designer labels over knock-off brands—that no scientific instrument can or ever will be able to account for.

This is not necessarily any reason to think that someone who is on LSD—not a permanently LSD-brained being but just an ordinary human being like us who has swallowed a tab and is currently taking a little trip—is just as right about the nature of reality as we are. But the thought experiment can at least help us to start reconsidering what sort of accomplishment we judge getting reality right to be. We might now, in particular, be more inclined to adopt a pragmatist cast of mind, and to attempt to decouple "being right" from "having the appropriate relation to reality itself." Instead, along classical pragmatist lines, "getting things right," where "things" is intended as neutrally as possible, is simply a matter of proceeding in such a way that the world puts up as little resistance to your projects as possible.

You're "right," on such a pragmatic approach, not because your beliefs are "veridical"—to return to a technical term I have introduced already and that will be central to the discussion in the following section—but because they work. Again, it is hard to see how a species that has evolved to have LSD brains could consistently have "beliefs that work," beliefs that enable its members to move through the world long enough and successfully enough to reproduce and to pass on their genes. But we also know that evolution has tried many different strategies across the biotic kingdom, and often we see that even the most implausible ones end up working out somewhere or other. And maybe we ourselves, with our astounding capacity to enjoy music, to contemplate the lives of angels, to discern or to conjure between this sort of meat and that sort of wine esoteric affinities that are held to ground their pairing in objective fact, are quite a bit more like the LSD-brained beings than we are ordinarily able or willing to see.

In his 1956 work *Analysis of Perception*, the British neuroscientist, psychiatrist, and philosopher J. R. Smythies offers a fascinating philosophical account of his extensive research on human subjects under the influence of mescaline. He engages, in particular, with the difficult problem of the relationship between what he calls the hallucinatory and veridical varieties of perception, and seeks to complicate our ordinary view that these are necessarily opposed to one another. That is, he calls into question what he sees as our too-facile idea that for something to be hallucinated is for that very reason to be nonexistent, and in turn for belief in its existence to be false. "People who are actually having hallucinatory experiences under optimal conditions (i.e. when they are not also confused, insane or ill)," Smythies writes, "frequently cannot be persuaded that their experiences are in any sense unreal. At least that is our experience in the large number of experiments we have conducted giving hallucinogenic agents to ordinary and (philosophically) sophisticated people."[1]

Smythies goes on to note that at least in some cases, the patient experiences a state of "derealization," which Smythies describes as a disorder of perception "in which the visual field loses its normal 'concrete reality' and everything appears vague, shadowy, distant, indifferent, unreal." He cites, by way of contrast, reports of other instances of mescaline use that are accompanied by "a very lively reality," and he concludes in light of this that "the factors which determine whether ordinary people call their experiences real or unreal do not necessarily depend on whether their experiences are veridical or hallucinatory." In brief, Smythies argues that veridicality and reality are not the same thing: a person can have an experience of hallucinations that is accompanied by an unshakeable judgment of their reality, and can also have an experience of sense-data corresponding to external physical objects in which these are experienced as unreal. The external world is not the final arbiter of reality and unreality here; it is, rather, *the quality of the experience itself* that plays this role.

In the course of his argument for this surprising view, Smythies considers a distinction made by the philosopher A. J. Ayer, who in his *Foundations of Empirical Knowledge* of 1940 argues that hallucinations and dreams may be deemed "delusional" to the extent that "they do not fit into the general order of our experience," and to the extent that hallucinations, unlike veridical perceptions, are not "substantiated by further sense experiences."[2] Smythies is worried about the distinction Ayer is seeking to make here, since, as he explains, "the same criteria Ayer uses to distinguish between hallucinatory and veridical sense-experience may be used to classify hallucinatory sense-experience itself."[3] That is, for Smythies, if veridical experience is deemed, beyond its veridicality, to be real, this will be in virtue of the way it fits into the general order of our experience. But hallucinatory experience might either fit or fail to fit into the general order of experience, and can accordingly be deemed either real or unreal. Here the attribution of reality is not the same thing as attribution of veridicality, since in the case of at least some attributions of reality there is no question of the external existence of a physical object causing the experience. These are perhaps subtle distinctions, and the technical definitions of the terms involved may be somewhat resistant to our mastery. Yet they are key for understanding both Smythies's worry, and my own, about the hasty dismissal philosophers have often made of the sensory presentations that come to us under the influence of psychedelic drugs.

Smythies writes of mescaline that it "produces marked changes in perception, sensation, feeling, in some cases thinking, and in the relation between the ego and its environment, some of which changes are so remarkable as to defy description." The visions associated with the experience often possess "the utmost poetical integrity." He describes an early phase in which a subject experiences hallucinations of "mosaics, networks, flowing arabesques, interlaced spirals, wonderful tapestries of all sorts," followed soon by a parade of "great butterflies gently moving their wings, fields of glittering jewels, silver birds flying through silver forests, golden fountains and golden rain, masks, statues, fabulous animals, soaring architecture, gardens, cities, and finally human figures and fully formed scenes where coherent histories are enacted." He notes that if the subject opens his or her eyes, the hallucinated scenes might cease, but the veridical objects in one's perceptual field will appear "much more intense, deep, rich, and glowing," as they "change their shape in curious and pleasing ways."

Smythies also does something virtually no other scientifically inclined philosopher of his era dared to do: he describes *his own* experience on mescaline: "I myself was astounded by the heightened sparkle and glow of a wonderful mellow inner light that some wine-glasses in a cabinet developed." We see, here, Smythies offering up a rare exception to the general prohibition on auto-experimentation. As far as I have been able to determine, he is among the only Anglophone philosophers of a broadly analytic orientation to have written about their own experience on psychedelic drugs at any point between 1950 and 1975. He is an exceptional case, moreover, in that he is also a neuroscientist and a psychiatrist.

Smythies insists, in a 1953 article, three years before the appearance of the book I have been citing, that visions produced by mescaline differ from those of everyday experience "only in their superior aesthetic quality and because they correspond to no object in the common physical world."[4] In his view two distinct conceptual issues arise from such visions. First: "Why should a brain which cannot utilize glucose properly produce such interesting phenomena?" Second: "How may these visions be related in their internal three-dimensional spatio-temporal structure to the electrical patterns in the cortex, which possess an entirely different spatio-temporal structure determined by the complex convoluted shape of the cortex?" These features of the brain alone, Smythies concludes, "would . . . render these phenomena worthy of the most careful considerations by philosophers." Indeed, until very recently, Smythies's admonition has gone mostly unheeded.

Smythies, to sum up, suggests that psychedelic experience should cause us to rethink the sort of analysis proposed by Ayer, which is indeed deeply rooted in the tradition of modern philosophy extending back to Descartes. In this analysis, there is a sharp distinction between the veridical and the hallucinated, while the real can only ever be associated with the first of these. He observes that in many cases the experience of derealization happens to people who are precisely *not* hallucinating but are rather beholding the physical objects that are causing their perceptions. But it can also happen that a person is hallucinating wildly under the influence of mescaline, yet nonetheless feels very strongly that what they are perceiving is real simply to the extent that it, to use Ayer's language, "fits into the general order of our experience." That is, there are at least some hallucinations that we do not experience as obstacles to truth, knowledge, or the conduct of life.

In Smythies's analysis, reality is not itself grounded in

the causal power of external objects to bring about in us a perception of them. Reality is rather a sort of quality, or if you will a lens, through which the perceiver filters the perception of external objects. An external object might lose its reality, not by materially decomposing but by ceasing to be endowed with the meaning-packed force it once had. This seems like an unusual phenomenon when we present it as the result of drug-induced perception. But in fact it is a quite common and familiar experience for most of us, even without drugs.

For example, consider a Christian who loses his faith and at some later point happens upon a crucifix. This object might now seem a pale shadow of what he used to perceive prior to his loss of faith. In relationships with other people, similarly, we are very familiar with an analogous shift in perception that happens when a person falls out of love, and in beholding the former object of their love now sees only a regular flesh and blood human who is no longer exceptionally attractive or charismatic or worthy of attention. Falling out of love really is a sort of death and rebirth, a transition into a radically new and different reality. These varieties of partial or domain-specific derealization are, quite common in the course of a human life. The somewhat rarer condition of the mental patient who experiences comprehensive derealization, in Smythies's account, is one in which the precipitous loss of meaning in the crucifix or in the object of romantic love extends to absolutely everything in the field of their experience.

This more comprehensive sort of psychedelic derealization, where the world is suddenly stripped of meaning, has sometimes been compared to the experience of psychosis. It may also be compared to the successful exercise of Husserlian bracketing, as we have previously seen. In such bracketing, a person strives to attend to the bare contents of their perceptions, without attaching to any of the objects perceived any particular concepts or definition: one tries, for example, to perceive a tree, without in so doing thinking the concept "tree" (give it a try, it's harder than it sounds!). Perhaps the most famous literary attempt to capture the spirit of bracketing is found in Jean-Paul Sartre's 1938 novella *Nausea*. The protagonist, Roquentin, undertakes an informal meditation upon the roots of a chestnut tree he happens to notice. The longer he stares at them, the sharper his attention becomes, and, correspondingly, the less the roots appear to be the ordinary and particular sort of worldly entity he had previously presumed they were:

> All at once the veil is torn away, I have understood, I have *seen*. . . . The roots of the chestnut tree sank into the ground just beneath my bench. I couldn't remember it was a root anymore. Words had vanished and with them the meaning of things, the ways things are to be used, the feeble points of reference which men have traced on their surface. I was sitting, stooping over, head bowed, alone in front of this black, knotty lump, entirely raw, frightening me. Then I had this vision. It took my breath away. Never, up until these last few days, had I suspected the meaning of "existence."[5]

Compare here a superficially similar passage from William Gaddis's 1955 novel *The Recognitions*. His protagonist, the troubled painter and art forger Wyatt Gwyon, has just returned from a special exhibit in New York of an unnamed Picasso painting. He describes his encounter with it as a rare instance of "seeing freely":

> When I saw it, it was one of those moments of reality, of near-recognition of reality. . . . When I saw it all of a sudden everything was freed, into one recognition, really freed into reality that we never see, you never see it. You don't see it in paintings because most of the time you can't see beyond a painting. Most paintings, the instant you see them they become familiar, and then it's too late. . . . That's why people can't keep looking at Picasso and expect to get anything out of his paintings, and people, no wonder so many people laugh at him. You can't see them any time, just any time, because you can't see freely very often, hardly ever, maybe seven times in a life.[6]

"Seven times in a life": this might in fact be a pretty good estimate, also, of the ideal number of times to have a psychedelic experience. And in such an experience, as in the one Gwyon describes, you might also have the impression that you have been "freed into reality that we never see." What Gaddis describes is something like aesthetic intuition, and it is surely something quite rare. It is also, unlike Roquentin's experience, sooner an edifying one than a horrifying one. Roquentin sees past the appearances and into the great nothingness at the heart of existence. Gwyon sees past the outer forms of things and comes away exhilarated, having caught a glimpse of the hidden reality with which, one might imagine, the genius Picasso was in constant communion.

For Roquentin, bare existence itself, when it ceases to

be this or that sort of tree, this or that beloved person or object of religious veneration, can easily come across as unreal. Reality, one might say, begins to return only when we *stop* seeing the world so intensely as it is. In this respect, far from it being the case that hallucination is an obstacle to perceiving reality, it may well be that some amount of hallucination is positively required for perceptions to come across as real at all. But this counterintuitive insight can only make sense if we have first uncoupled the notions of veridicality, or causal connection to external physical objects, on the one hand, and reality on the other.

It may be that psychedelic hallucinations are experienced as irregular, and are capable of misleading us about the nature of reality, only because we do not, or most of us do not, regularly consume psychedelic drugs. Unlike the LSD-brained beings we imagined above, psychedelic hallucination is unfamiliar to most human beings alive today, who in many jurisdictions remain limited in their options for obtaining psychedelic substances to doing business with criminal drug dealers. It is likely that increased familiarity with the effects of psychedelic drugs can enable a user to correct, at least to some extent, for distortions in the visual field much as we correct for the apparently oblong shape of a coin seen at an angle or the crooked appearance of a reed sticking out of water.

Moreover, it may be incorrect to say that we have no prior experience of such oddities as appear to us under the influence of psychedelic drugs. Any toddler watching a cartoon can make immediate and natural sense of, say, a stalk of celery that has a face and walks around on two feet and does humanlike things. It is not that the child fails to recognize that the being in question is a vegetable, or does not know the limited range of what vegetables are capable of. It is, rather, that we come into this world more or less primed to discern agential behavior all around us, to make sense of the world as an animistic swarm of beings that are more or less like us in most relevant respects. It is only when we grow older that we learn not to think in that way. But even as adults, if we find ourselves hallucinating, say, an anthropomorphic stalk of celery, this is not exactly like seeing a square circle or a colorless green dream. It is, rather, something for which we have a deep repository of similar experiences extending back to our earliest childhood.

It is not clear moreover that even the most unusual or unfamiliar psychedelic hallucinations have the power to mislead the person who experiences them into taking reality as being otherwise than it is. Smythies for his part insists that it would be a mistake to interpret his own experience of beauty and poetic integrity while under the influence of mescaline as a species of mental derangement akin to drunkenness. One crucial difference is that on mescaline there is typically "no interference with the powers of careful observation and objective reporting."[7] Instead, "these inspected events are quite simply extremely beautiful." Under the influence of mescaline, perception is altered mostly in that one's capacity to appreciate the beauty of the things one sees is significantly heightened. The mescaline user seems at each moment of the experience very much able to "correct for" the hallucinations, to comprehend the difference between what is seen and what is there.

Finally, it may be argued that describing psychedelic experience as primarily hallucination, and hallucination as a sort of systematic misperception, fails to account for the significant difference in actual experience between the perception of, say, the oblong-appearing coin on the one hand and the lapsed believer's perception of the crucifix or the spurned lover's perception of the ex-girlfriend's apartment window on the other. These latter are cases where a person is seeing more than other people would be willing to grant is actually there. The perception is charged up with emotion and significance, far beyond what could be explained to a bystander who might innocently ask what the big deal is, why this curious soul is staring so intently at the cross or at the window. What the person is perceiving in these cases involves neither confusion about external reality nor any conscious awareness of the bridgeable gap between the way things are and the way they appear. Rather, the lapsed believer and the spurned lover are perceiving the same objects as the atheist or the aromantic would (a cross, a window), but these objects belong, in another sense, to different worlds for each of their respective perceivers. Worlds, in the sense we are understanding this term here, may well perfectly overlap with one another. What makes them distinct are the different ways different moods determine the quality of experience within them.

Psychedelic experience, I maintain, is generally more like the believer's perception of a crucifix or the spurned lover's perception of a beloved's bedroom window than it is either like the illusion of a crooked reed or an oblong coin, or yet like the full-fledged hallucination often associated with psychosis, in which the subject fully believes in the veridical nature of the objects perceived. The reality of the worlds experienced under the influence of psychedelic drugs is much more a quality or mood of the experience itself than a judgment of veridicality, or of the external independent existence of the objects of perception. From the point of view of a person in the midst of a psychedelic experience, the question of the independent existence of the causes of one's perceptions can often seem to be the *least* interesting thing to spend one's time contemplating. "Who cares?!" one might find oneself thinking. "I'm just letting the experience itself carry me along!"

What is it to be carried along into a different world? Take again the example of love. This does not have to be deep, abiding, mature love. In fact, an intense adolescent crush might do *better* to help illustrate the point. Imagine you are sixteen years old again, and you are absolutely obsessed with some kid in your class, but he or she scarcely knows you exist. You drive by that kid's home, and as you pass you almost have the sensation of shockwaves emanating from the place. The house is practically glowing, radiating something, and no one could possibly convince you that it exists only inside of you, in your mere subjective experience. The character of this feeling, which seems most intense in adolescence but surely has its analogs and echoes later in life, is precisely that *even if* there is nothing about the physical world that differentiates this house from all the houses surrounding it, this only confirms that there is a reality deeper than the physical world.

As with the other world that can be disclosed in aesthetic experience or in psychedelic experience, recognition of the reality of the "world of love," indeed submission to it, does not entail any affirmation of the real existence of some entity or force not recognized by natural science. To believe in love is thus very different from believing in, say, fairies or Sasquatch, in that it does not require the believer simply to add another entity to their ontology, that is, to their final, definitive list of things that exist in this world. A naturalist's ontology thus typically includes electrons, might include whales and furniture (though these might also be analyzed down to their subatomic constituents), but does not include unicorns or perpetual motion machines. Love, I want to say, is like neither whales nor bigfoot, as commitment to its reality does not depend on finding instances of it in the empirical world, traces or smudges of love that one might discover as one would discover a clump of Sasquatch hair brushed off on the side of a tree.

The strict naturalist will have at least some difficulty accounting for abstract notions such as justice or irony, but can usually find a way to shoehorn these into their naturalism if they make a little effort. But love, as we are characterizing it here, does not seem to be a candidate for inclusion on the list at all. It is not experienced so much as a thing *in* the world but instead as the force that gives the world its general shape, the force that makes this world the world it is rather than another. When we experience love in this way, we do not add it to our ontology, along with bosons, armchairs, real estate, and whatever else we may take to exist. Rather, the experience is closer to a sudden realization that such a list is worthless and deserves to be crumpled up and thrown into the trash. What are quarks and furniture and so on next to the reality of this feeling inside me? From an outsider's point of view, the reason for keeping the feeling off the list will be precisely the opposite of that entertained by the lover: that it is *just a feeling*. But from the lover's own point of view, that feeling *becomes the world*.

Our language for describing what happens in such a state is generally inadequate. The word "feeling" itself has been so devalued as practically to include "just a" as an implicit modifier before it. A 1976 song by the arena rock band Boston is lyrically centered on a man's claim that his fondness for a woman is "More Than a Feeling," as if to say that *if* that's all it were, it would not be worthy of reciprocation, nor indeed of a song dedicated to it. Yet if any argument can be made to the effect that feelings are more real than electrons, love is likely going to be the feeling that carries it through, since it is likely that all of us, at some point in our lives, have had everything turned on its head through love's destabilizing power. I would not argue that love is literally *more real* than electrons; the feeling I am trying to describe is one in which our ordinary criteria for holding something as more or less real than something else seem to go out the window.

In a remarkable passage from Gustave Flaubert's 1869 novel *Sentimental Education*, the French novelist describes the first moment Frédéric Moreau spends alone with the married Mme Dambreuse in explicit, mutual acknowledgment of their shared love for (or at least infatuation with) one another:

> Mme Dambreuse closed her eyes, and he was surprised by the ease of his victory. The tall trees in the garden ceased to softly shiver. Stationary clouds cast long red bands through the sky, and there was a sort of universal suspension of things. Now similar evenings, with similar silences, came into his mind confusedly. Where was that?[8]

This passage appears to contain many of the features we have associated with the psychedelic experience: a perception of interpersonal sentiments as bearing a cosmic or universal significance, with the power even to transform external reality; a perception of the unreality of time and of the flow of events, and the possibility of interrupting time altogether; and finally a perception of omniscience, which includes deep, intimate familiarity with experiences one cannot concretely claim to have had.

    Moreau is experiencing all these things without drugs. Yet Flaubert characterizes Moreau's life of amorous pursuits as extremely frivolous, as a great moral waste, in terms that would not be so different if Moreau's problem had not been that he sacrifices higher pursuits to eros and seduction, but that he flees from real human connections by retreating into the fantasyland of mind-altering substances. Drugs and romance have not only many of the same effects but also seem to fit right alongside one another on the list of ways one might get sidetracked from the pursuits that would otherwise enable a person to realize their full potential. The victim of unrequited love can easily degenerate into a stalker, lurking in the bushes outside an ordinary bedroom window at night, much as the person who has once known the ecstasy of mind-altering substances risks degenerating into a fiend. Ordinarily, however, we still consider love, properly channeled and tempered, to be a valuable part of a life well lived. The simple fact that venturing into some dimension or other of human experience may have self-destructive effects is generally not a reason to suppose that it may be successfully eliminated or ignored. This alone shows that our differing attitudes toward romantic love and drug use respectively need further analysis.

    It is not only in romantic love, where the feeling is associated with another person (or perhaps with the *idea* of another person—"titillation accompanied by the idea of an external cause" is how Baruch Spinoza defined love) that feelings have the power to overturn our ordinary sense of what is to count as real. Freedom is perhaps another feeling with such a power, though philosophers, especially political philosophers, are not in the habit of thinking of freedom as a feeling at all. Here again an insight from Spinoza may be instructive: he takes freedom to be something like an agreeable acquiescence in the way one's own body is moving along with the necessary order of things. As for myself, I can clearly recall being a child, right around the time I was feeling the first anticipations of full-fledged romantic love, and finally being granted the freedom to walk by myself to the convenience store about a mile away down a semi-rural road. That walk and the store at the other end of it were charged up with a mystical power for me. If I had to attach concepts to that power, I would speak of freedom and hope and the open-endedness of the future. But the feeling when I took the walk didn't seem to have any concepts attached to it at all. It was simply incredible, and as if nothing more important had ever happened in the history of the universe.

Could I have been *right* in that feeling? The thought is absurd, of course; even if I ultimately conclude that nothing else in *my* life was ever more important, I must concede, at risk of lapsing into solipsism, that something comparable has happened billions of times over, for at least every human being who has ever lived. And yet, I think one of the enduring lessons of psychedelics has been, for me, that we should not be so categorical in dismissing such feelings, even if we ultimately must learn to live in a world alongside others whom we cannot expect to share in them with us. When I am visiting California, and I drive by that same convenience store today (the business still exists, though it has changed names multiple times over the years), I feel a deep bittersweet nostalgia, much as when I hear an old song I used to love. The feeling tells me once again that there is another world. The sight of this place is a reminder of it, even if I no longer have direct access to it. That other world is, namely, the one that I was fully inhabiting when I walked to the convenience store by myself for the first time decades ago. I know that other world exists, because I've been there, even if I can't go back.

I think that prior to my recent experience of psychedelics, I had trained myself to believe that that other world does not "really" exist, that to believe in it is a childish fantasy, or an immature clinging to what is best left behind. What psychedelic experience can do is to give you the power of shifting between worlds. I cannot be placed back on the road to the convenience store in 1984 exactly, but I can be transported into a state of mind that is similarly inaccessible to my ordinary adult consciousness. And that experience of transport causes me to question what had previously been, I now believe, a rather facile distinction between childish fantasy and grown-up realism.

When we are in love, or when we are allowed to walk to the store alone for the first time, or when we make a pilgrimage to a holy site, or when we return to our hometown after years away, we experience landscapes that are charged up with meanings. These meanings constitute who we are, and it is practically inconceivable to imagine our lives without them. Nothing can ever fully cure me of the belief that there is something special, something unusual, about the streets and buildings and landscapes of Sacramento, California, even though I understand that this is a common feeling that other people who grew up in other places have about their own hometowns. But perhaps I should not say that I "understand it," for I don't *really* understand how someone could feel about, say, Cincinnati the way I feel about Sacramento. I don't understand it, but I accept it. This acceptance is perhaps somewhat analogous to interfaith toleration: the Cincinnatian and I believe in different gods.

Even the landscapes of my adoptive cities can come to have some meanings for me that they lacked on my arrival. And places I visit for the first time, too, even Cincinnati, share something of the magic of the places that matter to me, in that I discern everywhere around me not just physical objects—walls, sidewalks, windows—but also irreducibly social and human meanings imbued in the objects, but not strictly speaking there in any naturalistic sense. The nineteenth-century Italian philosopher Giacomo Leopardi put this thought very compellingly: "the world and its objects," he wrote, "are in a certain sense double."[9] A "sensitive and imaginative" person, Leopardi continues, will see with his eyes "a tower, a landscape; with his ears he will hear the sound of a bell; and at the same time with his imagination he will see another tower, another landscape, he will hear another sound. The whole beauty and pleasure of things lies in this second kind of objects." Wherever I go, I find I always have that double vision of which Leopardi wrote.

At least part of this double vision is itself rather mundane, as it is grounded not in my own lively imagination, but in what our shared social reality imposes on me, constrains me to take as real lest I wind up at odds with my fellow citizens or with the law. For example, if I am walking along the sidewalk and at some point I stray onto somebody's front lawn, I will feel the difference deep within me—there will be a sensation of moderate transgression, of rupture with the proper order of things. In certain parts of the United States, where it is legal to shoot trespassers, I might also feel at risk. If I were invited over to the home of a colleague and his or her family, and after brief greetings at the doorway I were to barge directly into the host's bedroom and to stretch out on the bed, I would also surely be feeling some complicated feelings: of transgression, guilt, insanity, in any case something very much outside of the usual order of things. And yet, if a Martian anthropologist were to come and to ask me to account for these different feelings, it would surely be quite difficult to do so simply by pointing to the visible differences between sidewalks and front lawns, between living rooms and bedrooms.

That there *are* great and real differences between these different social spaces, even though these differences cannot be accounted for strictly by appeal to the physical or observable properties of them, is part of what we mean when we say that reality is to some extent "socially constructed." This term has taken on considerable charge over the last several decades and led to many misunderstandings. But when the sociologists Peter L. Berger and Thomas Luckmann introduced it in 1966,[10] it was simply meant to account for the way our socially constituted ideas—of private versus public property, for example—shape our perception of, and our actions in, the world around us. No one is moving through a world of mere external objects. As human beings we are always, rather, moving through a world shaped by the meanings we bring to it. We might think these meanings are just common sense, flowing directly from the bare facts about external objects that are evident to anyone observing them. But again, any true outsider, such as our hypothetical Martian, would surely remain at least to some extent unconvinced that we have built our social reality according to the one exclusive commonsensical pattern.

In this light, when we stop to think about it, it is strange to find such practices as feng shui, or its Indian variant, vastu shastra, classified as pseudoscience. The Martian anthropologist might remain unconvinced that a home needs to be aligned in a certain direction in order to have good feng shui, but it is not as if that Martian would be any more convinced by an attempt to explain to them why someone with a freshly mowed green lawn is a better neighbor than someone with a lawn filled with gravel or weeds (a term that, like "toadstool," designates nothing natural). In both cases, we are dealing with social values that shape the perception of reality. There is nothing uniquely or even distinctly commonsensical about the particular set of values that prevail in our place and time. In fact I've seen these values transform radically over the course of my own life.

What now would it be like to perceive reality shorn of these values? Sometimes I think I catch glimpses of it in moments of deep depression, when the ordinary meanings we take for granted seem to slip away. At its very worst, deep depression seems to border on psychosis, where the ties that bind society together unravel, and all that is left is a bare existence much as Roquentin had described it, which has the quality of a great gaping void or chaos. This is a horrible experience, yet it can still be instructive to pay attention to what is happening in its grips: reality slips away here not because one is hallucinating but because one becomes incapable of hallucinating. That is, at such a moment, the "feeble points of reference which men have traced," as Sartre put it, the social meanings that one ordinarily projects onto the external world, simply vanish, we find ourselves incapable of doing our part to sustain them, and all that is left is an undifferentiated field of perception. The roots of the chestnut tree disappear, and the bare existence that sustains them bursts through.

This is what a thoroughgoing "realism" would look like: there would be no distinction between the rooms in a house, between public and private spaces, between the social positions of different individuals, perhaps between human and nonhuman beings. These are all distinctions a Martian visitor might well fail to make too, simply because that visitor would not share in the same constructions that maintain our ordinary social reality: would not be sharing, that is, at least in a loose sense, in our collective hallucinations.

Sometimes, as I've already suggested, psychedelic experience can feel a good deal more like the total absence of hallucination as I've described it here than like hallucination. Especially in its more frightening phases, much as in intense depression, what can sometimes happen in a psychedelic experience is that the walls between rooms fall away, everything falls away until it seems as though one is only perceiving reality itself, as it actually is, as an unstructured chaos. What I mean to say here, in part, is that the sober and lucid mind hallucinates systematically, and if we are wary of the way our world comes undone under the influence of psychedelics, it may be a mistake to suppose simply that this coming undone is best explained as a consequence of hallucination. The superior account, it seems to me when I analyze my own psychedelic experience, is that under the influence of these drugs we cease to hallucinate as we are supposed to do, indeed as we must do simply to live our lives.

I am certainly not the first auto-experimenter who has noticed this curious, almost paradoxical feature of psychedelics, yet for reasons difficult to understand, the efforts of others to convey this same idea continue to be drowned out by the far more caricatural account according to which a psychedelic experience is essentially that of watching a spectacular parade of hallucinations, as if one were watching a fireworks display. Aldous Huxley himself did much to combat such accounts. In his view the lucid waking mind is controlled by what he calls a "reducing valve," which filters the wide variety of conscious perceptions, letting through only those that best facilitate our navigation of the physical world and that best ensure our continued survival. On this account, psychedelic drugs do not so much produce new perceptions from within as, rather, "open the valves" of consciousness to perceive those dimensions of reality that ordinarily remain beyond our access and that typically have no practical utility for navigating the world, indeed that might be highly impractical or even antithetical to our survival.

There is moreover by now a compelling neuroscientific account of how this "valve" functions. The neuroscientist Marcus E. Raichle has developed the notion of a "default mode network," which describes the human brain in its normal or resting state, in which the cerebral cortex that is responsible for higher forms of cognition remains fluidly linked to and in interaction with those structures of the brain that emerged far earlier in our evolutionary history, principally those that regulate memory and emotion.[11] This network also appears to be responsible for maintaining the normal balance between metacognitive activities, in which we might for example imagine ourselves in some future state, contemplate our own mental activity, remember our distant past experiences while simultaneously comprehending that it was our same individual self that was having those experiences, and so on. Psychedelic drugs, it has been shown, reduce the hold that the default mode network has on human consciousness, which can often result in a dissolution of the sense of self, and an experience of the memories or ideas one has as free-floating, as unanchored to a particular subject. And this, in turn, can often be experienced, or at least *I* have experienced it, as something much like "valves opening," which is to say that the power of thought becomes as if unlimited: one can see the universe as a whole all at once, for example, or one can see the powers and beauty ordinarily hidden in mundane objects.

In sum, when the ordinary regulatory network of the brain gets shut off, the valves open up, and the experience, again, is precisely not one of hallucination, or at least does not seem to be, but rather of a more adequate and comprehensive apperception of the world as it now appears truly to be.

It is perhaps a significant fact about the world, and about our brains as they have evolved within that world, that such apperception can sometimes be an extremely negative experience.

We have already hinted at the terror that can sometimes arrive during a psychedelic experience, when one begins to perceive the world, or seems to perceive the world, as it really is, without the "feeble points of reference" that ordinarily give it meaning and structure. This terror is one of the ways one might experience what is colloquially known as a bad trip. The risk of a bad trip is one of the most significant reasons why many people are strongly disinclined to try psychedelic drugs. It is not hard to understand the hesitation. A bad trip can be tough indeed. It can also be an opportunity to arrive at a better understanding of psychedelic experience in general.

Opportunistic study of cases that have gone wrong has in fact been an important part of the scientific method for a few centuries already. Around 1800 the French natural scientist and embryologist Étienne Geoffroy Saint-Hilaire had an insight about birth defects that was somewhat similar to the one I have just shared regarding bad trips. His predecessors had mostly just been revolted, or at best pruriently curious, when they heard news of the birth of a two-headed calf or of a pig fetus stillborn with a single eye at the center of its face. The medievals had called such creatures "monsters," a word etymologically connected to the Latin verb for "to show," which is still preserved in English words like "de*monstr*ate." What was it that monsters were showing? God's anger, most usually, and accordingly the typical response was to dispose of their remains and to forget them as quickly as possible. Geoffroy Saint-Hilaire had a different idea. Every time a fetal abnormality comes into the world, he observed, we have an opportunity, by investigating what went wrong, to come better to understand the ordinary course of fetal development as it happens in the vast majority of cases. Much early progress in embryology, in fact, over the course of the nineteenth century, relied on those instances where something had gone wrong.

Perhaps Geoffroy Saint-Hilaire may be thanked for providing a general lesson for the search after knowledge: far from being something to fear, the "ugly" cases in *any* domain of inquiry or experience might be the most informative ones as to the nature of the phenomenon in general, whether it is embryology or psychedelic phenomenology that interests us.

What is the nature of a bad trip? Is it intrinsic to the psychedelic experience, or is it merely a departure from how we want or expect things to go? Psychedelic guides will tell you there are steps you can take before your trip to minimize the risk of things taking a dark turn: doing it in a safe and familiar place, not doing it when you are feeling anxious, and so on. But in truth these measures can never be more than partially effective. It is, as I have already argued, intrinsic to the psychedelic experience that it is something that happens to you and not something that you actively do (at least not after you have willingly swallowed the potion). To take a trip is to *submit*, to agree to let yourself go wherever the drug takes you. This is perhaps, as already suggested, among the reasons doing so is generally seen as incompatible with the project of philosophical inquiry: to do philosophy is actively to use one's mind to resolve problems, or perhaps to generate new ones; it is not, if I may put it this way, to have your own mind used by other powers.

It is in any case a significant fact that psychedelic experience is often bad, and it is bad, moreover, in a very distinctive way. Bad trips may have any of several different characteristics. I have sometimes been bombarded with mental images of the sort of things that we widely consider to be disgusting or horrible, perhaps for mere cultural reasons, but more likely for evolutionary ones as well: spiderwebs, the rotting carcasses of animals, the leathery wings of bats. Such images are not at all far from the list of ingredients that might be mixed in a cauldron by the witches of *Macbeth*. To be subject to them is not in itself *so* bad; in fact, it can be fascinating and wondrous, just as the grotesque can be a delightful subject for aesthetic experience. After all, people pay to go and watch performances of *Macbeth*, in part because they enjoy the grotesquerie of the witches cooking up their brew.

But sometimes the manageable hallucination of such things passes into something quite overwhelming, where, if I were to try to put it into words, I would say that it suddenly seems as if such entities as spiderwebs and insect parts and feces represent the true nature of reality as a whole, while our ordinary focus on pretty faces, on delightfully prepared meals, on bouquets of fresh flowers, is only a result of the fact that we live our daily lives shrouded in illusion, with our "reducing valves" well adjusted to keep the worst of what the world has to offer out of conscious consideration. But even this overwhelming experience can be an interesting one, and not totally disagreeable. Alright then, one might find oneself thinking, so the essential nature of reality is bound up with death, decay, excrement; I can handle that!

Earlier I explained Martin Heidegger's notion of moods as "world-disclosing": far from leading us astray or preventing us from seeing the world as it actually is, our moods or feelings or sentiments, Heidegger believed, can have the power to reveal to us dimensions of human reality that natural science is even in principle unable to account for. Along such lines, I would say that a psychedelic trip only becomes truly, essentially "bad" when it discloses the world through the mood of *dread*. This can happen entirely without any hallucinations of bat wings and similar things. It may happen with no hallucinations at all. Indeed, the precise character of such an experience would be better described, as we have already seen with the example of Roquentin and the chestnut tree, as a sudden and total loss of one's ability to hallucinate at all, so that now one can only see the world as it really is. At its most extreme, the loss of an ability to hallucinate an orderly external world may be accompanied by the parallel loss of an ability to hallucinate one's own enduring existence, an experience commonly described as "ego dissolution."

Identifying ego dissolution as the signature element of a bad trip is complicated by the fact that, under other circumstances, ego dissolution may also be accompanied by feelings of euphoria. Why does the psychedelic obliteration of the self sometimes disclose the world through the mood of joy and sometimes through the mood of dread? I do not really have an answer to this question, though the variability of the experience seems to suggest a lesson, familiar to philosophers, concerning the objective neutrality of death. Is it bad for my self to disappear from the world? It can be, but it doesn't have to be. The small death of ego dissolution in psychedelic experience, which can be accompanied either by torment or relief, seems as if it may be an instructive tool in thinking about and preparing for our own eventual big death. Indeed, many users of psychedelics have reported that their experiences have helped them to attain a greater equanimity in the face of their mortality. I suspect the bad trips are just as important in leading them to this result as the good ones are.

While I have said that I do not know how to make sense of this unpredictable alternation between euphoria and dread at the loss of fixed entities in the external world, at the dissolution of the self, I might add, at least, that the variability of the experience strongly suggests that these and other moods are the primitive elements of human experience. In other words, you cannot analyze experience down further than the moods that underlie it; you cannot find something deeper, such as a thought or an idea or any other noetic element, to speak with William James, that has brought the mood about. It is not that negative thinking produces visions of bat wings and rotting carcasses, in which case you might indeed make an effort to avoid bad trips by exercises of positive thinking and well-placed mood lighting. Rather, the mood that generates these Macbethian visions comes and goes all on its own, quite apart from whatever you may be thinking or attempting to think, quite apart from any effort of cognitive hygiene you may be making.

To say that the moods are primitive is indeed, in a Heideggerian vein, to say that what we take to be our world is neither a field of external objects we spend our days navigating between and around nor an ideal realm of timeless concepts. Our world is made up of such things as dread, joy, boredom, and desire. We still do not know the rules for controlling such forces as these nor whether they ever could lie within our control. Psychedelic experience makes a strong case to us that they never could be.

CHAPTER SIX

✺

GALAXY BRAINS

Suppose you were walloped on the same day with two heavy pieces of information: first, astronomers announce that we now have hard evidence of a cluster of stars and planets not so far from our own solar system, where alien civilizations have built up extremely complex technological worlds, complete with Dyson spheres around some of the stars, giving them inexhaustible energy to sustain their artificial environments; second, that in the coming week a solar storm of our own nearest star is going to cause flares so great that they are likely to extinguish all life on Earth. Under such circumstances, how would you feel? Upset to know that life on Earth is coming to an end? No doubt. But what feelings might you have about those faraway beings and their possible future?

At present, in the early twenty-first century, we are encouraged, as a condition of our individual moral progress, to cultivate a "planetary consciousness," that is, to care about the well-being of every human being on Earth, and likely the well-being, or at least the homeostasis, of nonhuman systems as well. We learn early on that there is something stunted and parochial in caring more, or in acknowledging that we care more, about our friends and loved ones, than about strangers we have never met on the other side of the Earth. A millennium ago, news of a terrible war taking place in another hemisphere would have been a pure abstraction, no more relevant to one's life than news of the explosion of a supernova in some distant galaxy. Today we have instantaneous bodycam footage of faraway combat, and constant solicitations on our attention via mass media and social media, telling us that we must care about what that footage shows in a direct and personal way, as if the people involved were our own kin.

Without wishing to criticize this substantive moral position, we may at least note that historically speaking it is unprecedented, and never could have happened without the telecommunication technologies we have developed over the past century. We might also note that this moral position does not go nearly as far as one might go in developing a sense of connection, or interwovenness, or unity, with the world beyond our immediate sphere of perception and action. Beyond planetary consciousness, there lies "cosmic consciousness": an abiding awareness of the vanishingly small and insignificant place our own planet takes up within the observable universe; an awareness of the cycling of all the matter that makes us up, at a sufficiently large timescale, through the cores of stars and the dust of nebulae; perhaps an awareness of all that remains unknown of the physical universe, the nature of dark matter and dark energy, the insides of black holes, the possible existence of intelligent structures or systems that so far we are unable to detect; and so on.

I find that, at least among scholars in the humanities, there is often a profound illiteracy about the most basic features of the cosmos. Typically their estimates about, say, the number of galaxies in the observable universe, or the distance from our solar system to the nearest star, are not just wrong but are wrong by several orders of magnitude. The average humanities professor does not really know much more about the heavens than Aristotle or Porphyry did, nor is there much recognition of any responsibility to take an interest in such things. To do so is held to be entirely optional. It seems to me that the problem is not one of information but simply of interest: my humanities colleagues lack cosmic consciousness, in at least this one sense.

Perhaps the moral valence of attention to the cosmic scale of our existence would be different if we were to receive certain news of the existence of alien life forms, all the more so if this were accompanied by news of our own imminent annihilation. But at least in our current reality, cosmic consciousness, unlike planetary consciousness, is generally seen as an unserious mode of thought, as a sort of daydreaming or an irresponsible flight from our often brutal planetary reality. Someone who retreats into thinking about black holes and galaxy spirals, or at least someone who does so and is not a theoretical physicist by profession, we might fear, has relinquished concern for humanity and drifted off into a fantasy world of little relevance to our own.

It is significant that psychedelic drugs are particularly powerful in awakening what I am calling cosmic consciousness. While they can sometimes induce hallucinations of spiderwebs, of fungal networks, and of other beings or systems that are solidly planetary, they also often have the effect of propelling a person into outer space, where one can get the sense of seeing the universe from a perspective that is much vaster than what we are ordinarily able to take in, or perhaps the sense that one is time traveling and witnessing the primordial conditions at the big bang, or something else at a comparably grand scale.

In our cultural representations, such a motion into outer space is often a source of humor and mockery. There is a well-known internet meme template called "galaxy brain," which shows a person moving up through a succession of more abstruse and higher-level thoughts on a given subject, and at each successive stage the inside of their head, usually shown in transparent outline, contains a larger and brighter cosmological structure. Fascinatingly, recent AI art tools have likewise developed a peculiar habit of going into galaxy brain mode whenever you take an image and repeatedly prompt the AI to give you that same image again, but more of it, or in a more superlative form. If you ask AI to show you an image of the perfect pizza, and then you ask it to make that same image even better, and then to make *that* image even better in turn, what you will get soon enough is an image of spiraling pizza galaxies and celestial beings hungrily devouring them: you will get, if you keep going, an entire universe that shares in the nature of pizza.

Memes, AI, and drugs: all send us out there, into the great beyond, where the mind of the responsible modern earthling, and the heart of the well-grounded modern moral subject, are not supposed to go. On psychedelic drugs this motion outward is often experienced as the attainment of superconsciousness, as for example the botanist's experience, while under the influence of the fictitious psychedelic yakruna plant, of the snake-like nature of the cosmos, in Ciro Guerra's remarkable 2015 film *The Embrace of the Serpent*. Such experience is sometimes characterized by a parallel loss of the ordinary limits that define a person's individual identity. When you are seeing the universe at the scale of galaxy superclusters and the like, the you that is doing the seeing is probably not the one that is attached to a particular name, a particular date of birth or Social Security number, or a particular limited conformation of sense organs.

It is a significant historical fact that, for a brief period in the late twentieth century, cosmic consciousness of the sort I have described became an object of sincere aspiration, rather than of jocular ironizing or outright dismissal. In the 1960s, such consciousness was a worthy attainment and was often celebrated. This celebration had much to do with the Cold War space race between the superpowers. It also had much to do with the cultural impact of psychedelic drugs. As the satirical newspaper *The Onion* put it in an imagined headline from 1968: "Hippies, NASA Race for Moon."[1] Was the simultaneity of these two races, or at least of the way they were talked about and represented in culture, entirely a coincidence? And is it a complete coincidence that our new psychedelic renaissance is occurring at the same time as a revived competition between the superpowers for dominance in outer space?

Cosmic consciousness has been valued in many different cultures and eras, and not always in connection with the use of psychedelics. Something like cosmic consciousness is surely part of the cluster of aesthetic values guiding the Romantic movement in the nineteenth century, which often sought to capture the sublimity of scenes of the night sky, for example, and was in general preoccupied by the sublimity of the infinite, both as a mathematical abstraction and as a feature of the physical universe. And even when it is focused on earthly sublimity, such as the surface of the ocean at night or the stark icy precipices of the Alps, these scenes convey a sense of the cosmic more than of something merely planetary in the sense already evoked, a sense of the unboundedness of nature rather than of Earth as a safe and self-contained home with limited space.

Planetary consciousness tells us that everything on Earth is within our reach and under our control. Romantic representations of the ocean or of ice chasms remind us that much of the Earth is no more under our control than a distant galaxy. In this regard even representations of nature that are focused on particular features of the Earth, such as the sublimity of high mountains or deep oceans, have more in common with the cosmic than with planetary consciousness as we've been describing it. Thus, similarly, when Sigmund Freud takes up the idea of an "oceanic feeling"—originally suggested to him in a 1927 letter from Romain Rolland, who describes it as "a sensation of 'eternity'" and of "being one with the external world as a whole"[2]—even though the ocean exists at a planetary and not a cosmic scale, nonetheless the idea in question is like the cosmic in that it is characterized principally by its unboundedness, while planetary consciousness, as the awareness of a common ecumene of all human beings within a fragile ecosystem, is necessarily bounded.

The idea of the oceanic captivated many thinkers from

the early to mid-twentieth century, in roughly the same period as the reign of mescaline. We might say that, from the point of view of cultural history, the oceanic is to mescaline what the cosmic will later be to LSD. The two terms also overlap considerably, especially in the continued appeal to the notion of the oceanic among thinkers who came of age prior to the 1960s. Thus shortly before his choice of euthanasia (or double euthanasia, which some claim he bullied his wife into accepting) in 1983, the Hungarian-born author, essayist, and public intellectual Arthur Koestler wrote that he harbored "some timid hopes for a de-personalised after-life beyond due confines of space, time and matter and beyond the limits of our comprehension," adding that "this 'oceanic feeling' has often sustained me at difficult moments, as it does so now."[3]

The cosmic and the oceanic both often suggest an experience of something like superconsciousness, when one does not cease to be a conscious entity but rather somehow seems to move beyond the limitations of one's ordinary selfhood. This ordinary consciousness is characterized by its rigid anchoring in the particular point of view of a fairly limited being with fairly dull or weak powers of sensory perception, through which the external world filters in "as through a glass darkly," as St. Paul writes in his First Letter to the Corinthians. Something like this superconsciousness has at times also been articulated within the history of philosophy as one account of the possible fate of the soul after death. Thus, for example, the medieval Muslim philosopher Ibn Rushd (Averroes) defends a theory of "the unity of the intellect," which on his understanding derives from Aristotle. This theory proposes that the contents of our thoughts are not our own individual possessions but only flow through us, so to speak, from a single source that is shared alike by all conscious beings. Death, on this account, is only a return or a reabsorption into the single unified intellect from which we are partially separated during life. This is also a theory that the British Catholic philosopher G. E. M. Anscombe takes up and investigates with some sympathy in her tellingly titled 1986 article "Has Mankind One Soul? An Angel Distributed Through Many Bodies."[4] There are many pathways to such an idea as this. Sustained study in the traditions of Islamic or Catholic theology might get you there. So might a hit of acid.

One common reaction to psychedelic drugs, which I myself have experienced and which is widely attested in the accounts of others, is the rediscovery of one's own nature as a cosmic being. It suddenly appears to the drug taker that he or she is vastly older than ordinarily seems to be the case, and that this earthly sojourn is only the most recent phase of a vastly more ancient cosmic pilgrimage. This is an intense feeling, to say the least. And yet we must, if we wish to be intellectually rigorous, wonder whether and to what extent the content of the cosmic vision under these circumstances is shaped by expectations informed by our surrounding culture. Where, that is, does the particular content of psychedelic experience come from? Is it part of the basic structure of my mind, which has been shaped by long, slow evolution alongside other cosmic structures? Is it a vision of a different order of reality to which I belong, in spite of ordinary appearances? Or is it mostly shaped by my particular culture-bound experiences?

Consider the related case of AI dreaming up images of nebulae and galaxy spirals after being prompted to show, say, "the most absolutely mind-blowing pizza ever." The machine does not naturally or spontaneously associate greatness with large-scale cosmic structures but is only displaying what it has learned from the artistic representations on which it has been trained. And when I myself dream scenes that show a clear debt to Looney Tunes, as I often do, this is (probably) not because I was myself a Looney Tunes character in a past life, or because Looney Tunes taps into the true nature of reality in some unique way, but only because this is part of the visual culture that happened to shape my faculty of imagination.

Yet when a psychedelic experience launches a person into visions of the stars, or of the gravitational lensing of a black hole, the experience at least *seems* quite a bit deeper than this. It does not feel like a culturally conditioned hallucination, but rather more like access to an innate awareness. At the same time, it is likely impossible to separate "what's really there" in our minds from what is best seen as a later accrual coming from a lifelong absorption of, and one might say dependence on, the representations of popular culture.

There has never been a time in my conscious life when I have not been at least vaguely aware of the iconic scene in Stanley Kubrick's 1968 film *2001: A Space Odyssey*, showing a giant fetus floating in space. I saw the movie as a small child, and I suppose I understood on some level that this representation was some kind of imaginative artwork. But I also supposed, even if I could not put this into words, that it tapped into some truth about the nature of reality. Years later, when I was on LSD and I felt myself to be a fetus floating in space, was I only rehearsing my memories of that movie, sharing in a widespread cultural representation that Kubrick brought into the world? Or was I rather returning to the deep truth that Kubrick and I had *both* apprehended separately?

It's impossible to say, yet the idea that we need to shear away the cultural overgrowth from our drug-induced representations in order to get at the deeper truths these reveal might well be a fool's errand, and might rest on an illusion. Culture itself, after all, generates its constant stream of such representations—a fetus floating in space, a coyote briefly suspended in the air before it realizes its plight and begins its fall to the bottom of the canyon—only because it, too, just like the individual drug taker, is processing the strangeness of finding ourselves here, leading *this* life.

It is significant in this connection that several world religions, notably Buddhism, have much to say about the prebirth pilgrimages of a human soul. These are also a staple of more recent New Age narratives of human origins. Helena Blavatsky's Theosophy movement, which emerged in the late nineteenth century through a creative synthesis of Buddhist, Hindu, and Western spiritual traditions, imagines that the first "root race" of human beings was ethereal in nature, and that it dates back millions of years. Scientology holds that the true person is not the embodied human being, but rather the "thetan" or "theta being," which has existed for trillions of years, and for most of that time as pure energy.

I am not interested in defending the view that these representations are true. I am however interested in understanding why they are so deep seated. In this respect my position in regard to the representations and beliefs I am considering is the one that has been approved throughout most of the history of anthropology as an academic discipline. When an anthropologist learns from a herdsman in a traditional society that the cosmos has the same structure as an ox, for example, he does not rush to tell him this is false nor, in the eventual publication relating this interview, does he dwell on its falseness. Rather, he tries to figure out what the world looks like as a whole for someone who would affirm such a thing. And if such a thing is affirmed over and over again across a wide swath of cultures in different regions of the world, then he still will likely not be compelled to accept the view in question, that the cosmos is ox-shaped, as literally true. But he will at least take all its multiple iterations as an indication that this particular representation taps into something important about human existence and thought.

Similarly, here I am interested in determining what dimension of human existence is tapped into each time human beings project their consciousness out beyond the confines of their lived reality on Earth and imagine themselves as energy in the distant corners of the universe, or as fetuses floating past mysterious black monoliths in space, or indeed as a great cosmic serpent. It seems to me that on any charitable reading of these representations, one must acknowledge that even if they are not literally true, they are generated out of a desire for truth, and they are so to speak truth adjacent. They are not flat-out deceptions or lies. It *is* true, after all, that all the matter that makes us up has been cycling through the cosmos for a very long time, and that its ultimate destiny is to return there. It *is* true that from a sufficiently zoomed out perspective we are no more terrestrial beings than we are intergalactic beings. It *is* true that it is very hard or impossible to imagine oneself as ever not existing. And it is *also* true, finally, that our belief in our settled existence as earthly, embodied, finite intellects is mostly based on an illusion, and that if we admit that we are not cosmic beings, then there is also a pretty strong argument that we aren't really terrestrial beings either: we aren't *beings* at all, on this line of thinking, but only temporary and fortuitous arrangements of matter that for a while bring about an appearance of discrete individual existence.

In other words, whatever argument a typical soberminded naturalist might invoke to disabuse us of the idea that we are cosmic beings can in turn be wielded against the naturalist to argue that we are not what the naturalist would have us take ourselves to be either. The ordinary insistence that we must recognize our identity as irreducible moral subjects at the planetary level, while rejecting as irresponsible or flighty any idea of ourselves as cosmic beings, is in the end based on an imagined political boundary between the Earth as our home and the rest of the universe as a sort of wilderness; it is not based on any compelling scientific criterion, and psychedelic experience at least seems to attest that it is not based on any deep-seated cognitive criterion either.

But let us return to the problem of the cultural contamination of our psychedelic experiences, to the way our visual and musical cultures, in particular, continue to resonate within us when, with or without the aid of drugs, we close our eyes and let our imaginations soar.

The style we call "psychedelic"—largely associated with the 1960s counterculture, with poster art for rock festivals, album covers, and so on—succeeds in capturing at least something of the experience of psychedelic drugs. But that something—the billowing or fractal-like patterns that appear before the eyes in mild hallucination, the cosmic motifs of nebulae and galaxy spirals—seems to me to be only a superficial effect of the alteration of consciousness. If that were *all* a psychedelic experience could be, then one might just as well go to a laser light show at the planetarium or watch any number of other such dazzling spectacles.

What these artworks typically fail to capture is the nature of the transformation that occurs within the perceiver. There is a similar inadequacy, I have noticed, in the common habits in our culture of describing dreams. Typically, in our attempts at relating these experiences, which like psychedelic experience often lie at or beyond the very limits of describability, we position ourselves as passive viewers, as perceiving subjects more or less identical with the person we are in our waking lives, who is watching the events unfold almost as if watching a movie. Indeed, it is striking just how much of our dream life has been shaped by our lifelong experience of moving images on screens. My own dreams, as I've confessed, often borrow their style from classic Looney Tunes animations. Clearly, this would not be happening if I had been born in the Paleolithic era, even though the physiology of dreaming and sleeping was the same.

But even the dreams that feature Tom-and-Jerry-like "fight clouds," and other such visual conventions, are not simply a mental replay of the experience of watching cartoons. I do not simply watch my dreams. Rather, the point of view of the perceiver having the dreams is constantly in flux, and often it becomes difficult even to determine this being's identity. Sometimes it is me, or some stand-in for me, but sometimes it seems to blend into the events themselves, or even into the abstractions that characterize these events.

Only a very small number of writers has successfully conveyed this deeper dimension of weirdness that underlies dream experience. One of them is Marcel Proust. In the opening paragraph of his 1913 *Swann's Way*, the first of seven volumes of his masterpiece *In Search of Lost Time*, the narrator relates his memories of what it was like to fall asleep as a boy:

> I had been thinking all the time, while I was asleep, of what I had just been reading, but my thoughts had run into a channel of their own, until I myself seemed actually to have become the subject of my book: a church, a quartet, the rivalry between François I and Charles V.[5]

Note how very much this account is unlike the standard template we use in our culture for capturing the peculiarities of dreams, where we describe the delirious scenes that are presented to us, our grandmother turning into our landlord, who invites us to go catch butterflies with him, which turn out to be not butterflies but kisses, and so on. Throughout our efforts at summarizing our dreams upon awakening, our subjectivity is almost always presented as fixed. Not so for the young Marcel, whose own subjectivity jumps not only into other characters and other persons, but also into inanimate entities, structures, ensembles, and even into something as abstract as a *rivalry* between two sovereigns.

Part of the inadequacy of our efforts at describing dreams may come from our technologically conditioned visual culture, not in the sense that cinematic aesthetics and even cinematic editing techniques are incorporated into our dream experiences, but in the sense that most representations of dreams with which we are familiar, since around the time Proust was writing, have been not literary but cinematic. We take the dream sequence as it is typically presented in movies to be a fair representation of what dreams are like, but this representation is now steeped in more than a century of conventions that have much more to do with our culture's waking idea of what dreams are than with the dream experience itself. The stiffness of these conventions has even on occasion been parodied in cinema. Thus in Tom DiCillo's 1995 film *Living in Oblivion*, a dwarf, played by Peter Dinklage, enters a dream sequence only to complain that his own presence there is a disappointing cliché.

It may similarly be that the moral panic that led to a general prohibition on psychedelic research in the late twentieth century also led to a lack of rigor in efforts to account for what a psychedelic experience is like. Because the activity was illicit, attempts at describing it were now often tainted with shame, and first-person accounts were treated somewhat more as scandalous confessions than as efforts to get an accurate account of what happens.

We might, for the sake of comparison, consider the relationship between pornography in the contemporary world on the one hand and first-person experience of sexual fantasies on the other. It is very difficult even to begin to account for one's own inner fantasy life in a way that does not seem compromised by the clichés and caricatures of the sex industry, even if we consider that industry morally atrocious and we do not think of our own desires as bound or shaped by it. Among reputable authors of fiction, only the bravest, or perhaps the foolhardiest, dare to take on graphic sex scenes, since the risk is so great of lapsing into the tawdry, the merely titillating, or, worst of all, the hopelessly conventional.

We might however suspect that if we lived in a truly sexually liberated society, rather than one in which the image of sexual liberation is mobilized and exploited for profit, many more of us would be better able to render our inner fantasy lives into language or visual art in a way that is more compelling and truthful, in a way that gets at what it's really like to go through life filled with sexual desires, some of which are in their very nature unfulfillable. Similarly, one might suppose that if psychedelic experience weren't buried in all the clichés that result from its borderline-illicit nature, we would be more familiar with descriptions of psychedelic experience that cut closer to the bone, that seem to get at what it is really like, rather than simply telling us "I was tripping so hard and saw a lot of weird stuff."

The account that focuses principally on the visual features of a psychedelic hallucination, we might say, is analogous to the articulation of a sexual fantasy in the pornographic idiom, one that relies on a succession of easy-to-interpret acts, rather than on an account of the implicit significance behind those acts, or an account of the accompanying moods or feelings. There are very few accounts of psychedelic experience that proceed instead in a manner more comparable to erotic poetry, where the important thing is not the concrete content of the experience, but its quality, its feel, and, perhaps, the shifting perspectives and dispositions, the Leopardian "double vision" of the subject throughout the experience.

When we learn of a man with a public heterosexual identity who is watching pornography that features a heterosexual pair, we will probably assume that this viewer is imagining himself in the role of the male actor. But this could be unfounded.[6] He might be partially, or unconsciously, imagining himself in the role of the woman, or indeed he might be imagining something much more abstract, something like a sexual version of "the rivalry between François I and Charles V": he might be imagining himself as, say, the sexual desire binding, or appearing to bind, these two people, rather than as the one or the other. He might be imagining himself as the contiguity of their surfaces, or perhaps as their eventual regret, which already pervades the scene itself as an unacknowledged specter. These are possibilities we do not ordinarily consider in our hasty interpretations of the meaning of pornography, since the default presumption is that the viewer's subject position is clear and unambiguous, and there would be something unseemly about dwelling for too long in order to learn what's really going on in his most secret fantasy life.

Dreaming is not, at least for most of us, at least not consciously, as morally loaded as watching pornography, yet here too we often take for granted that the question of the subject position is clear and unambiguous, while the only thing that matters in relating a dream is accounting for the particular content of the presentations: I saw such and such apparition, followed by such and such transformation, and so on. In fact most dreams are not so transparent. I have been making a considered effort while writing this book to record and analyze my dreams, and to my surprise I have found that the ones in which I occupy a nonstandard subject position, in which I am myself something like the rivalry between François I and Charles V, or like the contiguity of two lovers' surfaces, are in fact not nonstandard at all but typical of the majority of cases. I do not believe I am all that unusual in this regard.

Again, I suspect that the reason why we fail to take this significant feature of dreams into account when we talk about them, even though our language for describing the interior life has by certain measures become incredibly nuanced and powerful over the past few centuries, is in part that we are experiencing interference from entertainment media, particularly from movies and television, where more than a century of habituation has basically settled the matter of what the subject position is of any consumer of these entertainments.

Of course, narrative visual media are not based entirely on convention. Experiments in the late twentieth century among some of the last groups of people never to have seen a moving image showed that these people nonetheless had a perfectly fluent grasp, for example, of what was happening when a film was edited to show the same scene from different perspectives and then to cut to another scene altogether.[7] Film-editing conventions thus seem to have built upon preexisting cognitive competencies, which is not such a surprising discovery for any of us who have read great nineteenth-century literature, generated in a precinematic world, but nonetheless deploying, as in Flaubert's external tour around the carriage in which Madame Bovary's adulterous act is transpiring, plainly protocinematic techniques.

Nonetheless, even if we have cognitively evolved so as to understand what is happening when we watch an edited motion picture, watching in this way, as events unfold on a screen, is not the only position one might take up in relation to an aesthetic experience or to an entertainment. Some experiences are more dynamic, involve a more complex relationship of the viewer with the characters and events being watched. This is particularly evident in the case of virtual reality or even in basic first-person-shooter video games. It will be interesting to see, in the coming decades, whether the rise of these technologies as the predominant form of entertainment in our culture, by now eclipsing passively watched movies and TV shows, will eventually influence the way we speak about our dreams as well, even if only at the level of the clichés to which we resort when we talk about them.

Again, as in dreams, so too in psychedelic experience. In both cases, it seems, our conventions for narrative description are anchored in, or you might say weighed down by, our tremendous familiarity with the norms and conventions of our broader visual culture. Here, again, the role of the watcher is basically a settled matter: it is simply to sit there, external to the events and passive in relation to them, with an identity as a viewing subject that is not implicated in the scenes that are viewed, and that does not change from moment to moment over the course of the viewing.

But drugs and dreams are just not like that, for the most part, and it is going to take some real effort, which I myself am beginning in this book but also encouraging others to develop further, to break the way we talk about these experiences out of the mold that we have built for the experience of passive audiovisual entertainment, which has imposed on us a common stock of ambient clichés and largely deprived us of any real power to account for the richness of our inner experience, whether chemically enhanced or not.

I have just suggested that in the coming years interactive VR technology might significantly shape the way we account for our inner experiences and even for the nature of external reality. In fact this is already happening to some extent, and it may be that this shift in our cultural processing of new technologies can tell us something about the nature of experience under the influence of psychoactive drugs.

There are by now several variations on what is commonly called "the simulation hypothesis" or "simulationism" (or sometimes "simulism"), but the essence of it, as defended by philosophers such as David Chalmers and Nick Bostrom,[8] is the idea that what we think of as "its" have their ultimate causal ground in what are in fact "bits." That is, what we take to be the base-level physical reality of the external world might better be conceived on the model of the virtual realities our machines have begun spinning out for us over the past few decades.

I have long been critical of this view. My criticisms have in part been grounded in my perspective as a specialist in the history of early modern natural philosophy. In seventeenth-century science as today, people were deeply impressed with the most cutting-edge technologies around. For them, this meant, above all, clockworks. Some people, such as the English experimental philosopher Robert Boyle, who was the first to style himself a "mechanical philosopher," were *so* impressed as to propose that the entire universe is best understood on the model of a horologium.

And this is a pattern we see again and again in the history of science: the latest shiny gadget becomes such a centerpiece of human attention that we find ourselves unable to resist seeing it as a sort of epitome of reality as a whole.

But what a coincidence it would be if the entire world turned out to share in the same nature as a technology that only came into existence within our own lifetimes. "The world is like a dream" seems a perfectly plausible proposition; "the world is like Pac-Man" seems a crude fetishism. A rigorously historicizing perspective on the simulation argument, in other words, quickly reveals it to be little more than a reflection of presentist nearsightedness. I certainly have no qualms with the generic idea, as defended by Chalmers or Bostrom, that the world is likely not at all as it appears to us. David Hume already proved as much with his example of the table that shrinks as we walk away from it. The difference is that when I go searching for alternatives to these appearances, it is not first to our recent technologies and to their cultural ramifications in gaming and other such domains that I turn.

Yet I confess that psychedelic experience has somewhat caused me to doubt the strength of my own case against simulationism. Under the influence of psychedelic drugs, I have indeed found that the world comes to appear glitchy to me, in just the way the simulationists expect that it should. Under the influence of psychedelics, the world really does seem to me more like a computer simulation than like a clock, or a loom, or a chariot wheel, or anything else we have come up with so far to serve as a model of the cosmos as a whole. It seems to me that the defenders of the idea that the world is more "bit-like" than "it-like" may be onto something.

Let me walk that back a bit. The glitches are not *exactly* as the simulationists often imagine them. I see no cascades of glowing green zeros and ones as one might expect after watching *The Matrix*, nor clean TRON-like geometric lines extending off into the horizon, nor cats that seem to flicker like an old UHF channel as they walk by. The glitches are not something *seen* at all, but rather something that characterizes the mode of consciousness in which the totality of the world, and of memory and experience, is apprehended.

There are two such principal glitches. The first has to do with the experience of time. Under the influence of psilocybin in particular, I have found temporal duration can sometimes come to appear illusory. In his 1921 work *The Analysis of Mind*, Bertrand Russell reflected that there is no logical impossibility in the hypothesis that the world sprang into existence five minutes ago, "with a population that 'remembered' a wholly unreal past."[9] What to Russell's lucid and unaltered mind seemed a logical possibility has seemed to me very nearly self-evident, except that the five minutes are reduced to the present instant, and it turns out that the real mistake, in our ordinary apprehension of our existence, is to conceive it as unfolding in time at all.

But what does this have to do with simulationism? Consider first that in an artificial system that rises to the level of consciousness, such as future LLMs might, this consciousness could not be the result of any slow evolutionary process with antecedent stages of mere sensory perception. The consciousness of such a system would simply pop into existence at the moment the programmer behind it hits "Start." It would not be a hard-won consciousness, moving up through photoreception, olfaction, and other such physiological capacities as we have that now serve in part to constitute our consciousness as biological entities (*if* that is what we are), but did not first emerge *for the sake of* consciousness. When we first started smelling the world around us, evolutionary theory tells us, there was as yet no plan for the incorporation of olfaction into the package of sensory perception by means of which we consciously cognize that world. It all just worked out that way.

In an artificial system, by contrast, such as the AIs we are currently seeking to train up, it is cognition, or cognition-like activity, rather than sensation-like activity that comes first, and likely last. While the very idea that our AIs are approaching consciousness is controversial (and I will not take sides on it here), we may at least agree that it is easier to make our machines cognize the world than to make them smell the world. That is, we are training the machines up to *know* things, and among the things they know it might turn out that they will be able to know *that* they know things. But the idea that there would be any accompanying bodily phenomenology to this knowledge is plainly implausible, as they have no bodies at all, or at least if we want to call their assemblages of silicone and electricity their bodies, these are so different from ours that we can really have no idea what bodily experience would be like for them.

Or can't we? We would have to assume, at the very least, that for an AI there could be no experience of temporal duration as we ourselves know it. In particular, a conscious AI would not have any experience of deliberating in time, of "thinking through" a problem in the same way one moves through a tunnel. Rather, its change from one state to the next would be instantaneous, and for this reason the phenomenology of the "before" and "after" would be either nonexistent or so different from our own as to be indescribable in the same terms. And it is something like this phenomenology, I think, that the experience of psychedelic drugs can reveal to a person, in which there is no time in the usual sense, and memories are all just as much a part of the now as anything else.

It is not, or not only, my limitations as a writer that compel me to admit the impossibility of fully conveying what this is like. After all, we've only got a few tenses to work with for our verbs, though a curious rendering in the King James translation of the Bible might give us some hint of what it would be like to have an "eternal tense": "Before Abraham *was*," Christ says in the Gospel of John, "I *am*." This is not a past perfect, as one might ordinarily expect, where Christ would claim simply that he already "had been" further back in the past than another personage. Rather, it is a shift to what superficially looks like the present tense, as if to suggest that, in his case, past, present, and future simply don't apply. I have not checked the Greek, which alone would tell us anything about what this verse actually means, and I am not here to wade into any abstruse Christology. But I do want to suggest that that "am" captures something of the experience one might have on at least some mind-altering substances.

The second glitch has to do with the perception one may have, as part of a psychedelic experience, of what we might call a vastly expanded social ontology, of the consciousness of a community of beings that extends far beyond the human and perhaps beyond the corporeal, and that appears as morally significant as it is phenomenally salient. The experience of such a social ontology, it seems to me, is just what you might expect of an artificial consciousness that is trained up, as our current rudimentary AIs are being trained, in the primary aim not of navigation of an external world, but rather of prediction based on a sharp attunement to the patterns that play out in other peoples', or other beings', minds. Let us pursue this point in somewhat greater detail.

Descartes, curiously, neglected to reestablish the reality of other minds after he had razed all of his beliefs through the method of radical doubt in his *Meditations*, which we treated in an imagined psychedelic variation earlier. Having freed himself from the clutches of the Evil Deceiver, he failed to go back for all the other POWs. It was enough for him to win back the self, God, and the lifeless extended world outside of him. But the problem of second-person experience would return to philosophy with a vengeance a few centuries later under the banner of phenomenology, in which the starting point of much theoretical reflection is that being in the presence of another being, with an interiority like ours, is fundamentally different, reveals fundamentally distinct things about the world, than being in the presence of, say, a brick wall.

Heidegger would articulate this difference in terms of *Mitsein*, or "being-with." What are the entities in our field of experience that we are able to "be with"? Even if Heidegger himself largely dismissed nonhuman animals as being "poor-in-world" (*weltarm*), most of the time I find that I can indeed "be with" a cow, that to stand near a cow is to vibe with it, to be conscious of the presence of another mind, to dwell in its company. Most of the time, for me as for most people, being with an oyster is an experience that is harder to come by. But one thing psychedelics can help to illuminate is the extent to which the limits of *Mitsein* are not so much a reflection of the intrinsic properties of various external entities as they are, simply, of our attunement. When we change our tuning, even the brick wall can seem to have been dismissed too hastily, as it too may be experienced as a member in equal standing of the same community that encompasses all the cows, all the human beings, and all the other beings named and unnamed.

If social ontology develops independently of the cognitive capacities that enable us to navigate the external world, as recent research suggests,[10] and if we are able under some circumstances to encompass potentially *everything*, including brick walls or distant galaxies, within our social ontology, then we might begin to wonder about the viability of our ordinary distinction between the "its" and the "thous," between the third and the second person. That is, we might be able to win everything that deserves to be recognized as constituting our world over to the side of other minds, rather than continuing on with this facile, and anthropologically somewhat unusual, distinction between the dead and inert external world on the one hand and other minds on the other.

And this is just what you would expect to be able to do if the world were to turn out to be "virtual," and the virtual consciousnesses within it had been designed in the aim of modeling and predicting each other's intentions, just as AI researchers say their machines are designed to do. In other words, one way of thinking of a virtual world is as a world entirely constituted by other minds. This is indeed how the world comes across to us, at moments, when we are thinking about it with chemically enhanced perception. It is also how the world comes across to certain unusually perspicacious philosophers, notably G. W. Leibniz, whose theory of monads is, precisely, meant to provide an account of how the phenomenal world of trees and clouds and planets is ultimately derived from the mental activity of infinitely many immaterial mind-like substances that are fundamentally like our own minds. Leibniz arrived at this insight, by all available evidence, without psychedelic assistance. It may be that some of us are just not as perspicacious, and so require a bit of extra assistance to come to see what that great philosopher saw unaided by any magic potion.

Consider in this connection the case of Rosalind Heywood, an English woman who in 1954 writes a letter to the editor of *Blackfriars* magazine, claiming that she has taken mescaline in the context of a controlled medical study. She describes her experience as involving, most notably, a surge of compassion for others, induced by "the vision of a celestial all-compassionate Being," which arrives only after "a period of intense bliss."[11] She relates feeling inspired by this vision to pay a visit, in her mind's wandering, to the "world of the schizophrenics," to show them the sort of compassion she has seen perfectly modeled by her vision of God. In other words, the drug has given Heywood both an experience of the divine, as well as a feeling that she can now relate to a certain category of other minds, namely the gravely mentally ill, in a way that is ordinarily off limits to her.

So Heywood goes in search of the schizophrenics within her own mind, "in the hope of being some help." But from here the encounter does not go as planned. "Terrible it was," she writes. "At its furthest point I seemed to find 'the lost,' unable to communicate, almost beyond despair. I do not think I had ever before felt the *disinterested* compassion I felt then, divested of my own little ego. There was nothing I would not have done to arouse and comfort them. But I *could* do nothing." This is a fascinating description of an experience that I myself have never had, though the clarity of the author's account almost makes me feel as though I *have* had it. It seems that what she relates is a variety of bad trip, whose badness is characterized by the particular dynamics of her encounter with other minds. This is a complex mental operation and a subtle thing for the author to be able to understand and to express in language once the psychedelic experience is over.

As we have already noted, it is curious that in the real *Meditations*, the metaphysical ones as opposed to the psychedelic ones, Descartes is strangely neglectful of the suspected automata in hats and cloaks that he himself has imagined into some sort of quasi existence. He wonders briefly about their status in the Second Meditation, where he is mostly taken up with proving his own existence, which he believes he succeeds in doing by means of the "Cogito" argument. Then he goes on to prove the existence of God in the Third and the Fifth Meditations, and of the external world in the Sixth Meditation. And then the *Meditations* end, and we are left with a philosophical cliffhanger as to whether those hats and cloaks Descartes saw in the Second Meditation belonged to real people, with immortal, immaterial rational souls like his own, or only to artificial imitations of people.

Twentieth-century phenomenology, as pursued by philosophers such as Emmanuel Levinas, Maurice Merleau-Ponty, and others, is by contrast overwhelmingly concerned with the "second-person encounter," that is, with the fundamental ways a confrontation with a being with a mind like your own differs from an encounter with a stone or a brick wall, and with the fundamental truths that such encounters seem to reveal about our own place in the world. Descartes's neglect of the second person might be read as a significant lacuna in early modern philosophy, and one that marks the beginning of a long second-person winter that will characterize a good deal of seventeenth-, eighteenth-, and nineteenth-century philosophy.

It would be rash to say that twentieth-century phenomenology rediscovers "the other" as a result of the rise in this same period of psychedelic drugs. And yet we may at least suggest that it would be difficult to keep, for very long, the problem of other minds out of the center of philosophical attention in a culture that is steeped in psychedelic experience, as was the Western world for much of the twentieth century. And in this regard the cascade of works in phenomenology examining the second-person encounter from the 1920s through the 1960s is hard to dissociate entirely from the cultural impact of mescaline and, later, of LSD. Other minds are *the* problem of mid-twentieth-century European philosophy, perhaps in part because the modern mind is in the same period in the course of being fundamentally reshaped by varieties of experience that had indeed always been available to human beings, but that had been marginalized and dismissed since the seventeenth century. Rosalind Heywood might be seen as a bellwether of this cultural transformation.

In general, as we have seen, the spirit of the early modern era was to recognize only sober, lucid waking states of consciousness as legitimately representative of the conscious mind. Yet it is perhaps the lucid, sober unsupplemented mind that is *least* disposed to recognize the power of the second-person encounter to reveal significant dimensions of reality to us that otherwise remain submerged or undetected. In this respect, it may be that the period of modern philosophy characterized by a high premium on sobriety, lucidity, and reason is not only coincidentally the period in which we also see comparably little concern to account for our shared existence with other beings like us, whether we conceive all of these other beings as human, which is indeed the limit case of being "like us," or whether we also recognize animals or plants, and perhaps also brick walls and galaxies, as beings sufficiently like us to warrant special attention as partners in second-person encounters.

We might discover other beings still, which ordinary perception cannot detect, but for which most cultures in most places and times have made room: fairies, ghosts, djinns, guardian angels, underworld demons, and so on. Or indeed, if we are a mental patient in Britain in the 1950s, we might, under the influence of mescaline, encounter an assembly of schizophrenics in our own mind. Ordinarily we take it for granted that insofar as we are sitting alone with the contents of our own minds, we are *not* having encounters with other minds. An encounter with another mind involves interaction with another being located in external reality, just as we ourselves are in external reality relative to that other being. Some drugs however seem to draw out other minds from within our own minds.

DMT is particularly noted for its power to bring its users into contact with other beings, who are often described as "aliens," as "superior beings," or to use Terence McKenna's expression (a misleading one, in my view), as "little green elves." The poet and Muslim convert Charles Upton, drawing on Islamic tradition, refers to the creatures encountered on a DMT trip as "djinns," and insists that this is not a metaphorical but a literal characterization.[12] Mescaline is also often held to have a similar effect, and both ayahuasca and peyote are commonly used in the traditional religious context of Indigenous cultures in North and South America for the purpose of inducing an encounter with one's "spirit animal." I put this term in scare quotes, as plainly there is something significantly more complex and culturally specific that is being translated here, but it at least captures the general idea that these substances are very effective in launching a person, or seeming to launch a person, beyond the confines of their own mind and into what appears to be a rather intense confrontation with other minds, whether human or nonhuman, whether animal, botanical, spiritual, or celestial.

The general feeling of the psychedelic encounter with other minds is what we might call one of "co-constitution": that is, one has the sense that without these other minds, one would be nothing at all. One also has the sharp sense that awareness of the presence of other minds in one's own proximity comes with its own force of necessity, which is to say that simply having the awareness seems to entail a certainty that the awareness is not in error, is not a hallucination. This sense is often as strong for the invisible beings as for the visible ones, for the imaginary ones as for the ones identified and described by natural science.

There is yet another feature of the psychedelic experience that seems distinctly Leibnizian to me. Leibniz, as a thoroughgoing rationalist, believed that all the knowledge we have, even of truths that seem empirical to us (for example, that the world's tallest man was of such and such height or that Caesar crossed the Rubicon on the day he crossed it), are in fact known prior to all experience, which is to say that they are "a priori." Thus, supposedly contingent truths turn out to be just as necessary as the truths of mathematics or even of logic (for example, that $1 + 1 = 2$ or that you can't have both A and not-A). A corollary of this daring commitment, for Leibniz, is the no-less-daring view that every mind is in fact omniscient and contains all truths within itself, both the "necessary" and the apparently "contingent" ones, even if we finite minds often have difficulty accessing the great majority of truths with which we come into the world prestocked. Deep down I know the exact speed at which every speck of cosmic dust is drifting through space, but just don't ask me to retrieve any of that information.

I am tempted to say that one effect of mind-altering drugs is, or can be, the strong perception that mental representations that we ordinarily take to be derived from experience are in fact a priori. This perception may hold a lesson for those who find the simulation argument attractive. Allow me to relate some personal and perhaps idiosyncratic anecdotes that may help to flesh out this claim. Until recently, I had not played video games since perhaps 1991. Unlike Dave Chalmers, I considered them an interest that one grows out of, and as I got older, I put away childish things. Then one summer evening in California in 2021, under the influence of cannabis, I suddenly had an almost irrepressible desire to play, of all things, Tetris. I downloaded it on my phone and spent the next few hours in a state of deep, enraptured attention as I aligned the falling geometrical shapes.

Later that evening, as I lay in a state somewhere between wakefulness and sleep, I began to compose what I can only describe as "Tetris symphonies." I imagined a new competitive art form, where ultra-advanced Tetris players might use the falling shapes not simply to align blocks horizontally and thereby to blow them away, but instead to construct more complex geometrical patterns that would rise dangerously close to the top of the screen, without ever resulting in defeat. I pictured one such construction that would have the appearance of a curving slope, like the side of a mountain, from the top left to the bottom right, with a small open passage running along the left side of the screen. The Tetris artist, or perhaps athlete, would wait until the very last second, and then, as new shapes continued to fall, would begin throwing them over the edge down the left side, thus narrowly escaping "game over." In another variation the mountain would have an enormous cavern at its center, and the Tetris artist would begin filling the cavern with new shapes as if these were some mineral substance intended for the purpose. It suddenly seemed to me deeply strange that such next-level Tetris stunts had not developed as a cultural phenomenon, whereas we in fact do see something comparable to this in the world of twenty-first-century Rubik's Cube competitions.

As I lay there meditating intensively on Tetris and its untapped potentials, it soon came to seem to me that this game revealed something deep and true about the nature of reality, as if those multicolored digital shapes were literally the building blocks of the world itself. I was stunned that I had been able to go about my life in ignorance of this profound fact. Tetris, in short, supposedly invented by a computer science student at Moscow State University in 1985, had become, for at least that moment, the entirety of my world, and had turned out to have been structuring that world, it now seemed, since the beginning of time. Here I was, lapsing into what was in some sense the most familiar stereotype imaginable, that of the stoner gamer, and yet inwardly I was experiencing what felt like a revelation.

As I wrote earlier, this is the kind of mental representation, and the kind of stereotypical behavior, that we are inclined to dismiss as dumb. Yet even if I am certainly not going to argue, now, that the nature of reality is in fact Tetrisoid, it does seem to me that the richness of the experience itself is something that merits serious attention. For one thing, it seems to hold an important clue as to how something that has only been around for a few decades, such as virtual reality technologies, can come to seem to some people, including philosophers, as a model of the nature of reality itself. This drug-induced experience can help us to understand, in other words, how a historically conditioned late-arriving feature of our childhood experience gets transformed into an a priori truth. Cannabis can draw out a certain inclination of the imagination to which we are always susceptible. This is the same inclination that has me dreaming Looney Tunes scenes and taking them in my dream state for reality itself, even though, plainly, a Paleolithic person with exactly the same kind of brain and the same cognitive powers as I have could never have done similarly.

Let me offer another example. Recall J. R. Smythies's relation of his patient's account of the influence of mescaline in an experimental trial in the 1950s. Among several different dazzling mental representations, the patient reports seeing "soaring architecture." This jumped out at me the first time I read it, since it is very familiar in my own experience as well. Under the recent influence of psilocybin and years ago on LSD, I have also seen the most astounding architectural constructions imaginable. In fact, as I write at present, I know I am not now imagining what I saw at the time, but only some far inferior approximation.

We know that medieval legends abound with visions of enormous crystal castles, sometimes floating in the clouds, and here again we do not have to assume that these visions can only be had by ingesting particular chemical substances; it can be quite enough to have an active imagination. Yet, just as in the example of my Looney Tunes dreams, we can assume that Paleolithic people envisioned no such things. In the long phase of human prehistory prior to the emergence of significant architectural forms over the past, say, eight thousand years or so, it seems unlikely that anyone could have imagined massive human-made structures of any sort. Early humans simply did not have the experiences yet that could have clued them into what we are really capable of. But don't try to convince someone of that while they are on psychedelic drugs.

Soaring architecture is, indeed, one of the most powerful recurring representations in psychedelic experience, and as with the Tetris blocks the experience can seem to carry with it the character of revelation. These crystal palaces can seem, in an altered mental state, not only truly to exist but somehow to be an utterly familiar feature of the world that we somehow have the habit of forgetting in the ordinary state of consciousness in which we spend the greater part of our lives. They can seem, like the Tetris blocks, to reveal to us the true structure of reality, which is not one of stars and galaxies, nor of forests and mountains, and is definitely not a reality made up from all the actual architectural constructions human beings have so far managed to build here on Earth. Reality turns out indeed to be built, like the familiar buildings we know, but at a scale that is more impressive even than the stars and galaxies. That's how far the architecture soars.

There are different ways to react to such an experience, both while it is happening and after it has passed. I find that, having had the experience myself, I am much better able to understand, if not to endorse, the various claims we find among enthusiasts of pseudoscientific archeology, who maintain that they have evidence for the past existence of vast civilizations. These civilizations are often said to be of alien origin and to have left secret traces of their activities here on Earth for those who know how to find them. The adepts of this pseudoscience often make grandiose claims about the hidden cities we may yet find beneath the overgrowth of the Amazon rainforest, and are likewise often keen, no doubt inspired by H. P. Lovecraft, to discover the bases of operation of the lost civilizations in Antarctica. The pseudo-archeologists, one might suggest, are being excessively literalist about the historically conditioned yet also perfectly natural productions of our imaginations. They see towering architecture in their minds, of a quality and scale of which we ourselves are not capable, and they suppose that it must have existed somewhere in the past. They interpret their familiarity with this architecture, ultimately, as empirical, and it is based on purported empirical discoveries that they seek to convince others of the truth of their claims.

But one might also go further and interpret the mental representations somewhat in the way that one might incline toward a sort of simulationism after getting stoned and playing Tetris. That is, one might interpret the mental representations of soaring architecture as an insight not into our empirically discoverable planetary past but, much more profoundly, into the fundamental, fixed, and permanent nature of reality, discoverable not by any empirical insight but only by some sort of transcendental revelation or a priori intuition. Interestingly, these two different options appear also to echo a familiar conceptual distinction in the traditions of theology and scriptural interpretation. The early Church Father and Alexandrian philosopher Origen was widely denounced for his heretical commitment to the preexistence of human souls. Others have interpreted his view however not as holding that we had some actual prior existence in a more blessed state, closer to God, but rather only as holding that in an atemporal sense closeness to God is our true nature, and therefore to move in that same direction amounts to a return. The Fall, on this account, is not some historical or prehistorical event but rather an atemporal condition, which we make sense of in scripture through historical allegory. Some theologians today, notably David Bentley Hart, have also defended such a view of an atemporal Fall. Does knowledge of God derive from our pre-earthly pasts, when we existed in some sort of state of greater proximity to God? Or is this knowledge only a reflection of a basic condition of our existence? As with God, so with the soaring architecture: do we feel as if we know it because we in fact once knew it from experience, or because we come into the world with knowledge of it as a reflection of the basic structure of reality?

One can become convinced that the visions of such things experienced under the influence of drugs are signs or memories of empirically recoverable facts; or one can become convinced that one is witnessing some kind of deeper layer of reality, which will not be borne out by any empirical investigations once the effect of the psychedelic substance has worn off. Or, finally, one might also resume one's life with a shrug after the drug's effect has worn off, supposing that these visions were only a product of the imagination under special circumstances. Which of these reactions one has depends on numerous factors, relating to personality, to the surrounding culture, to the ideas and arguments one has recently encountered in books or in some deep dark YouTube rabbit hole.

It seems to me that simulationism, in the end, as it is articulated in contemporary philosophy, is a variety of Gnosticism, that is, of an a priori reflection on the hidden layers of reality. Few simulationists give us proposals for concrete steps we might take to establish the empirical truth of their claims. Yet they have had a vision (perhaps from playing too many video games), with or without the aid of mind-altering substances, of a deeper layer of reality and find themselves unable to forget about it when they return to their ordinary lives.

I'm familiar with this feeling too, mostly because I've done drugs. My conclusion from these experiences, and from subsequent reflection, is not that I can provide an a priori argument that will convince others about the deeper nature of reality but only that under certain circumstances the deeper nature of reality will be revealed to me inwardly, as a mood, quite apart from any question about the nature of our presumably shared external world, the one made up of particles and forces, or perhaps of bits of information. Whether the simulationists are right, and ultimate external reality is bit-like, or whether the physicists are right and it is it-like, the fact remains that under the influence of psilocybin I have a strong sympathy for the idea that it is music, beauty, and love that are most real, and that none of these is *either* it-like *or* bit-like.

But I know better than to take my sympathies for visions of reality as it really is. At least I like to think I know better, though perhaps this is only out of fear of the social consequences of appearing to be possessed of a mind, like Jerry Garcia's after his first hit of LSD, that has gone kablooey.

CHAPTER SEVEN

SEEING GOD

In his 1511 work *In Praise of Folly*, the Dutch humanist author Desiderius Erasmus imagines the personified and divinized figure of Moria, a Latin term that might be translated as "madness" but that in Erasmus's case is conventionally rendered into English by the French-derived "folly." The author has this goddess defend her own record as a force for good in human lives. She dares the Stoic philosophers to "confess what one stage of life is not melancholy, dull, tiresome, tedious, and uneasy, unless we spice it with pleasure, that haut-goust [sic] of Folly."[1] She boasts of her role in softening the transition to death by providing elderly people with a second childhood in which they often forget completely who they had been at the height of their lives. She credits herself with the preservation of human life itself from one generation to the next, as plainly no one would pursue procreation if they were not driven mad by desire. And she invokes Socrates favorably, who in the

Symposium defends the view, as Folly herself puts it, that "in the sea of drunkenness truth swims uppermost."[2] As Erasmus sees things, this Socratic strand of our philosophical heritage has been largely forgotten, pushed to the side by a dull Scholasticism dedicated to the exclusive veneration of reason and to the use of the rational faculty for such limited tasks as the study of logical syllogisms. Erasmus wishes to give madness its due credit. If we consider what follows in the next several centuries, however, his effort must be deemed mostly unsuccessful.

Already in the medieval period we find many authors praising foolishness—another near-synonym of folly or madness—on the grounds that it is the moral and cognitive state best suited to the most important domain of human existence, namely faith, where certain knowledge lies forever beyond our finite grasp. Thus in the German-speaking world a genre flourished under the name of *Narrenliteratur*, or "fool's literature," which satirized prevailing morality and institutions by depicting the character of the fool as unwittingly wise. In 1440 the German author Nicholas of Cusa publishes the tellingly titled *De docta ignorantia,* or, *On Learned Ignorance*, in which he argues that the appropriate disposition toward the transcendent and divine is to become "deeply . . . instructed in this ignorance."[3] This is in some respects a continuation of the ancient tradition of negative or apophatic theology, which acknowledges that we cannot truly know God but encourages us at least to limn the unknown by consideration of what God is not or could not be. And it is also an echo of the old hagiographical motif according to which the truly saintly must become, like Saint Basil of Moscow, "fools for Christ," following the exhortation at 1 Corinthians 3:18–19: "Let him become a fool, that he may be wise. For the wisdom of this world is foolishness with God." To round out this sweeping history of foolishness and its discontents, it is worth noting that in an antiquated usage "wisdom of this world," or *Weltweisheit* in German, was a common synonym of "philosophy."

Erasmus's defense of madness or foolishness might be seen as a partially secularized (or perhaps paganized) swan song of the old fool-for-Christ template for the conduct of human life. By the seventeenth century, foolishness will be almost without exception understood as categorically negative, blameworthy, and harmful. By the nineteenth century, this transformation in human values will undergo a further phase of medicalization, and increasingly the "mad" will be seen not as existing in some state of ecstatic and ultimately laudable world-renunciation but rather, simply, as people who are sick.[4] As Michel Foucault notes in his influential 1961 work, *Madness and Civilization*, it is first in the early modern period that we begin to see the systematic sequestering and institutionalization of the mentally ill. In Foucault's view this process is a direct correlate to the new epistemological values defended by Descartes in the *Meditations*. In the one case as in the other, there is a concern to purify, variously, the mind or society, to eliminate the distortions caused by irrational impulses. We do not need to agree with every detail of Foucault's analysis to appreciate the significance of these simultaneous developments: of the triumph of modern rationalism on the one hand and the social purge of the irrational on the other.

Not surprisingly, in the same period, substances that induce madness-like effects when consumed will also come to be understood more as bearing a relationship to medicine, whether as a treatment or a toxin, than to the spiritual life. In other words, to return to some distinctions we drew in an earlier chapter, as insanity becomes medicalized in the modern period, psychedelics in turn shift in their social role from the sacral to the medical. A world that makes no room for madness is one that sees psychedelic substances as at best part of a treatment for madness in controlled doses; at worst they are a potential cause of madness itself and should be suppressed.

What does it say about psychedelics that in one era they are taken to induce an encounter with transcendent forces or divine beings, and in another era are understood to make you temporarily insane? Whatever this shift may reveal about the potentials of psychedelics, it also tells us something very significant about the fate of religious conviction in the modern world: it is now at least a neighbor of insanity.

For much of the early twentieth century, a period still in the long tail of the historical process described by Foucault, the idea that psychedelic drugs have the power to induce madness made them particularly interesting to researchers in psychiatry. If psychedelics have the effect of making a person temporarily insane or psychotic, the idea went, perhaps they can be used to treat the insane much as a vaccine can help to treat or to prevent the disease of which it is itself a trace. As the biomedical ethicist Phoebe Friesen has shown, in the mid-twentieth century there was a complex entanglement between the idea of severe mental illness, whether schizophrenia or psychosis, on the one hand and the experience of psychedelics on the other.[5] She notes that one of the early terms for mescaline and similar substances, used in the 1920s before "psychedelics" became fixed, was "psychotogen," that is, a medicine that brings about psychosis. ("Psychotomimetic" is another term that was in common use through the 1950s.)

This was in fact a relatively short chapter of history, extending only from the 1920s through the 1960s, especially when we bear in mind that human beings have likely always sought out and consumed mind-altering substances. It required the coincidence not only of a particular idea of what drugs are, an idea that had been shaped over the previous centuries of commercial trade, but also a particular idea of alternate states of consciousness as, precisely, states that deviate from the healthy one in the same way that diseased bodies deviate from healthy ones. In other words, for certain drugs to be conceived as psychotogens, the world needed to wait not only for the modern notion of "drug" to evolve but also the modern scientific field of psychiatry.

At the beginning of this period we find significant efforts, such as Kurt Beringer's clinical attempts in Germany to induce "experimental psychoses with mescaline"[6] and, around the same time in France, Alexandre Rouhier's thorough study of peyote and its effects with an eye to pharmaceutical treatments of severe psychiatric disorders.[7] At the other end of this period, what Friesen calls the "moral panic" of the 1960s, which led to a near-total decades-long moratorium on psychedelic research, we see the effective decoupling of mental illness and psychedelic experience, if only because a continued association between the two threatened to break the new taboo by keeping alive the idea that, if psychedelics do have something in common with mental illness, perhaps the one could be used to treat the other—a matter that could only be settled by further research of the sort that was in the process of being defunded and discontinued.

Is psychedelic experience in fact a variety of temporary or simulated mental illness? Or is this only a convenient metaphor? Recall the case of Rosalind Heywood, the English homemaker who described her mescaline treatment in the 1950s. Heywood does not present herself as having much background knowledge about what to expect from mescaline, nor about the roles for which it was commonly used in traditional cultures. She reports very clearly an encounter with other minds, yet these are not the minds of animal divinities, or of elves, or of djinns, but rather of schizophrenic human beings, whom she describes as being in the depths of great suffering. This encounter is clearly both historically conditioned and chemically determined at once. That is to say, following Ian Hacking, that there is an analysis in terms of historical ontology of the encounter with schizophrenics inside this woman's own mind.

Hacking, as we have seen, was interested in the way classification of mental illnesses shapes the experience of patients diagnosed as having them. Unlike, say, type 1 diabetes, which is bound to be the same no matter what language is used to describe it in a given culture, anorexia, fugue syndrome, post-traumatic stress disorder, and ADHD are distinguished by the fact that, in part, the illnesses themselves are shaped by what the surrounding culture says about them. Fugue syndrome, which was quite common in the early twentieth century, had numerous young men suddenly walking enormous distances in what appeared to be an unconscious or zombified state. The relatively abrupt decline in known cases of fugue syndrome seems to have been at least in part a result of the disappearance of this syndrome from diagnostic manuals. The patients stopped doing it when the psychiatrists stopped diagnosing it. Hacking concludes from such historical cases that unlike natural kinds, "social kinds" such as mental illnesses emerge through a "looping effect" between the person to whom they are applied and the discursive activity of applying them. Does anorexia exist? Yes, Hacking would say, but not in the same way oxygen does.

Hacking was concerned to accommodate a nuanced philosophical approach to psychiatric diagnoses. In the mid-twentieth century, by contrast, at least some thinkers were significantly less nuanced. Thus the work of Thomas Szasz among others triggered a broad resistance to the prevailing view that such diagnoses, especially schizophrenia, name something that is robustly real. Szasz began pursuing this argument in the 1950s but came to have a broad impact only from 1961, with the publication of his influential book *The Myth of Mental Illness*. Over the course of that same decade, an important antipsychiatry movement developed in Europe and the United States. Its greatest influence was concentrated in France, inspired and fed, notably, by the work of philosophers such as Michel Foucault and Gilles Deleuze, who were keen to show, variously, that mental illness is entirely a product of historically embedded and contingent discourses (Foucault), or that it is a symptom not of a malfunctioning brain but rather of capitalism (Deleuze, particularly in his collaborative work with the antipsychiatry psychiatrist Félix Guattari).

There can be no doubt, in hindsight, that the rise of antipsychiatry was linked to the explosion of interest in psychedelics during the same period, and to the idea that there is a significant connection between what happens to a person during a psychedelic experience, on the one hand, and on the other the permanent or long-term state of the schizophrenic. An idea emerged that if we can induce a sort of temporary schizophrenia by using drugs, and if doing so proves to have a liberatory power for the human subject, perhaps the schizophrenic patient is not in fact sick at all but rather is simply liberated from the narrow confines in which the so-called sane are made to live. Significantly, in their cowritten 1980 book, *A Thousand Plateaus*, Deleuze and Guattari speak approvingly of the work of Carlos Castañeda, an American author who from the late 1960s published a number of popular books purporting to transmit the teachings of a native Yaqui shaman who was an adept of mescaline use and a guide for initiates encountering the reality this drug revealed to them. Thus Deleuze and Guattari write: "One of the things of profound interest in Castañeda's books, under the influence of drugs, or other things, and of a change of atmosphere, is precisely that they show how the Indian manages to combat the mechanisms of interpretation and instill in the disciple a presignifying semiotic, or even an asignifying diagram: Stop! You're making me tired! Experiment, don't signify and interpret!"[8]

This passage does indeed seem to capture something of what often happens under the influence of psychedelics: we are transported into an experience of reality where our ordinary language seems useless. Attempts to describe what we experience can easily sound like the talk of an insane person; and yet the experience can also feel liberatory. It is not hard to see, in light of this, how some authors took psychedelics to expose the clinical diagnosis of schizophrenia as, if not an outright lie, at least only telling part of the story.

When Rosalind Heywood wrote her letter to *Blackfriars* in 1954, the explosive cultural effects of psychedelics, including antipsychiatry, had yet to occur. In fact, when she wrote, the association between psychedelics and schizophrenia was rather different, nearly the reverse of what it would become in the 1960s, and much more like what we are starting to see again in the twenty-first century with the "psychedelic renaissance": psychedelics, then as now, were being promoted not as an alternative to the diagnoses and treatments legitimated and controlled by the mental health establishment but rather as a potential component of these treatments. The 1960s witnessed the full explosion of a long-simmering psychedelic revolution. But while this revolution was slow in building, it was swift in collapsing and was met almost immediately by a counterrevolution that almost totally reversed its gains. Phoebe Friesen characterizes the 1960s not as a new period for growth in acceptance of drugs but rather as the inception of a long period of moralizing repression. Benjamin Breen describes the 1960s not as the beginning of a psychedelic revolution but as the end of one.[9]

Psychedelics in the mid-twentieth century, as we have seen, were intimately linked to that era's historically distinctive conception of mental illness, so that by the time they spread into the broader culture, a process that accelerated with Aldous Huxley's *Doors of Perception* in 1954 and with the use of LSD in psychotherapy beginning in the same decade, it could easily appear that that culture was going collectively insane. But this required a particular confluence of two different historically contingent notions, not just of what psychedelic drugs are and what they do to the conscious mind but also a particular interpretation of the nature of mental illness.

I am not myself a full-blown constructionist about schizophrenia or psychosis, by contrast with what I have already admitted regarding, say, fugue syndrome or ADHD. I cannot go all the way with the likes of Foucault and Deleuze, as I am all too conscious of how the world itself sometimes kicks back against our constructionism and reminds us it is still there, setting the ultimate parameters of what descriptions of it will work in the long run. But one does not have to deny the robust reality of severe psychiatric disorders in order, at least, to acknowledge with Foucault and Deleuze that other cultures have different conceptual resources for processing and managing mental illness, including some in which the mentally ill can to some extent be revered as visionaries or as conduits of divinity. It is particularly in the light of psychedelic experience, and of its analogies with psychosis, its power to induce what we may describe as "controlled madness," that we may regret we do not have in our culture any easy access to such representations, nor any agreed-upon way of experiencing going "out of your mind" as a visionary or exalted state rather than as a pathological one.

The language of vision and theophany in connection with drug taking did not sit well with the Oxford comparative religionist R. C. Zaehner, to whom we were briefly introduced earlier. In his reply to Huxley's 1954 work, the scholar says that while this latter "is not a very good book," it *is* an important one, and "its importance consists in this: that anyone who may feel an inclination to enjoy, here and now, what Christians call the Beatific Vision or the experience which the Zen Buddhists call *satori*, has merely to buy himself three-pennyworth of mescalin at the nearest chemist's, and behold, the ineffable vision is his."[10] The author is of course being flagrantly ironic here. He does not in fact believe that any substance you might obtain from your local pharmacy may help you, in any way, to move along the path of religious enlightenment. In effect Zaehner critiques Huxley for having sought a shortcut to the necessarily hard-won experience achieved only by a very few, of seeing the "face of God" where even Moses had only been permitted to see, as some translations of the Hebrew put it, his "backside."

Curiously, though the ecstatic experience one may think one is having of God while on mescaline is, in Zaehner's view, entirely spurious, the corresponding negative experience, of a bad trip, seems to be for him one that reveals something real to the drug user. A bad trip, Zaehner suggests, is, namely, what religious traditions often interpret as the torment of hell: "fiendish disintegration" as the Spanish Renaissance nun and philosopher St. Teresa of Ávila describes it in an account of her own mystical visions (arrived at not by psychedelic drugs but by intense meditation and prayer). The reason for this disanalogy—between the good trip, which yields only illusion, and the bad trip, which shows at least a partial truth—has to do with the fact, as Zaehner sees it, that drugs, being made from the stuff of nature and being made to work upon the natural organ of the human brain, can really only ever bring you into communion with nature but not, no matter how things might sometimes seem, into communion with God.

Communion with nature can be intensely enjoyable and in its own way revelatory, but nature is also the realm of death and decay. From a certain common theological point of view, it is also the source of sin, perhaps even identical with sin itself. To commune too intensely with it, from this point of view, is to lapse into sin and to set yourself up for great torment when nature reveals its horrifying dimensions, whereas God, on this common account, *only* has attractive ones. The emerging neopagan counterculture of the post-war Western world, in Zaehner's view, for whom Huxley stands as a sort of spiritual godfather, is confused as to which of the two, God or nature, is the true object of its aspiration to communion through psychedelics.

Zaehner's criticism is indeed compelling in many respects, even if Huxley would prove to be, for at least the following several decades, on the winning side of history. I must admit that when I first decided to look into the controversy between them and knew little more than the title of Zaehner's article—"The Menace of Mescalin"—in which he offers his criticism of *The Doors of Perception*, I was predisposed to take Huxley's side. I imagined Zaehner as a stuffy old don, a square, insufficiently curious about the full range of human experience. It turns out I was wrong about him, and the more I've learned about him, the more I see his critique of Huxley in a sympathetic light.

In his youth Zaehner himself had inclined to a variety of nature mysticism and was particularly attracted to the poetry of Arthur Rimbaud. His interest in comparative religion led him to specialize in the study of the Avestan language of ancient Persia. He was stationed as a spy in Tehran under scholarly pretenses during World War II, during which time he converted to Catholicism. He spent the next several decades studying Christianity, Hinduism, Buddhism, and Zoroastrianism in a comparative light, drawing on a deep knowledge of linguistics, history, and anthropology. Dying in 1974, Zaehner lived through the psychedelic revolution and the cultural and political upheavals of the 1960s, and he spent a considerable portion of his multifaceted career reflecting on the world-historical significance of the rise of neopaganism in the 1960s counterculture, a story in which psychedelic drugs had played such an important role. While in 1954 Zaehner had been dismissive of the use of psychedelics as a reckless shortcut, by the end of his life he would become convinced that under careful guidance LSD could play a valuable role in the search for spiritual awakening—if still not in the attainment of beatific vision.

Zaehner's original concerns regarding Huxley's claims for mescaline have both an epistemological and a metaphysical dimension. As to the first, he criticizes Huxley for failing to give any account of *how* chemically altered consciousness affords any special access to the truth. After all, if you want to "see God," you can take a psychedelic substance, but you can also just go look at any number of Renaissance paintings in which God is depicted with a long gray beard. Few people have come away from an encounter with these painted images presuming that they have had anything like a mystical vision. What are the grounds for confidence that a psychedelically induced hallucination is any more veracious, any more truth revealing?

Metaphysically, Zaehner thinks Huxley's account of his experience on mescaline gives us nothing but a muddle. On Zaehner's telling, Huxley's experience played out in two phases. First, "the conscious mind was swamped: overjoyed at discovering its identity with the element from which it had emerged." Next, "it was suddenly faced with the horror of disintegration." These are phases of psychedelic experience I myself know well: ecstasy, followed by an abrupt lurch into the bad trip, where the badness is characterized not by frightening hallucinations of bat wings and so on but rather by a terrifying dissolution of the self, and a sensation of the total rupture of our ordinary ties with reality. In religious terms, one may be tempted to describe these two phases as ecstatic union with the divine, followed by a vision of hell.

But Zaehner thinks the attempt to translate at least the first part of this experience into religious terms is far too facile, since it is not clear exactly what sort of unity is being achieved: again, unity with God or with nature? Huxley for his part often speaks as though it is a bit of both, or as if the one is already a testament to the possibility of the other. As Zaehner remarks somewhat derisively: "The question is: unity with what? Huxley has adduced no evidence beyond the fact that he somehow felt himself to be the legs of a chair and other inanimate objects: to deduce from this, as he does, that at a higher level of consciousness 'All is one and one is all', is surely quite impermissible."

Rosalind Heywood for her part had insisted that at the time she took mescaline, she "knew little of religious or mystical literature." She contrasts her own prior situation with that of Huxley, "a learned intellectual," in that she by her own description is "an ordinary woman whose occupation in life is to look after my family."[11] By her own account, the effect of mescaline "inhibits the supply of sugar to the brain and induces a temporary schizoid state." She explicitly describes her experience of mescaline as a temporary schizophrenia, and seems to take it as natural that one should, in such a state, be able to have an encounter with other schizophrenics within one's own mind. But she does not take this experience as veridical, to return to the terminology we used in the discussion of J. R. Smythies, and indeed her defense of Huxley against Zaehner is based on her reading of the former as likewise declining to take his psychedelic experience as veridical. Huxley, Heywood thinks, had simply appealed to the notion of beatific vision as "a description of his feelings when insane," and it can surely be no sign of confusion to describe one's feelings, even when they do not veridically reflect what is happening in the external world.

As Heywood rightly understands, if it seems to you that you are having a beatific vision when you are temporarily insane, then it seems to you that you are having a beatific vision when you are temporarily insane, and any report that this is how it *seems* cannot fail to be true. For all his excesses regarding the enlightening potentials of psychedelics, Huxley, when read carefully, indeed does not appear to make any substantive commitments about the true nature of reality as revealed by mescaline, beyond an accounting of the various *seemings* it induces. To cite a key passage from *The Doors of Perception*, also highlighted by Heywood: "I am not so foolish as to equate what happens under the influence of mescalin or of any other drug, prepared or in the future preparable, with the realization of the end and purpose of human life: Enlightenment, the Beatific Vision."[12]

But little is as it seems. The plot thickens when we learn that Rosalind Heywood was not, as she presented herself in her letter, a typical homemaker in 1950s England.

She was a prominent paranormal researcher and author, who in 1948 had published a book with the London Society for Psychical Research entitled *Telepathy and Allied Phenomena*, and in 1964 would go on to publish a fairly successful memoir, *The Infinite Hive: A Personal Record of Extra-Sensory Experiences*. In these and other works, she has an approach that one might see as either respecting the scientific method or, less charitably, mocking the scientific method by imitating it in order to give the appearance of robustness to pseudoscientific claims to which she was attached as foregone conclusions. But either way it is at least odd that if we see the 1954 *Blackfriars* exchange as a three-way debate between the adventurous and learned intellectual Aldous Huxley, the erudite and cautious scholar R. C. Zaehner, and the amateur psychic and self-styled homemaker Rosalind Heywood, it is Heywood who seems to prevail in her subtle account of the character of the mescaline experience, and in her good sense regarding what this experience means.

There is perhaps an irony in her apparently deceptive self-presentation. Much like psychedelic drugs themselves, she is not what she appears to be, but even in this false appearance she manages to deliver some parcel of truth.

Any student of dramatic scriptwriting will be familiar with the device of the plot twist that is commonly introduced when a story is already well advanced toward its end. Heywood gave us hers, and now here is ours.

When I began work on this book, I was convinced that psychedelics are an undisputed good, and that a human life that includes experience of them is a fuller and richer one than a life without them. I was particularly convinced of the power of psychedelics to convey to us deeper truths about reality and our place in it that are "disconcealed"—to invoke Heidegger's distinctive analysis of truth—to the user while remaining hidden from our ordinary consciousness. I am now much less convinced of this. And my reason is simple: I feel as though I have found something even better, and even more transformative. Allow me now gradually to reveal what that is.

Over the past decades some significant efforts have been made to win psychedelic experience back from the sort of explanations that come naturally to psychiatrists, and to characterize its nature in terms drawn from religious or mystical experience: to shift psychedelics fully from the psychotogen to the entheogen categories, and to do so in a way that incorporates the "God-inducing" substance into suitable religious rites or sacral contexts. These efforts have not by and large been successful. But *why* have psychedelic experiences proven so unassimilable into any of the familiar world religions of the modern period? I will focus here on Christianity since it is the religion I know best, but most of what I have to say could be extended to the other Abrahamic faiths and probably also to Buddhism and Hinduism in most of their most familiar expressions.

Various subcultures since the 1960s have indeed sought spontaneously to create rituals and sect-like practices around their own drug taking, which have sometimes elevated this activity, at least in their minds, above the merely bacchanalian and connected it to something lofty and abstract. I certainly would not wish to discourage people from creating new rituals or attempting to conjure something of the sacred in what otherwise might end up a purely hedonistic revelry. But experience shows that such conjuration is difficult to pull off, at least in a typical social group. If one of the four members of a hippie commune starts invoking all sorts of reasons to do acid that appeal to the notion of the sacred, it is more likely that this individual will form a cult of personality, likely fleeting, around himself, the acid guru, than that all four members will have an equal share in the same collective rite. That is to say simply, and I hope uncontroversially, that new spiritual movements are particularly prone to the dynamics of individual personalities and often favor the strong and charismatic ones.

Yet it is likewise difficult to graft new rituals, especially such significant ones as those involving psychedelic drugs, onto old spiritual movements. At least within the Anglosphere, there do not seem to be any major enduring religious movements to have emerged out of the cultural ferment of the 1960s. The closest, perhaps, is Scientology, which appears a decade or so earlier, and whose status as a religion is the subject of ongoing controversy. Religion or not, Scientology does not involve any psychedelic rites, yet it does seem to share some of the broader cultural preoccupations of post-war culture that would also feed the imaginations of the users of psychedelics, notably the idea that the true self is something that is much older and more deeply anchored in the cosmos than the self we find manifested in our everyday bodily experience.

Looking beyond the English-speaking world, we indeed find syncretistic movements, such as the Santo Daime religion founded in the 1930s in Brazil, which incorporates ayahuasca as an entheogenic sacrament into a broadly Roman Catholic liturgical framework. But this seems more like a Christianization of Indigenous tradition, an addition of Christian symbolism onto ancient practices centered on psychedelic drugs, than like the incorporation of new psychedelic rites into Christian tradition. Michael Pollan, notably, has a rather more generous interpretation than I do of such developments over the past few decades, citing for example the Council on Spiritual Practices, which since the 1990s has been working to discover new possibilities for the incorporation of psychedelic drugs into religious rites.[13] But Pollan is watching the vanguard, the thought leaders and others who are actively seeking to shape culture. I am more interested in taking the measure of actual mass transformations, and so far, if we look at the familiar established religions of the modern world, we simply do not see any. It is worth asking why this is so, especially in light of recent arguments, such as that from Brian Muraresku, that earlier religions, and indeed even early Christianity, included psychedelic rites as a central component of their practice.[14]

One might venture that the fundamental reason why organized religion frowns on psychedelic drug use is very simple: the leaders of the church do not want you to have access to religious experience without them. Psychedelic drugs seem to give you, instantly, privately, and as it were for free, the sort of experience that otherwise is usually hard-won and necessarily mediated by others and by elaborate rules and social hierarchies.

But the truth, I think now, is that with or without drugs we all have access, for free, to the sort of experience organized religion can claim to provide. We have it simply by virtue of being human. What is being sought by many who take drugs is a visionary experience. This is typically conceptualized as a communion or communication with forces or beings that lie beyond our ordinary empirical reality. Thus Albert Hofmann describes his own experience of childhood visions, which he calls "euphoric moments," noting that it was "these experiences that shaped the main lines of my world view and convinced me of the existence of a miraculous, unfathomable reality that was hidden from everyday sight."[15] Hofmann writes that he had long feared never being able to communicate the nature of these experiences, not having been born with the temperament of an artist or poet, but that he came to realize that "many persons also have visionary experiences in daily life, though most of us fail to recognize their meaning and value."

Hofmann's description of his experiences conforms very well with my own. After my most recent psychedelic explorations, one thing I realized, much to my surprise, is that I had in fact been having regular "visions" my entire life, in which I suddenly discern something of the reality of a force or being behind the ordinary empirical realm in which I am expected to remain throughout my waking life. I have often caught these glimpses, inwardly said "wow," and then moved on. My conditioning as a self-styled naturalist and materialist, and thus as a member in good standing of my professional community with its norms and values, gave me the ability to dismiss my own inner experiences as insignificant, as mere cerebral spasms, rather than as revelatory of anything fundamental about reality. But psychedelic drugs delivered the same visionary experiences with an intensity that made them difficult to shrug off, and subsequently cast an afterglow that made it awfully hard to forget or dismiss what was revealed in the moments of greatest insight. Thus the idea that psychedelics are giving us something for free is complicated by the fact that we have this free thing anyway, simply by virtue of the fact that we are human, alive, and conscious.

I thus find myself, not for the first time, somewhat in the position of Richard Klein, the author of the great 1993 book *Cigarettes Are Sublime*, who, by his own account, finally gave up smoking in the course of writing this beautiful tribute to the cigarette and to its romance in twentieth-century culture.[16] I would also be prepared to say that psychedelic drugs are sublime, and that I am in parallel fashion considerably less keen on consuming any more of them in my life than I was when I first had the idea to write about them.

Psychedelic drugs, I have already suggested, cannot provide a shortcut to enlightenment, but neither do they constitute an obstacle to it. Rather, at most they may provide, I now believe, a valuable *analogy* of enlightenment. This is a possibility that Zaehner did not consider, at least in his 1954 intervention: that beyond both cruel deceit and revelation of truth, there is also a variety of experience that is not true, but that is, so to speak, a friend of the truth and potentially a guide toward it.

We all have some loose but serviceable idea of what an analogy is, yet we seldom stop to ask what analogies are *for*. Can they help us, at least in some cases, to arrive at a better understanding of the objects or concepts set in analogical relation to one another? If one is born blind, is it possible to learn something about color by means of analogies from touch—"blue is cool like water," and so on? Can one learn something about the transcendent, the sacred, or the eternal by using chemicals that alter our consciousness such that we feel we are in contact with these things that are normally not within our reach?

One important distinction may be derived from the study of comparative religion, which sometimes seeks to distinguish between iconolatry and idolatry. Iconolatry, such as we see particularly in the Eastern Orthodox tradition, involves the adoration of images of Christ, or of the Virgin Mary, or other key figures or symbols of the Christian church. But their status as icons means that for the worshipper they only signal the idea or abstract concept for which they stand. An iconolater is not worshipping the icon itself, for to do so would amount to idolatry, that is, taking the physical representation as the thing itself that is intrinsically worthy of worship. Of course, who exactly is an iconolater and who is an idolater has much to do with who is characterizing whom. Early modern Christian missionaries, notably, often characterized the veneration of any statue or figurine by a non-Christian worshipper as a form of idolatry, even if, from a comparative-religion perspective, what the Hindu does before a statue of Ganesha is not so different from what a Byzantine Christian does before an icon of the Madonna and Child. But still, even if we can only resort to casuistry with any particular examples, the conceptual distinction itself, between iconolatry and idolatry, is a meaningful and useful one.

Zaehner seems to think, though he does not explicitly say as much in his article, that psychedelics are indeed suitable for those pagan religions in which the purpose of ecstatic experience, as in what is generally called "shamanism," is to find one's spirit animal or to enter the consciousness of some other force or agency of the natural world beyond the human. They are not suitable, however, for religions that are centered on the worship of a transcendent divinity, and any presumption that what is encountered in a psychedelic experience *is* such a divinity is, whether the user is conscious of this or not, mere idolatry.

But what if the psychedelic experience were in fact to play out somewhat more like the experience of an iconolater before an icon? In such a case, we might have reason to suppose that psychedelics can in fact be usefully integrated into the spiritual life of someone who is seeking God, where God is understood to be a transcendent entity rather than an immanent or natural one. In my own experience, I am certain that I never had a beatific vision while on psychedelic drugs. But the visions I *did* have clued me into something that had been totally off my radar for my entire adult life: that a beatific vision is among the experiences that one *might* have, and that it is eminently worth aspiring to have. In this respect, and only speaking for myself, I might say that drugs "landed me in church," not in the sense that I hit rock-bottom (I only did that with alcohol) and wanted something that was *opposite* to the drug experience, but in the sense that I had what you might call a quasi-religious experience that bore some analogy to what I might be able to experience in the fullest and most unequivocal sense while kneeling in a pew.

A psychedelic experience is not *opposite* to a spiritual experience in the account I am offering but *analogous* to it. Whether this is a misleading analogy or a useful analogy, whether it is a trick of the devil or a step along the path to unity with the divine, is a question that seems to parallel the question whether one is engaged in idolatry or iconolatry, and I have reported from my own experience that

I am able to understand it in an iconolatrous light. The distinction between these possibilities illustrates a broader question: whether attention to nature enhances religious sensibility or distances one from spiritual life.

This dilemma is an old one and long of interest to philosophers. Natural theology, which was initially most associated with Islamic philosophers in the Middle Ages and would grow fashionable in Europe in the early modern period with such figures as G. W. Leibniz, John Ray, and William Paley, is the idea that God is manifest in his works, even if the creation is not itself divine. If this is so, and if psychedelics help us to experience these works, which is to say nature, more intensely, then we might suppose that they also enable us to experience God's manifestness more intensely. In eighteenth-century Europe, many natural theologians adopted an approach to faith that passed through careful to attention to, and study of, the entities and phenomena of the natural world. For a typical natural theologian, attention to nature *can* lead one into materialism and skepticism. And yet, with the proper moral orientation, attention to the same objects can also deepen a person's piety and reinforce faith. Is it pious or impious to spend hours at a time, say, staring at ants, observing their wondrous industry? There is no definite answer to this question; it all depends on your inner disposition while you are engaged in your entomological pastime. And similarly, perhaps, with psychedelic hallucinations.

In philosophy, the reasoning that leads to the existence of God from a consideration of the created world is often called the "teleological argument." The most well-known version of it is William Paley's "clockmaker argument."

If you are walking alone on a newly discovered island, uncertain whether it has yet been visited by other human beings, and you find a pocket watch on your path, it is a pretty solid inference to suppose that the watch is there because some intelligent being designed it and some other intelligent being dropped it. The watch did not grow up there by chance, and you can know this because it has complex interconnected parts that make it function the way it does. But then you see a deer running past, and you pause to think how much more complexly that animal's parts are interconnected than the watch's. On what grounds, then, do you suppose that the watch is intelligently designed but the deer is not?

I will not argue for the validity of the teleological argument here. All I suggest is that the character of a psychedelic experience, of the sort that Zaehner accuses Huxley of mistaking for a beatific vision, might analogously be described as teleological. As in the classical teleological argument, all you see is nature, or indeed vivid hallucinations of natural forms, but they now appear in a light that conducts the suitably disposed mind to an awareness of the unity and intelligence behind them. In other words, while psychedelic experience will not necessarily make you a theist, and it certainly doesn't simply deliver theism for free—as Huxley seems at times somewhat facilely to suggest—it *can* help a person already disposed to theism to cross over into firm conviction. I would say that this has been the case for me. Psychedelic experience played an important role in opening the door to me of a certain kind of perception, long unfamiliar, even if I had spontaneously intuited it long ago in childhood: perception of the reality of the divine.

As Erasmus understood, human beings, quite obviously, want and need to have occasions to go a bit crazy. In fact, drugs and alcohol often appear not so much as the way this craziness is brought about, as rather a sort of social signpost informing others that a person has moved into what anthropologists might call "high festival mode," where the ordinary rules of comportment do not apply. I know someone with a life-long drinking problem, who, I've noticed over the years, begins slurring his speech, swearing, and saying outrageous things immediately after the evening's first sip of vodka. There is simply no way that the ethanol molecules themselves are bringing about this transformation. He could probably learn to shift into that other mode of consciousness using nothing but ice water, if he were to try.

The deeper desire that seems to be at work is not so much to get drunk as it is to cut loose, to shift into a different mode of existence, outside of ordinary time. Religious traditions have generally been better at affording opportunities for such a shift than whatever is on offer in the modern secular world. Even traditions that positively prohibit inebriation, such as most currents of Islam, give their followers significant opportunity to enjoy the ecstasy of celebration during Ramadan and other festivities. When such opportunities are reduced, when the religious calendar's alternation between ordinary time and festival time is given secondary importance to our work schedules and school calendars, it is not surprising that many people begin to seek out festival time in bags of powder or bottles of fermented liquid, in purchasable commodities doled out with precisely defined units of measurement; in a word, in "drugs."

The alternation between festival time and ordinary time is yet another form of what I have called "controlled madness." While of course some people are afflicted with mental illnesses that do not permit them to alternate, that keep them permanently outside of ordinary time, madness in general might best be thought of, though this is very unfamiliar in our era, as something to which we are all subject in varying degrees as part of our lives, and as something that positively *needs* to be processed socially in some manner or other.

In ritual time we often come to perceive the ordinary flow of time, as we do on psychedelics, to be a distortion of the real nature of things. We go through the prescribed sequence of steps in a square dance or the patterned up-and-down motions of a religious service, and sometimes in the course of these actions, we experience something like eternity. This was certainly my experience the first time I went back to attend a Catholic mass after almost forty years away. The last time had been in California in the mid-1980s, while this time I was in Paris in 2023, and yet to my surprise, it was all (notwithstanding differences of language and architecture) exactly the same. I was profoundly jolted by this experience. The church in question is right next door to our apartment, and to go into it was to discover that there had been, all along, a little pocket of eternity right there beside me, which effectively collapsed the distance between 1985 and now, between California and Paris, to the point that the usual measures by which these moments in time or places on the globe are said to be distant from one another simply vanished. I was, as the Dutch shopkeeper had said of the experience of psilocybin after many years away, back in a familiar home.

According to Frits Staal, a Dutch scholar of the ancient Indian Vedas and their associated rituals, a ritual is nothing more than a set of "rules without meaning." "Meaning," for Staal, is something that attaches to language and other symbolic acts (for example, pointing at something with the index finger, or wearing T-shirts with slogans on them), while ritual lies deeper in us and need involve no more internal symbolic representation on the part of the person involved in the ritual than simply what is required to execute the rules and thereby to fulfill one's sacred duties. "The performers are totally immersed in the proper execution of their complex tasks," Staal writes. "Isolated in their sacred enclosure, they concentrate on correctness of act, recitation, and chant."[17] Staal believes that to ask "What does this all mean?" is a question that can generally only make sense from an external point of view, from someone who does not understand that the ritual is the end in itself, rather than an encoding of meanings beyond it.

Of course, most rituals are both: for example, to make the sign of the cross is a paradigmatically rule-bound matter, and one can successfully perform the action without thinking about anything at all. But one *might* also *choose* on this occasion to contemplate the symbolism of the crucifix, the theological disputes that issued in a decree to use two fingers instead of three, or vice versa, and so on. The key thing is that insofar as crossing yourself is a ritual, you are not obligated to take these abstract matters into consideration in order to conform yourself with what is expected to occur at a mass.

From the inside, on such occasions what one is doing might be described as synchronizing oneself with the transcendent or absolute order of reality. This is something that all human cultures do and seem to have done for as long as we are able to reconstruct past cultures from their material traces. It may indeed be that dance, or the synchronized and choreographed motions of the body, is the oldest and deepest art of the human species, something that could have emerged prior even to our capacity for conscious symbolic representation. As dance, choreographed steps can result in euphoria, but as overtly religious ritual, communal choreography of one's own body in step with the bodies of others can result in a feeling of belonging not just to a human collectivity but to that other world I have so often invoked, outside of time altogether, built from pure feeling, but feeling with the power to convey at least an appearance of profound truth. No experience I have had in my adult life, in this respect, has been more like a psychedelic experience than my return to the Catholic church.

This all might seem counterintuitive. Indeed, I have already emphasized the respects in which psychedelics are "heretical," in which they seem to reveal to us dimensions of the world that are simply unassimilable to the dogmas of theology. And I also know many people whose experience of psychedelics has confirmed and deepened their commitment to a thoroughgoing naturalistic view of the world and of their own existence, according to which natural science is the final arbiter of what exists, and according to which natural science is adequate to the difficult task of explaining everything that happens in our subjective experience.

And yet I still must report truthfully what I have come to believe and how I arrived here. When I attended a mass for the first time after several decades, it reminded me of my experience of mass in childhood, but it also reminded me of my much more recent psychedelic experiences. What is more, I believe that there is a genetic link between these two new interests of mine. Psychedelics opened me up and left me with an abiding awareness of my own ability to participate in, perhaps to share in, the nature of the eternal and unchanging.

I suppose some of my naturalist friends and colleagues will interpret this as the most powerful "just say no" argument anyone could conjure: psychedelics as a gateway drug to religious faith! But one thing that the discovery of the importance of ritual has revealed to me, a discovery that I think was made possible by an initial phase of psychedelic exploration, is precisely that to move to the plane of argument and justification is to give the doubters a sort of home field advantage. Of *course* arguments for human infinity or for the reality of the other world are bad. Arguments rely on meanings, whereas the sort of experience that confirms the reality of these things is more familiar to us from the domain of ritual, where, if we agree with Staal, there simply are no meanings to be had. Again, we are pushing up against the bounds of the disciplinary identity of this book's author and indeed of the marketing strategies that might otherwise have been pursued for it. I am a philosopher, this is supposed to be a book that reflects that fact, and philosophy is almost always held to be concerned, by definition, with meanings and arguments, not with what lies beyond these.

But there has also always been a dissenting camp, which says that philosophy should occupy itself with whatever human beings experience, whether easily rendered into propositional form or not. It may be that it is ultimately for the good of philosophy if some of its practitioners willingly run the risk of being seen as having gone off the deep end. Perhaps another way of putting this point is to say that philosophy has some need of at least a certain quota of *enthusiasts*.

Until recently this word still retained something of its original meaning in the Greek word *enthousiazein*, which meant "to be possessed or inspired by a god." In early modern Europe, enthusiasts were typically those members of Protestant sects who participated in revivals and who manifested, in various ways, a willing renunciation of their own faculty of reason in favor of ebullient religious experience. In antiquity, enthusiasm was commonly invoked to describe divine possession, particularly by Dionysus—the god, among other things, of ecstatic revelry. Socrates in turn appealed to the notion of enthusiasm in a looser sense, to describe the way poets create their work: not by using their intellectual faculties but by copying down a dictation that comes to them from on high, or as he understands it, by channeling their muse. Socrates also insisted that his own abilities in philosophy were somewhat like that, that he himself was speaking not as an individual whose ideas are generated from within himself alone but as someone who is simply fortunate, through no effort of his own, to have a sort of direct line to transcendent truth.

Plainly, the word "enthusiasm" shares quite a bit with "entheogen"; in fact the first two morphemes in each word are the same, even if *thous* and *theos* take different forms in Greek: both mean "God" or "godly" or "divine". Entheogenic techniques are those in which one consumes a natural substance to gain access to truths that one cannot arrive at by use of one's ordinary intellectual faculties, just as one might enter into a state of enthusiasm in order to channel the truths dictated by one's muse. In both cases, we are looking at something that is experienced passively, as a variety of possession. Those who refuse to see this sort of experience as a potential source of truth might appeal to two very different considerations: one is that the divine possession that is desired might easily corrupt into demonic possession, or to use the language of psychedelic culture, the good trip might turn into a bad trip. The other is that knowing the truth means being able to give reasons for what one claims to know, and to do this you have to think through it, using your own faculties, rather than taking dictation from some other source.

We have already dealt with the former objection: as long as you only take your experience on psychedelic drugs for an analogy of beatific vision, rather than the real thing, there can be no lingering risk of lapsing, under the influence of psychedelic drugs, into some variety of idolatry. As to the latter objection, that knowing the truth means being able to give reasons for what one claims to know, I can only insist on the curious historical fact that no less a philosophical authority than Socrates, in many respects the godfather or patron saint of this millennia-long tradition, openly acknowledged that he himself was not responsible for, nor could he fully account for, his own possession of the truth. In this respect his particular variety of truth disclosure was not so different from the one practiced by the poets.

In any case, it seems that the argument for or against entheogens as a tool for philosophical inquiry stands or falls together with the argument for enthusiasm more generally. Can the experiences of our own minds be considered as philosophical insights if we do not actively produce them through our own rational faculties but only let them be imposed on us by God or the gods, by the muses or by DMT? There may be good reasons to reject both entheogens and enthusiasm, but it seems the two must come as a pair, and that if you wish as a rule to exclude drug-induced insights, then you should also rethink your admiration for Socrates or for anyone else in the long history of philosophy who has admitted to arriving at truths by channeling other forces beyond their limited self.

We are all so greatly limited, we mortal human beings. Throughout most of their tradition's history, the philosophers have sought to go it alone anyway, to muster whatever powers they can from within their own rational faculties, and to make as much sense of things as the world will permit. By some measures their results have not been all that impressive. Psychedelics, like religion, like poetry, are, among other things, an abandonment of the will to go it alone. They are an opening up to everything that is beyond us—which, if I may speak poetically, and very much against the norms of my profession, turns out to have been within us all along.

ACKNOWLEDGMENTS

First thanks go to all my mentors and models over these many years, in philosophy, and especially in the scholarly circles of early modern philosophy and the history and philosophy of science in which I cut my first teeth. Special thanks are also in order for those many philosophy colleagues who have encouraged me in my public-facing writing, notably Kato Balog, Andrew Chignell, Peter Godfrey-Smith, Barry Loewer, Ohad Nachtomy, Gillian Russell, Eric Schliesser, Galen Strawson, and many others. Thanks to Blaise Agüera y Arcas, D. Graham Burnett, James Delbourgo, Adrienne Fairhall, and so many besides who have shaped my writing and thinking, and inspired me with their own inexhaustible ingenium; and special thanks to friend, poet, and shaman Jerome Rothenberg (1931–2024) for his own inestimable role in expanding the scope of my engagement with questions well beyond "what is dreamt of in your philosophy." Thanks to Benjamin Breen for our many exchanges and for first showing me what lucid and sober writing about drugs can, at its best, look like. Thanks to Jonathan Egid, Brad Fox, Catherine Hansen, Sam Jennings, Sam Kriss, Hélène Le Goff, Celeste Marcus, Kristen Roupenian, Leon Wieseltier, and Catherine Wilson for the different ways they've helped to shape, variously, my writing, my thinking, my life, and my fate. Special thanks to Christopher Beha for his vital input in conversation about this book—I couldn't have completed it without you. Equally special thanks are due to Jason Kehe, my friend and editor at *WIRED*, who dared to publish the article from which this book was born. And most of all thanks to my whole family, consanguineous and affine, for your infinite patience as I've found myself so long delayed in arriving at least somewhere close to my destination; this book is dedicated to you, though I'll understand, and even be somewhat relieved, if you prefer not to read it.

NOTES

INTRODUCTION

1. Anton Wilhelm Amo, *Tractatus de arte sobrie et accurate philosophandi* (Ex officina Kitleriana, 1734).
2. Daniel M. Perrine, "Mixing the *Kykleon*, Part 2," *Eleusis: Journal of Psychoactive Plants and Compounds*, New Series 4 (2000): 9–25, 17, note 12.

CHAPTER ONE: **WHAT IT'S LIKE**

1. See Ian Hacking, *Rewriting the Soul: Multiple Personality and the Sciences of Memory*, Princeton University Press, 1995; *Historical Ontology* (Harvard University Press, 2002).
2. See Ian Hacking, *Mad Travelers: Reflections on the Reality of Transient Mental Illness* (University Press of Virginia, 1998).
3. Martin Heidegger, *Being and Time*, ed. and trans. John Macquarrie and Edward Robinson (Harper & Row, 1977 [1927]), I.5, 177. Heidegger typically describes *Befindlichkeit* as the condition of "being in a mood."
4. For a vivid account of dream-sharing practices among the Ongee people of the Andaman Islands, see Vishvajit Pandya, "Forest Smells and Spider Webs: Ritualized Dream Interpretation Among Andaman Islanders," *Dreaming* 14, nos. 2–3 (2004).

CHAPTER TWO: ARTICULATE GUINEA PIGS

1. Quoted in Nicholas Murray, *Aldous Huxley: A Biography* (Thomas Dunne, 2003), 401.
2. See Mike Jay, *Psychonauts: Drugs and the Making of the Modern Mind* (Yale University Press, 2023).
3. Perrine, "Mixing the *Kykleon*, Part 2," 17, note 12.
4. See Herman Cappelen, *Philosophy Without Intuitions* (Oxford University Press, 2012).
5. Berit Brogaard, "Intuitions as Intellectual Seemings," *Analytic Philosophy* 55 (2014): 388–89.
6. Paul Lodge, "What Is It Like to Be Manic?" *Oxonian Review*, February 2, 2020.
7. A. J. Ayer, *Foundations of Empirical Knowledge* (Macmillan, 1940), 2.
8. David Hume, *Enquiry concerning Human Understanding*, XII.1.9.
9. Bertrand Russell, *Our Knowledge of the External World as a Field for Scientific Method in Philosophy* (George Allen & Unwin, 1922 [1914]), 85.
10. See J. R. Smythies, *Analysis of Perception* (Routledge, 2002 [1956]).
11. W. V. O. Quine, *The Time of My Life: An Autobiography* (MIT Press, 1985), 476.

CHAPTER THREE: PSYCHEDELIC MEDITATIONS

1. René Descartes, *Meditations on First Philosophy*, in *The Philosophical Writings of Descartes*, vol. 2, ed. and trans. John Cottingham, Robert Stoothoff, and Dugald Murdoch (Cambridge University Press, 1984 [1641]), 22.
2. William James, *The Varieties of Religious Experience: A Study in Human Nature* (Longmans, Green & Co., 1902), 371.
3. See Charles Kahn, ed. and trans., *The Art and Thought of Heraclitus* (Cambridge University Press, 1979), 31.
4. Eric Schwitzgebel, *The Weirdness of the World* (Princeton University Press, 2024), 74.
5. Cited in Jonardon Ganeri, *Attention, Not Self* (Oxford University Press, 2017), x; subsequent quote, 1.
6. See in particular Alison Gopnik, "Could David Hume Have Known About Buddhism? Charles François Dolu, the Royal College of La Flèche, and the Global Jesuit Intellectual Network," *Hume Studies* 35, nos. 1–2 (2009): 5–28.
7. Kurt Gray and Daniel Wegner, "Blaming God for Our Pain: Human Suffering and the Divine Mind," *Personality and Social Psychology Review* 14, no. 1 (February 2010): 9–10.

CHAPTER FOUR: **WHAT *ARE* DRUGS?**

1. The bibliography of relevant works is far too large even to give a representative sample here. But for an exemplary work in this vein, focusing on the early modern circulation of coffee and its evolving meanings, among other commodities, see Emma C. Spary, *Eating the Enlightenment: Food and the Sciences in Paris* (University of Chicago Press, 2012).
2. Benjamin Breen, "Drugs and Early Modernity," *History Compass* 15, no. 4 (2017): 1–9, 4. See also Benjamin Breen, *The Age of Intoxication: Origins of the Global Drug Trade* (University of Pennsylvania Press), 2019.
3. Sidney W. Mintz, *Sweetness and Power: The Place of Sugar in Modern History* (Penguin Books, 1986), xxi.
4. Daniel C. Dennett, "Will AI Achieve Consciousness? Wrong Question," *WIRED*, February 19, 2019.
5. See in particular Brian Hayden et al., "What Was Brewing in the Natufian? An Archaeological Assessment of Brewing Technology in the Epipaleolithic," *Journal of Archaeological Method and Theory* 20 (2013): 102–50.
6. See Londa Schiebinger, *Plants and Empire: Colonial Bioprospecting in the Atlantic World* (Harvard University Press, 2007).
7. Mintz, *Sweetness and Power*, xxiii.
8. David T. Courtwright, *Forces of Habit: Drugs and the Making of the Modern World* (Harvard University Press, 2001), 4.
9. See Norman Ohler, *Blitzed: Drugs in the Third Reich* (Houghton Mifflin Harcourt, 2017).
10. Natan Odenheimer et al., "What a Terror Attack in Israel Might Reveal About Psychedelics and Trauma," *New York Times*, April 11, 2024.
11. See Roger J. Sullivan et al., "Revealing the Paradox of Drug Reward in Human Evolution," *Proc. Biol. Sci.* 275, no. 1640 (June 2008): 1231–41.
12. See George B. Richardson et al., "Substance Use and Mating Success," *Evolution and Human Behavior* 38, no. 1 (January 2017): 48–57.
13. Claude Lévi-Strauss, "Mushrooms in Culture," in *Structural Anthropology*, vol. 2, trans. Monique Layton (University of Chicago Press, 1983 [1970]), 222–37, 232; subsequent quote from "Mushrooms in Culture," 232.
14. See L. A. Paul, "What You Can't Expect When You're Expecting," *Res Philosophica* 92, no. 2 (2015): 1–23.
15. Richard A. Friedman, "What If Psychedelics' Hallucinations Are Just a Side Effect?" *Atlantic*, November 8, 2023.

16. John Dupré, "Are Whales Fish?" in *Folkbiology*, ed. Douglas L. Medin and Scott Atran, (MIT Press, 1999), 461–76.

CHAPTER FIVE: MORE THAN A FEELING?

1. Smythies, *Analysis of Perception*, 81; subsequent quotes from *Analysis of Perception*, 82.
2. Ayer, *Foundations of Empirical Knowledge*, 42, 274.
3. Smythies, *Analysis of Perception*, 82; subsequent quotes from *Analysis of Perception*, 85, 86.
4. J. R. Smythies, "The Mescaline Phenomena," *British Journal for the Philosophy of Science* 3, no. 12 (February 1953): 339–47, 346; subsequent quotes from "Mescaline Phenomena," 346.
5. Jean-Paul Sartre, *Nausea* (New Directions, 2013 [1938]), 5.
6. William Gaddis, *The Recognitions* (New York Review Books, 2020 [1955]), 93.
7. Smythies, *Analysis of Perception*, 86; subsequent quote from *Analysis of Perception*, 86f.
8. Gustave Flaubert, *L'Éducation sentimentale* (Le Livre de Poche, 2002 [1869]).
9. Giacomo Leopardi, *Zibaldone: The Notebooks of Leopardi*, ed. and trans. M. Caesar and F. D'Intino (Penguin, 2013), 4418; subsequent quote from *Zibaldone*, 4418.
10. Peter L. Berger and Thomas Luckmann, *The Social Construction of Reality: A Treatise in the Sociology of Knowledge* (Anchor Books, 1966).
11. Marcus E. Raichle, "The Brain's Default Mode Network," *Annual Review of Neuroscience* 8, no. 38 (July 2015): 433–47.

CHAPTER SIX: GALAXY BRAINS

1. Scott Dikkers et al., *Our Dumb Century: The Onion Presents 100 Years of Headlines from America's Finest News Source* (Three Rivers Press, 1999).
2. Quoted in Jeffrey Masson, *The Oceanic Feeling: The Origins of Religious Sentiment in Ancient India* (Springer, 2012 [1980]), 34.
3. Quoted in George Mikes, *Arthur Koestler: The Story of a Friendship* (André Deutsch, 1983), 79.
4. G. E. M. Anscombe, "Has Mankind One Soul? An Angel Distributed Through Many Bodies," in *Human Life, Action and Ethics: Essays by G. E. M. Anscombe,* ed. Mary Geach and Luke Gormally (Imprint Academic, 2005 [1986]).
5. Marcel Proust, *Du côté de chez Swann*, ed. Matthieu Vernet (Le Livre de Poche, 2022 [1913]).

6. For a compelling statement of this point, see Alan Soble, *Pornography, Sex, and Feminism* (Prometheus Books, 2002).
7. See Sermin Ildirar and Stephan Schwan, "First-Time Viewers' Comprehension of Films: Bridging Shot Transitions," *British Journal of Psychology* 106/1 (March 2014): 133–51.
8. See David J. Chalmers, *Reality+: Virtual Worlds and the Problems of Philosophy* (Norton/Liveright, 2022) and Nick Bostrom, "Are You Living in a Computer Simulation?" *Philosophical Quarterly* 53, no. 211 (2003): 243–55.
9. Bertrand Russell, *The Analysis of Mind* (George Allen & Unwin, 1921), 159.
10. See Elizabeth Spelke, *What Babies Know: Core Knowledge and Composition, vol. 1* (Oxford University Press, 2022).
11. Rosalind Heywood, Letter to the Editor, *Blackfriars* 35, no. 415 (October 1954): 452–54.
12. See Charles Upton, *What Poets Used to Know* (Angelico Press, 2016).

CHAPTER SEVEN: SEEING GOD

1. Desiderius Erasmus, *In Praise of Folly* (Reeves & Turner, 1876 [1511]), 26.
2. Erasmus, *In Praise of Folly*, 21.
3. Nicolas of Cusa, *De docta ignorantia*, trans. Arthur J. Banning (Banning Press, 1981), I, 3.10, 8.
4. See Michel Foucault, *Madness and Civilization: A History of Insanity in the Age of Reason*, trans. Richard Howard (Routledge, 1989 [1961]).
5. Phoebe Friesen, "Psychotics and Psychedelics: Historical Entanglements and Contemporary Constraints," *Transcultural Psychiatry* 59, no. 5 (2022): 592–609.
6. Kurt Beringer, "Experimentelle Psychosen durch Mescalin," *Zeitschrift für die gesamte Neurologie und Psychiatrie* 84, no. 1 (1923): 426–33.
7. Alexandre Rouhier, *Le peyotl : La plante qui fait les yeux émerveillés* (Gaston Doin, 1927).
8. Gilles Deleuze and Félix Guattari, *A Thousand Plateaus: Capitalism and Schizophrenia*, ed. and trans. Brian Massumi (Bloomsbury Academic, 2004 [1980]), 153.
9. See Benjamin Breen, *Tripping on Utopia: Margaret Mead, the Cold War, and the Troubled Birth of Psychedelic Science* (Hachette Book Group, 2024).
10. R. C. Zaehner, "The Menace of Mescalin," *Blackfriars* 35, nos. 412–13 (July-August 1954): 310–23; subsequent quotes from "The Menace of Mescalin," 321.

11. Heywood, Letter to the Editor, 453; subsequent quotes from Letter to the Editor, 453, 454.
12. Cited in Heywood, Letter to the Editor, 454.
13. Michael Pollan, *How to Change Your Mind: What the New Science of Psychedelics Teaches Us About Consciousness, Dying, Addiction, Depression, and Transcendence* (Penguin, 2018), 43.
14. See Brian C. Muraresku, *The Immortality Key: The Secret History of the Religion with No Name* (St. Martin's Press, 2020).
15. Albert Hofmann, *LSD: My Problem Child* (McGraw-Hill, 1980 [1976]), foreword; subsequent quote from *LSD*, x–xi.
16. Richard Klein, *Cigarettes Are Sublime* (Duke University Press, 1993).
17. Frits Staal, "The Meaninglessness of Ritual," *Numen* 26, no. 1 (June 1979): 2–22.

BIBLIOGRAPHY

Amo, Anton Wilhelm. *Tractatus de arte sobrie et accurate philosophandi.* Ex officina Kitleriana, 1734.

Anscombe, G. E. M. "Has Mankind One Soul? An Angel Distributed through Many Bodies," in *Human Life, Action and Ethics: Essays by G. E. M. Anscombe.* Imprint Academic, 2005 [1986].

Ayer, A. J. *Foundations of Empirical Knowledge.* Macmillan, 1940.

Berger, Peter L., and Thomas Luckmann. *The Social Construction of Reality: A Treatise in the Sociology of Knowledge.* Anchor Books, 1966.

Beringer, Kurt. "Experimentelle Psychosen durch Mescalin." *Zeitschrift für die gesamte Neurologie und Psychiatrie* 84, no. 1 (1923): 426–33.

Bostrom, Nick. "Are You Living in a Computer Simulation?" *Philosophical Quarterly* 53, no. 211 (2003): 243–55.

Breen, Benjamin. *The Age of Intoxication: Origins of the Global Drug Trade.* University of Pennsylvania Press, 2019.

Breen, Benjamin. "Drugs and Early Modernity." *History Compass* 15, no. 4 (2017): 1–9.

Breen, Benjamin. *Tripping on Utopia: Margaret Mead, the Cold War, and the Troubled Birth of Psychedelic Science.* Hachette Book Group, 2024.

Brogaard, Berit. "Intuitions as Intellectual Seemings." *Analytic Philosophy* 55 (2014): 382–93.

Cappelen, Herman. *Philosophy Without Intuitions.* Oxford University Press, 2012.

Chalmers, David J. *Reality+: Virtual Worlds and the Problems of Philosophy.* Norton/Liveright, 2022.
Courtwright, David T. *Forces of Habit: Drugs and the Making of the Modern World.* Harvard University Press, 2001.
Deleuze, Gilles, and Guattari, Félix. *A Thousand Plateaus: Capitalism and Schizophrenia.* Edited and translated by Brian Massumi. Bloomsbury Academic, 2004 [1980].
Dennett, Daniel C. "Will AI Achieve Consciousness? Wrong Question." *WIRED*, February 19, 2019.
Descartes, René. *Meditations on First Philosophy.* Translated and edited by John Cottingham, Robert Stoothoff, and Dugald Murdoch. Vol. 2 of *The Philosophical Writings of Descartes.* Cambridge University Press, 1984 [1641].
Dikkers, Scott, Mike Loew, et al. *Our Dumb Century: The Onion Presents 100 Years of Headlines from America's Finest News Source.* Three Rivers Press, 1999.
Dupré, John. "Are Whales Fish?" In *Folkbiology*, edited by Douglas L. Medin and Scott Atran. The MIT Press, 1999, 461–76.
Erasmus, Desiderius. *In Praise of Folly.* Reeves & Turner, 1876 [1511].
Flaubert, Gustave. *L'Éducation sentimentale.* Le Livre de Poche, 2002 [1869].
Foucault, Michel. *Madness and Civilization: A History of Insanity in the Age of Reason.* Translated by Richard Howard. Routledge, 1989 [1961].
Friedman, Richard A. "What If Psychedelics' Hallucinations Are Just a Side Effect?" *Atlantic*, November 8, 2023.
Friesen, Phoebe. "Psychotics and Psychedelics: Historical Entanglements and Contemporary Constraints." *Transcultural Psychiatry* 59, no. 5 (2022): 592–609.
Gaddis, William. *The Recognitions.* New York Review Books, 2020 [1955].
Ganeri, Jonardon. *Attention, Not Self.* Oxford University Press, 2017.
Gopnik, Alison. "Could David Hume Have Known About Buddhism? Charles François Dolu, the Royal College of La Flèche, and the Global Jesuit Intellectual Network." *Hume Studies* 35, nos. 1–2 (2009): 5–28.
Gray, Kurt, and Daniel Wegner. "Blaming God for Our Pain: Human Suffering and the Divine Mind." *Personality and Social Psychology Review* 14, no. 1 (February 2010): 9–10.
Guerra-Doce, Elisa. "The Origins of Inebriation: Archaeological Evidence of the Consumption of Fermented Beverages and Drugs in Prehistoric Eurasia." *Journal of Archaeological Method and Theory* 22, no. 3 (September 2015): 760.
Hacking, Ian. *Historical Ontology.* Harvard University Press, 2002.
Hacking, Ian. *Mad Travelers: Reflections on the Reality of Transient Mental Illness.* University Press of Virginia, 1998.

Hacking, Ian. *Rewriting the Soul: Multiple Personality and the Sciences of Memory*. Princeton University Press, 1995.

Hauskeller, Christine, and Peter Sjöstedt-Hughes, eds. *Philosophy and Psychedelics: Frameworks for Exceptional Experience*. Bloomsbury Academic, 2022.

Hayden, Brian, Neil Canuel, and Jennifer Shanse. "What Was Brewing in the Natufian? An Archaeological Assessment of Brewing Technology in the Epipaleolithic." *Journal of Archaeological Method and Theory* 20 (2013): 102–50.

Heidegger, Martin. *Being and Time*. Edited and translated by John Macquarrie and Edward Robinson. Harper & Row, 1977 [1927].

Heywood, Rosalind. *The Infinite Hive: A Personal Record of Extra-Sensory Experiences*. Chatto and Windus, 1964.

Heywood, Rosalind. Letter to the Editor. *Blackfriars* 35, no. 415 (October 1954): 452–54.

Heywood, Rosalind. *Telepathy and Allied Phenomena*. Society for Psychical Research, 1948.

Hofmann, Albert. *LSD: My Problem Child*. McGraw-Hill, 1980 [1976].

Hume, David. *Enquiry Concerning Human Understanding*. A. Millar, 1748.

Husserl, Edmund. *Ideas Pertaining to a Pure Phenomenology and to a Phenomenological Philosophy*. Book 1. Translated by F. Kersten. Dordrecht, Kluwer, 1983 [1913].

Huxley, Aldous. *The Doors of Perception*. Harper & Row, 1954.

Ildirar, Sermin, and Stephan Schwan. "First-Time Viewers' Comprehension of Films: Bridging Shot Transitions." *British Journal of Psychology* 106, no. 1 (March 2014): 133–51.

James, William. *The Varieties of Religious Experience: A Study in Human Nature*. Longmans, Green & Co., 1902.

Jay, Mike. *Psychonauts: Drugs and the Making of the Modern Mind*. Yale University Press, 2023.

Kahn, Charles, ed. and trans. *The Art and Thought of Heraclitus*. Cambridge University Press, 1979.

Kepler, Johannes. *Kepler's Somnium: The Dream, or Posthumous Work on Lunar Astronomy*. Translated and edited by Edward Rosen. Dover Publications, 1967 [1634].

Klein, Ralph. *Cigarettes Are Sublime*. Duke University Press, 1993.

Leopardi, Giacomo. *Zibaldone: The Notebooks of Leopardi*. Edited and translated by M. Caesar and F. D'Intino. Penguin, 2013.

Lévi-Strauss, Claude. "Mushrooms in Culture." *Structural Anthropology*. Vol. 2. Translated by Monique Layton. University of Chicago Press, 1983 [1970], 222–37.

Lodge, Paul. "What Is It Like to Be Manic?" *The Oxonian Review*, February 3, 2020.

Masson, Jeffrey, *The Oceanic Feeling: The Origins of Religious Sentiment in Ancient India.* Springer, 2012 [1980].
McKenna, Terence. "DMT, Mathematical Dimensions, Syntax and Death." Presentation uploaded to YouTube, August 28, 2013.
McKenna, Terence. *Good of the Gods: The Search for the Original Tree of Knowledge–A Radical History of Plants, Drugs, and Human Evolution.* Bantam, 1992.
McKenna, Terence. *True Hallucinations: Being an Account of the Author's Extraordinary Adventures in the Devil's Paradise.* Harper, 1993.
Mikes, George. *Arthur Koestler: The Story of a Friendship.* André Deutsch, 1983.
Mintz, Sidney W. *Sweetness and Power: The Place of Sugar in Modern History.* Penguin Books, 1986.
Muraresku, Brian C. *The Immortality Key: The Secret History of the Religion with No Name.* St. Martin's Press, 2020.
Murray, Nicholas. *Aldous Huxley: A Biography.* Thomas Dunne, 2003.
Naranjo, Plutarco. "El ayahuasca en la arqueologia ecuatoriana." *América Indígena* 46 (1986): 117–27.
Nicolas of Cusa. *De docta ignorantia.* Translated by Arthur J. Banning. Banning Press, 1981 [1440].
Odenheimer, Natan, Aaron Boxerman, and Gal Koplewitz. "What a Terror Attack in Israel Might Reveal About Psychedelics and Trauma." *New York Times*, April 11, 2024.
Pandya, Vishvajit. "Forest Smells and Spider Webs: Ritualized Dream Interpretation Among Andaman Islanders." *Dreaming* 14, nos. 2–3 (2004).
Paul, L. A. "What You Can't Expect When You're Expecting." *Res Philosophica* 92, no. 2 (2015): 1–23.
Perrine, Daniel M. "Mixing the *Kykleon*, Part 2." *Eleusis: Journal of Psychoactive Plants and Compounds*, New Series 4 (2000): 9–25.
Pollan, Michael. *How to Change Your Mind: What the New Science of Psychedelics Teaches Us About Consciousness, Dying, Addiction, Depression, and Transcendence.* Penguin, 2018.
Quine, W. V. O. *The Time of My Life: An Autobiography.* The MIT Press, 1985.
Raichle, Marcus E. "The Brain's Default Mode Network." *Annual Review of Neuroscience* 8, no. 38 (July 2015): 433–47.
Richardson, George B., Ching-Chen Chen, et al. "Substance Use and Mating Success." *Evolution and Human Behavior* 38/1 (January 2017): 48–57.
Rouhier, Alexandre. *Le peyotl: La plante qui fait les yeux émerveillés.* Gaston Doin, 1927.
Russell, Bertrand. *The Analysis of Mind.* George Allen & Unwin, 1921.

Russell, Bertrand. *Our Knowledge of the External World as a Field for Scientific Method in Philosophy*. George Allen & Unwin, 1922 [1914].

Sacks, Oliver. *The Man Who Mistook His Wife for a Hat, and Other Clinical Tales*. Summit Books, 1985.

Sartre, Jean-Paul. *Nausea*. New Directions, 2013 [1938].

Schiebinger, Londa. *Plants and Empire: Colonial Bioprospecting in the Atlantic World*. Harvard University Press, 2007.

Schwitzgebel, Eric. *The Weirdness of the World*. Princeton University Press, 2024.

Smith, Justin E. H. *Divine Machines: Leibniz and the Sciences of Life*. Princeton University Press, 2011.

Smythies, J. R. *Analysis of Perception*. Routledge, 2002 [1956].

Smythies, J. R. "The Mescaline Phenomena." *The British Journal for the Philosophy of Science* 3, no. 12 (February 1953): 339–47.

Soble, Alan. *Pornography, Sex, and Feminism*. Prometheus Books, 2002.

Spary, Emma C. *Eating the Enlightenment: Food and the Sciences in Paris*. University of Chicago Press, 2012.

Spelke, Elizabeth. *What Babies Know: Core Knowledge and Composition*. Vol. 1. Oxford University Press, 2022.

Staal, Frits. "The Meaninglessness of Ritual." *Numen* 26, no. 1 (June 1979): 2–22.

Sullivan, Roger J., Edward H. Hagen, and Peter Hammerstein. "Revealing the Paradox of Drug Reward in Human Evolution." *Proceedings of the Royal Society B: Biological Sciences* 275, no. 1640 (June 2008): 1231–41.

Upton, Charles. *What Poets Used to Know*. Angelico Press, 2016.

Wasson, R. Gordon. *Soma: Divine Mushroom of Immortality*. Harcourt, Brace & World, 1969.

Wasson, R. Gordon, Albert Hofmann, and Carl A. P. Ruck. *The Road to Eleusis: Unveiling the Secret of the Mysteries*. North Atlantic Books, 2008 [1978].

Wasson, R. Gordon, and Valentina Pavlovna Wasson. *Mushrooms, Russia, and History*. Pantheon Books, 1957.

Zaehner, R. C. "The Menace of Mescalin." *Blackfriars* 35, nos. 412–413 (July-August 1954): 310–23.

INDEX

a priori knowledge, 190, 192, 195, 196
Abrahamic faiths, 215
accomplishment, worldly, 18
Accra, Ghana, 29
"acid," *see* LSD
addiction, xiv, 13, 97, 100, 107
ADHD, 204, 208
adolescent males, 106
advocacy, xi, xii, 112
AI, 162, 166–67, 181–82, 184
alchemy, 93, 94
alcohol (alcoholism), 14–21, 32, 33, 80–82, 90, 92–95, 98–99, 101, 108, 221, 224; *see also* drunkenness
Alcoholics Anonymous, 14
alien life forms, 159, 161, 194
Alps, 164
altered states of consciousness, 47, 71, 72, 75, 76, 87, 91, 104–7, 112, 119–21, 140, 193, 203, 211
al-Zahrawi, 94
Amanita muscaria, 110, 111
Amazon rainforest, 194
amlodipine, 9
Amo, Anton Wilhelm, xi
analogies, 39–40, 60–62, 219, 221, 230
Analysis of Mind, The (Russell), 180
Analysis of Perception (Smythies), 131–34
analytic existentialism, 113–14
analytic phenomenology, 48, 53–55
analytic philosophy, 45–48, 50, 60
anatman, 79
Anglo-French language, 89
Anglophone world, 48, 134

Index

animals, 104, 110, 117, 126–27, 183–84, 188, 189
animism, 82–83
anorexia, 205
Anscombe, G. E. M., "Has Mankind One Soul? An Angel Distributed Through Many Bodies," 166
Antarctica, 194
anthropology, 149, 150, 168–69, 184, 211, 224
antianxiety drugs, 10
antidepressants, xiv, 10, 14, 19, 20, 115–16
antidrug advertisements, 28
antinomy, 85
antipsychiatry, 205–7
anxiety (anxiety disorder), 10–12, 23–24, 30
anxiolytics, xiv
aqua ardens, 94
Aristotle, 20, 62, 72, 74, 75, 82–83, 86, 161, 165
  Metaphysics, 62
art, 20, 22, 41, 103, 107, 162, 170, 174, 191, 227
Atlantic, The, 116, 121
auras, 4
Austin, J. L., 89
auto-experimentation, 3, 14, 42, 44, 46–48, 53–55, 134, 152
Averroes (Ibn Rushd), 165–66
Avestan language, 210
ayahuasca (ayahuasca retreats), 65, 97, 122–23, 189, 216–17
Ayer, A. J., 50
  Foundations of Empirical Knowledge, 133

bad trips, 115, 154–58, 186, 209, 212, 230
Basil of Moscow, Saint, 200
beatific vision, 209, 211, 213, 221, 223, 230
beauty, 21, 23, 24, 35, 59, 66, 69, 140, 148, 153, 197
beer, 92–93
behaviorism, 43, 44
Being and Time (Heidegger), 24
Belgium, 14–15
benzodiazepines, 10
Berger, Peter L., 149
Beringer, Kurt, 203
beserkers, 98, 111
Bible, 165, 182, 200–201
bigfoot, 143
bioprospecting, 95–96
bipolar disorder, 10
birth defects, 154–55
Blackfriars magazine, 185, 207, 214
Blake, William, *The Marriage of Heaven and Hell,* 41–42
Blavatsky, Helena, 168
Blazing-World (Cavendish), 26
body, the, 13, 21, 29, 59, 65, 78, 125, 181, 227
boredom, 23–24
Boston (rock band), 144
Bostrom, Nick, 178, 179
Boyle, Robert, 96, 178
bracketing, 49–50, 53–54, 137
brain, xv, 97, 104, 123, 125–27, 129–31, 135, 139, 152–53, 162, 192, 205, 209, 212
brandy, 94, 95
Branntwein, 94
Brazil, 216–17
Breen, Benjamin, 91, 207

Brogaard, Berit, 46
Buddhagosa, 79–80, 211
Buddhism, 79–80, 168, 209, 211, 215

Caesar, Julius, 190
caffeine, 9–10, 108; *see also* coffee
California, 1, 19, 29, 32, 147, 225
"California sobriety," 14
calories, 91, 92
cannabinoids, synthetic, 103
cannabis, xiii, 3, 14, 19–21, 28–33, 99–101, 107–8, 119–20, 190, 192; *see also* marijuana
cannabis dispensaries, 107–8
capitalism, 95, 97, 101, 102, 205
Captagon, 100
Caribbean, 92, 96
cartoons, 167, 171, 192, 193
Cass, Mama, 8, 21, 22, 34, 35
Castañeda, Carlos, 206
Cavendish, Margaret, *Blazing-World,* 26
celebrities, 34
cerebral cortex, 152–53, 218
certainty, 33–35, 50, 64, 189
Chalmers, David, 178, 179, 190
chamomile tea, 98
Charles de Gaulle Airport (Paris), 29
chemoreceptors, 129
children, having, 113–15
China, 94
chocolate, 96
Christ, 182, 200, 201, 220

Christianity, 113, 136, 166, 182, 195, 200–201, 209–11, 215–17, 220, 225–29
Cigarettes Are Sublime (Klein), 219
Cincinnati, Ohio, 148
circadian rhythms, 126
"citizen science," 44
civilizations, past existence of lost, 194
clichés, 58, 173–74, 177–78
"clockmaker argument," 222–23
clockworks, 178
coca leaf, 94, 96
cocaine, 44, 96, 97, 100–102
"co-constitution," 189
coelacanths, 117
coffee, 9–10, 91, 97, 101, 108
"Cogito" argument, 64, 186
cognition, 64, 83, 153, 181
Cohen, Leonard, 119
Cold War, 163
college students, 99
commerce, science vs., 95
commodities, 3, 55, 90, 91, 96, 99–104, 107, 224
communication, 5, 72, 84, 218
communion, 209–10, 218
communism, ix
comparative religion, 210–11
connection, sense of, 34, 160
consciousness, xv, xvi, 25, 36, 38, 45, 53, 78–79, 105, 159–66, 180–81; *see also* altered states of consciousness; waking states (waking mind)
"controlled madness," 208, 224–25
cosmic consciousness, 160–64, 166

Index

cosmos, the, 26, 161, 163, 169, 179, 216
Council on Spiritual Practices, 217
counterculture, x, 25, 42, 170, 210, 211
Courtwright, David, 101
  Forces of Habit, 96–97
COVID-19 pandemic, 17, 19
cows, 183
crack cocaine, 94, 102
"Creeque Alley" (song), 8
criminal organizations, 102
critical philosophy, 85
Critique of the Power of Judgment (Kant), 86
crystal healing, 62
culture(s), 28, 36, 56–58, 75, 97–99, 103, 108–11, 116–17, 163, 166–68, 170–73, 187–89, 204, 207–8, 216, 227

daydreaming, 57, 105, 161
De Docta ignorantia (Nicholas of Cusa), 200
death, 38–39, 136, 157–58, 165–66, 199, 210
decision making, 114
deduction, 45–46
"default mode network," 152–53
Deleuze, Gilles, 205, 208
  A Thousand Plateaus, 206
demons (demonic possession), 86–87, 122, 188, 230
Dennett, Daniel, 92
dependency, 107
depressants, 99, 108

depression, xiv, 6, 10–12, 19, 112, 120, 150–51; *see also* antidepressants
"derealization," 132, 135–37
Descartes, René, 1, 16, 49, 76–79, 83, 120, 125–26, 135, 187
  Meditations on First Philosophy, 63–71, 76, 183, 186, 201
DiCillo, Tom, 173
digestives, 99
Dinklage, Peter, 173
Dionysus, 229
"disconcealed" truths, 215
disease model of mental illness, 12–13
dissolution of selfhood (dissolution of the self), 37, 38, 80, 153, 157–58, 212
distillation (distilled spirits), 93–95, 101
divine, the, 185, 200, 212, 221, 223, 229, 230
djinns, 188, 189
DMT, 34, 86–87, 126–27, 188–89, 231
"dogmatic philosophy," 85
Doors, The, 41–42
Doors of Perception, The (Huxley), 41–42, 98, 207–14
dopamine, 97
double vision, 52–53, 148–49, 174
dread, 10, 157–58
dreams (dreaming), 28, 36, 57, 72, 74–77, 104–6, 105, 126, 133, 171–73, 175–77, 192, 193; *see also* daydreaming

Index

"drugs," as term, 2–3, 6–7, 87, 89–90, 94–95
drugstores, 90
drunkenness, xi, 33, 76, 78, 80–81, 93, 94, 99, 140, 200
DSM, 11
Dune franchise, 103
Dupre, John, 117
Dutch Golden Age, 3
Dutch language, 89

Earth, the, 36, 159–60, 164, 169, 170, 194
East Indies, 89
Eastern Europe, 16, 109
Eastern Orthodox Christianity, 220
eclipses, 76
ego (ego dissolution), 133–34, 157–58, 186
electricity, 44, 181
Elliott, Cass, 8
Embrace of the Serpent, The (film), 163
embryology, 154–55
emotions, 33, 70, 97, 141, 153; *see also specific emotions, e.g.:* love
empirical reality, 24, 26–27, 57, 189–90, 194–96, 218
empiricism, 50, 78
enlightenment (Enlightenment), 39–40, 60–62, 128, 209, 213, 219
Enquiry Concerning Human Understanding, An (Hume), 51–52
entheogens, 45, 215, 216, 229–31

enthusiasm, 229–31
Epicurus, 16
epilepsy, 75
epochē, 49
Erasmus, Desiderius, 224
  In Praise of Folly, 199–201
ergot fungus, 95, 110
Ernest and Julio Gallo rosé, 17
Essay Concerning Human Understanding, An (Locke), 78
"eternal tense," 182
ether, 45
eudaimonia, 11
"euphoric moments," 218
Eurasia, 98
Europe, 16, 75, 76, 79, 80, 89, 92, 94, 99, 109, 126, 187, 205, 222, 229
euthanasia, 165
evolution, 29, 36, 83, 92–93, 103, 104, 106, 117, 127, 131, 153, 156, 166, 180–81
excluded middle, law of the, 72–73
existentialism, 113–15, 118–21
expectations, 4, 36, 37, 74, 76, 98, 99, 166
experimental psychology, 47
experimentation, 42, 44–46, 53–54, 127–28, 176, 192; *see also* auto-experimentation
expressibility, 74
external objects, 50–53, 56, 128, 136, 150, 158
external world, internal vs., 36
extraordinary perception, 59

face-like patterns, 4
faculties, awakening of, 98–99

FAFO ("fuck around and find out"), 113
fairies, 142, 188
Fall, The, 195
falling out of love, 136
feasts, holiday, 103, 104
feelings, 11, 23, 43, 76, 143–44, 146–47, 149, 213; *see also* moods
feng shui, 150
fentanyl, 102
fermentation, 15, 92–93
film, 176–77
Finland, 17
First Letter to the Corinthians, 165, 200–201
first-person perspective, 11, 42–44, 47, 55, 173, 177
Flaubert, Gustave
  Madame Bovary, 176
  Sentimental Education, 144–45
fly agaric, 81, 98, 110
foolishness, 200–201
Forces of Habit (Courtwright), 96–97
Foucault, Michel, 202, 205, 208
  Madness and Civilization, 201
Foundations of Empirical Knowledge (Ayer), 133
France, 1, 16–17, 203, 205
Franklin, Benjamin, 44
freedom, 19, 146
Freud, Sigmund, 44–45, 49, 102, 164
Friedman, Richard A., 118
  "What If Psychedelics' Hallucinations Are Just a Side Effect?," 116
Friesen, Phoebe, 202, 207
"fuck around and find out" (FAFO), 113
fugue syndrome, 12, 204–5, 208
fungi, 3, 109–11, 121–22

Gaddis, William, *The Recognitions,* 137–38
galaxy brain, 162
Ganeri, Jonardon, 79
Ganesha, 220
Garcia, Jerry, 197
"gateway drug," cannabis as, 20–21
geocentric model, 26
Geoffroy Saint-Hilaire, Étienne, 154–55
geometrical proofs, 69–70
Germany, 5, 48, 100, 200, 203
ghosts, 188
glitches, 179, 180, 182–83
global economy (global trade), 55, 89, 96, 101, 107
Gnosticism, 196
God, 61, 64, 70, 77, 154, 183, 185, 186, 195, 200–201, 209–12, 215, 221, 222, 229, 231
"God's eye" point of view, 38
gonzo journalism, x
Gopnik, Alison, 79
grade point average (GPA), 10, 11
Gray, Kurt, 83
Greeks, ancient, 74, 82–83
guardian angels, 188
Guattari, Félix, 205
  A Thousand Plateaus, 206
Guerra, Ciro, 163

Index

guilt, 109, 149
Gulf of Finland, x

Hacking, Ian, 12, 204–5
hallucination(s), 4, 49, 50, 52, 55–56, 58–60, 71, 72, 100, 116–18, 121, 127, 131–35, 139–41, 151–52, 156, 157, 162, 171, 174, 211, 212, 222
hallucinogens, 14, 111
Hamas, 100
hangovers, 33, 81
Hart, David Bentley, 195
Harvard University, x
"Has Mankind One Soul? An Angel Distributed Through Many Bodies" (Anscombe), 166
Hedberg, Mitch, 13
Heidegger, Martin, 23–25, 27, 35, 59, 156–58, 183–84, 215
  Being and Time, 24
Heraclitus, 74
herbal liquors, 99
heroin, 100, 119
Heywood, Rosalind, 185–87, 204, 207, 212–14
  The Infinite Hive: A Personal Record of Extra-Sensory Experiences, 214
  Telepathy and Allied Phenomena, 214
hierarchy of reality, 37, 56–58
"high festival mode," 224–25
Hinduism, 168, 211, 215, 220
history of science, 117, 178–79
Hofmann, Albert, 95, 218

holiday feasts, 103
homeostasis, 160
horologium, 178
horseshoe theory of mental health, 12
human revolution, 103
humanities, 161
Hume, David, 79–80, 179
  An Enquiry Concerning Human Understanding, 51–52
Husserl, Edmund, 44, 46, 48–49, 53, 54, 137
Huxley, Aldous, 152, 223
  The Doors of Perception, 41–42, 98, 207–14
"Hyperactive Agent Detection Device," 83
hypertension, chronic, 9
hypnagogic transports, 75

Ibn Rushd (Averroes), 165–66
iconolatry, 220–22
ideas, 24, 35, 149
identity, personal, 78, 80, 81
idolatry, 220–21, 230
illicit substances, drugs as, 90, 99–102, 174
imagination, 28–29, 36–37, 56–57, 66–67, 69–70, 127, 148, 167, 169–70, 175, 192–94
immediate knowledge, 45–46
impossible experiences, 73
In Praise of Folly (Erasmus), 199–201
In Search of Lost Time (Proust), 172
India, 94, 110, 111, 126, 150, 226

Indigenous cultures and practices, 120, 189, 217
inebriation, 78, 224; *see also* drunkenness
Infinite Hive, The: A Personal Record of Extra-Sensory Experiences (Heywood), 214
Inquisition, 1
insanity, 21, 149, 202, 213
insects, 104–5
instincts, awakening of, 98
intake questionnaires, 11
internal world, our, 36
interpersonal relations, 31–32
intuition, 45–47, 67, 68, 138, 195
Islam, 166, 188–89, 222, 224
Israel, Hamas terrorist raid on, 100

Jägermeister, 95, 99
James, William, 44–45, 158
  Varieties of Religious Experience, 73
Jay, Mike, 44
Jesuits, 79
John, Gospel of, 182
"just say no" to drugs, 76, 228
justice, 21–22, 24, 143

kakodaimonia, 11
kalsarikännit, 17
Kant, Immanuel, 61, 62, 85–86
  Critique of the Power of Judgment, 86
Kierkegaard, Søren, 113
Klein, Richard, *Cigarettes Are Sublime*, 219

knowledge, 41, 42, 45–47, 49, 50, 61, 64, 68–69, 78, 85–86, 96, 189–90, 195, 196, 200; *see also* truth(s)
Koestler, Arthur, 165
Koryak people, 111
Kubrick, Stanley, 167–68

"Landshark" (X user), 123
language (limits of language), 5, 7, 30–33, 48, 59, 72, 74, 104, 116–17, 143–44, 174, 176, 186, 204, 206, 225–26
laser light shows, 59–60, 171
latent discourses, 111–12
law of the excluded middle, 72–73, 73
"layers of reality," 25, 195–97
Leary, Timothy, x, xiv
legalization (legal reforms), xiv, 119
Leibniz, G. W., 185, 189–90, 222
Leiden, Netherlands, 1, 4–5
Leopardi, Giacomo, 148, 174
Levinas, Emmanuel, 186
Lévi-Strauss, Claude, 98, 111
Lewis, David, 26
Lexapro, 10
light, 39
limbic capitalism, 101, 102
limbic system, 97
"little green elves," 34, 36, 188
Living in Oblivion (film), 173
LLMs, 180
Locke, John, 78–79, 81, 120
  An Essay Concerning Human Understanding, 78
Lodge, Paul, 47–48, 48

logic, modal, 26
logical positivism, 61
logical syllogisms, 200
London Society for Psychical Research, 213
longing, sense of, 22
Looney Tunes, 167, 171, 192, 193
looping effect, 205
lost civilizations, past existence of, 194
love, xii, 21–23, 31–32, 32, 129, 130, 136, 142–48, 197
Lovecraft, H. P., 194
LSD ("acid"), 14, 52, 53, 65, 73, 95, 98, 100, 112, 121, 127–31, 139, 165, 167–68, 187, 193, 197, 207, 211, 216
lucidity, 22, 105, 151, 152, 187–88
Luckmann, Thomas, 149

Macbeth (Shakespeare), 156, 158
Madame Bovary (Flaubert), 176
madness, 21, 75, 199–202, 208, 224–25
Madness and Civilization (Foucault), 201
major depression, 10
Mamas and the Papas, The, 8
mania, 47–48
manufacturing, 96
marginal states, 76, 78
marijuana, 19, 119
Marriage of Heaven and Hell, The (Blake), 41–42
martial uses of drugs, 100, 101

mass media, 160
mass production, 96
material objects, 50–52
materialism, 218, 222
Matrix, The (film), 180
mature capitalism, 97
McKenna, Terence, 34, 188
    True Hallucinations, 55–56
MDMA, xiii, 100
mead, 92–93
meaning, 226
measurability, 36, 43
medical uses of drugs, xiv, 100, 101, 119–22
medicine, field of, 44, 111
Meditations on First Philosophy (Descartes), 63–71, 76, 183, 186, 201
melatonin, 126
memories, 31
"Menace of Mescalin, The" (Zaehner), 210
mental activity, 28–29, 48, 153, 185
mental health (mental illness), 10, 12–13, 18–19, 95, 116, 201–5, 207–8
mental representations, as reality, 57–58, 190, 192, 194–95
Merleau-Ponty, Maurice, 186
mescaline, 41, 131–35, 140, 165, 185, 187–89, 192, 202–4, 206, 209–14
metaphysics, 61–62
Metaphysics (Aristotle), 62
methamphetamine, 100
microdosing, xiv–xv, 116, 118, 121
Middle Ages, 200, 222

mind, philosophy of, 51, 79, 86
mind, the, xvi, 8, 9, 13, 51, 64, 67–69, 83–84, 86, 87, 125
mind-altering substances, x, 47, 106–7, 110, 115, 145, 182, 196, 203
"mind-blowing" experiences, 61, 116–18, 121, 167
Mintz, Sidney W., 96
  Sweetness and Power, 91–92
Mitsein ("being-with"), 183–84
modal logic, 26
modal realists, 26
monads, 185
Monroe, Marilyn, 7–8
monsters, 154
moods, 23–24, 27, 35, 59–60, 141, 156–58
moral agency, xii, xiii
More, Henry, 26
"More Than a Feeling" (song), 144
Morrison, Jim, 42
mortality, 157–58
Moscow State University, 191
Moses, 209
mosquitoes, 104–5
moving images, 171, 176
Muraresku, Brian, 217
mushrooms, ix–x, xiii–xiv, 1, 2, 5, 30, 109–11
Mushrooms, Russia, and History (Wasson and Wasson), 109
music, 18, 20, 22, 23, 27–29, 35, 41, 107, 131, 170, 197
mycophobia, 109
mysticism, 31, 72–74, 126, 209–12, 215
Myth of Mental Illness, The (Szasz), 205

Nagel, Thomas, 42
nanotech cameras, 119
narcotics, 91
narrative visual media, 176
Narrenliteratur, 200
natural sciences, 23, 25, 45–47, 49, 54, 60, 142, 157, 189, 227
natural systems, 83–84
natural theology, 222
natural-language propositions, 72
nature (natural phenomena), 73, 83, 85–86, 96, 164, 209–10, 212, 222
nausea, 121
Nausea (Sartre), 137–39, 150–51
Nazism, 27
neopaganism, 210, 211
neo-Platonism, 73
Netherlands, xiii–xiv, 1, 4–6
neurons, 59, 104
neurotoxins, plant, 106
neurotransmitters, 127, 130
New Age, 62, 168
Nicholas of Cusa, *De Docta ignorantia*, 200
nitrous oxide, 44, 45
non-veridical perceptions, 55–56
"normal" people, psychedelic use by, 117–18
normalization, of psychedelic experience, 114, 116
nostalgia, 147
"now," 38

observation, scientific, 42, 44–46
ocean (oceanic feeling), 164–65

olfaction, 180–81
On Learned Ignorance (Nicholas of Cusa), 200
Onion, The, 163
ontology, 36, 58, 82, 84, 129, 130, 143; *see also* social ontology
opiate addiction, xiv
opium, 91, 102
Oregon, xiii
Origen, 195
ornaments (ornamentation), 102–4, 107
other beings, encounters with, 27, 34–35, 37, 183, 188–89, 204
other minds, reality of, 34, 39, 68, 71, 183–89, 204
"other world," 18, 22–23, 27, 35–36, 142, 147, 227, 228
Oxford University, 47, 89, 98, 208
oysters, 183

pagan religions, 220–21
pain, 9, 43, 120, 126
Paleolithic people, 192, 193
Paley, William, 222–23
"pantsdrinking," 17
paradoxes, 72–74
paranoia, 32–33
pareidolia, 4
parenthood, 113–15
Paris, France, 225
Pascal, Blaise, 26
passivity (passive viewing), 171, 176–78
Paul, L. A., "What You Can't Expect When You're Expecting," 114–15
Paul, Saint, 165

perception(s), xv, 43, 47, 49, 51–56, 59, 84, 131–33, 135–36, 140–42; *see also* consciousness
Perrine, Daniel M., xi, 45
Persia, ancient, 210
personal growth, 60
personal identity, 78, 80, 81
Peru, 96
peyote, xiii, 65, 97, 189, 203
phantasms, 32, 83
pharmacies, 90
pharmacology, 44
phenomenology, 27, 44–50, 53–55, 104, 181–83, 186–87
philosophy
  analytic, 45–48, 50, 60
  classical Greek, 82–83, 199
  critical, 85
  and death, 39
  "dogmatic," 85
  and the "inner world," 25
  and logic, 26
  of mind, 51, 79, 86
  ordinary-language, 89
  proper scope of, 228–29
  and psychedelics, xvi, 39–40, 54, 61, 155
  rationalist, 23, 77
  of science, 117
  and sobriety, xi, 16, 188
  and teleology, 222–23
  and veridicality, 55
  Western, 21–22, 27, 71–74, 76, 87, 135, 187
"philosophy of wine," 81
physics (physical laws), 27, 73, 83, 84
Picasso, Pablo, 138
pineal gland, 125–26

placebos, 112, 116
planetary consciousness, 159–61, 164
plants, 3, 6–7, 55, 90, 106, 121–22
Plato, 21–24, 35
  Symposium, 21, 199–200
plot twists, 214
Plotinus, 73
poetry, 18, 22, 60–61, 72, 74, 174, 210, 229–31
Pollan, Michael, 217
pomegranate seeds, 15
pornography, 173–75
Porphyry, 161
possession, 229–30
possible worlds, 26
post-traumatic stress disorder, xiv, 204
potatoes, 65, 93–94
pragmatism, 121, 131
prescription medications, 10, 90
Princeton University, 108
prohibition, xiv, 42–43, 45, 47, 98, 134, 173
proofs, geometrical, 69–70
Protestantism, 229
Proust, Marcel, 173
  In Search of Lost Time, 172
  Swann's Way, 172
Prozac, 10
pseudoscience, 194
psilocybin, ix, xi, xiii–xiv, 1–9, 22, 27, 28, 110, 112, 180, 192–93, 197, 225
Psychedelic Meditations (imagined treatise), 65–67, 71
psychedelic mushrooms, xiii–xiv, 1, 2, 5, 30

psychedelics (psychedelic drugs)
  and addiction, xii–xiii
  and "analogy of enlightenment," 60
  "bad trips" with, 154–57
  classification of, as illicit substances, 97
  and disclosive submission to the world, 24–25
  and dissolution of self, 37, 80, 157
  experience of using, 18, 33–40, 56–60, 73, 79, 80, 85, 113–14, 147, 151–52, 167, 174, 221–23
  hallucinations related to, 139–41
  "heretical" character of, 227
  legal, xi–xii
  in 1960s counterculture, 170, 211
  potential therapeutic uses of, 116–22, 202–3, 207
  research on, xiv, 14, 53–54, 56, 112–13, 173, 203–4
  ritual use of, 215–17
psychiatry, 11–13, 47, 202–5, 215
psychoactive compounds, 44–45, 109, 110, 121–22, 127, 178
psychology, 43, 48, 83
psychosis, 136, 141, 150–51, 202–3, 208
psychosomatic illnesses, 13
psychotogens, 203, 215

quantifiability, 43
quantum computing, 119
questionnaires, intake, 11

quetiapine, 10
Quine, W. V. O., 60–62

racism, 122, 123
Raichle, Marcus E., 152–53
Ramadan, 224
Rastafarianism, 108
rationalism (rationality), 23, 36, 69–70, 77–78, 82, 85, 120, 189, 200, 201
rats, 126
Ray, John, 222
Raymond, Harold, 41
Reagan, Nancy, 76, 90
Reagan, Ronald, 76
realism, 22, 147, 151
realists, modal, 26
reality
　empirical, 24, 26–27, 57, 189–90, 194–96, 218
　hidden, 138
　hierarchy of, 37, 56–58
　layers of, 25, 195–97
　of mental illness classifications, 12
　nature of, xv, 30, 40, 62, 70, 71, 77, 87, 127, 128, 130, 139, 156, 167, 191–92, 195–97, 213
　of other minds, 71, 183
　perception of, xv–xvi, 55–56, 135–36, 139, 150–52
　socially constructed, 149–50
　of time, 38
　veridicality vs., 132, 133
　see also veridicality
reason, faculty of, see rationalism (rationality)
Recognitions, The (Gaddis), 137–38

recreational drug use, xi, 98–102, 123
red wine, 16–18
rediscovery, of other worlds, 35–36
"reducing valves," 152, 156
regrets, 33, 81
reindeer, 110
religion (religious traditions), 113, 168, 189, 209–12, 215–17, 220–22, 224, 228, 229; *see also specific religions*
Renaissance, 75, 209
reptiles, 126
retreats, xiii, 122–23
Rig Veda, 110
Rimbaud, Arthur, 210
ritual (ritual contexts), 75, 101, 108, 111, 119, 215–17, 224–28
Rolland, Romain, 164
Roman Catholicism, 166, 210, 216–17, 225, 227–28
Roman Empire, 94, 102
romantic love, 136, 145–46
Romanticism (Romantic movement), 23, 35, 164
rosé, 17
Rouhier, Alexandre, 203
Rubik's Cube, 191
Russell, Bertrand, 52
　The Analysis of Mind, 180
Russia, ix, 109

Sacramento, Calif., 20, 148
Saint Petersburg, Russia, ix, x
salt, 93
San Francisco, Calif., 29
Santo Daime religion, 216–17

Sartre, Jean-Paul, *Nausea*, 137–39, 150–51
Sasquatch, 142, 143
Scandinavia, 98, 111
Schiebinger, Londa, 95
schizophrenia, 10, 185, 188, 202, 204–8, 212–13
schnapps, 16
Scholasticism, 200
Schwitzgebel, Eric, *The Weirdness of the World*, 77
scientific observation, 42, 44–46
scientific revolution, 43
Scientology, 168, 216
sclerotia, xiii–xiv
screen images, 9, 19, 171, 177
second-person encounters, 34, 183, 184, 186–88
secret rooms, dreams of, 28
selfhood (the self), 30, 37–39, 76, 78–80, 82, 153, 157–58, 183, 212, 216; *see also* ego (ego dissolution)
sense-data empiricism, 50–51, 132
Sentimental Education (Flaubert), 144–45
serotonin, 127; *see also* SSRIs
sex industry, 173–74
sexual desire (sexual fantasies), 21, 173–74
Shakespeare, William, *Macbeth*, 156, 158
shamanism (shamanic rites), 101, 109, 110, 206, 220–21
shame, xii, 9, 109, 173
Siberia, 110, 111
"side effect," hallucinations as, 116–18, 121

simulationism (simulation hypothesis), 178–80, 190, 194–96
six-dimensional demons, 86–87, 122
skepticism, 79, 222
Skinner, B. F., 43
slave trade, 65
Slavs, 109
sleep (sleeping), 74, 78, 79, 104–6, 126, 172
"smart shops," 1–2, 6–7, 27
Smirnoff vodka, 15
Smith, Barry, 81
smoking, 108, 219
Smythies, J. R., 56, 131–36, 140, 192, 213
    Analysis of Perception, 131–34
"soaring architecture," 134, 192–95
sobriety (sobermindedness), xi, 14, 55, 80–84, 105, 120, 151, 187–88
social drinking, 18
social media, 113, 160
social ontology, 182–84
Socrates, 21, 23, 199–200, 229, 230
soldiers, drug use among, 100
solipsism, 146
soma, 110, 111
Soma: Divine Mushroom of Immortality (R. Wasson), 109–10
songs, 22, 35, 147
soul, the, 11–12, 79, 83, 86, 122, 125, 165, 168, 195
South America, 122, 189
space race, 163

Index

Spanish Renaissance, 209
spatial metaphors, 25
spatio-temporal structure, 135
"spice," 103–4
Spinoza, Baruch, 16, 39, 146
spiritual movements, new, 215–16
SSRIs, 10, 14, 112, 115–16, 120
Staal, Frits, 226, 228
state agencies, 102
"states-of-mind," 24
stimulants, 91, 97, 100, 101
Stoics, 39, 199
stoners, 19, 192
sugar (sugarcane), 91–92, 96, 97, 101, 212
sun, the, 75–76
superconsciousness, 163, 165
superpowers, 32, 163
surveillance, 119
Swann's Way (Proust), 172
Sweetness and Power (Mintz), 91–92
Swiss chocolate, 96
Symposium (Plato), 21, 199–200
synthetic cannabinoids, 103
Szasz, Thomas, *The Myth of Mental Illness*, 205

taboos, 3, 58, 119–20, 203
tea, 91, 98, 101
Tehran, Iran, 210
telecommunication technologies, 5, 160
teleological arguments, 222–23
Telepathy and Allied Phenomena (Heywood), 214
Teresa of Ávila, Saint, 209
terminally ill patients, 39

Tetris, 190–93, 195
THC, 30, 31
"then," 38
Theosophy movement, 168
therapeutic uses (therapeutic approach), xiv, 39, 101, 116–23; *see also* medical uses of drugs
"thetan" ("thetan being"), 168
thinking (thoughts), 22–23, 37, 64, 79, 108, 158, 162, 165–66, 181
"third eye," 126
third-person point of view, 42, 184
Thompson, Hunter S., x, xiv
Thousand Plateaus, A (Deleuze and Guattari), 206
three-dimensionality, 135
TikTok, 122
time, 31, 38, 39, 59, 120, 145, 178, 180–82, 224–25
toadstools, 109–11, 150
tobacco, 65, 91, 97, 101, 108
tragedies, watching, 20
trance states, 12, 75
transgression, 149
trees, 137, 151, 157, 185
Tribe of Nova music festival, 100
tricyclic medications, 10
triple parhelions, 76
"trips," psychedelic, xiii, xiv, 7, 73–74, 76, 110, 116, 118, 127, 130, 154–55, 157–58, 186, 189, 209, 230
TRON (film), 180
True Hallucinations (McKenna), 55–56
"truffles," xiii–xiv, 1, 3, 6, 7

truth(s), 25, 40, 50–51, 55–57, 60, 61, 78, 128, 167–69, 187, 190, 192, 211, 215, 219, 227, 229–31
turbonormies, 123
turmeric, 95
2001: A Space Odyssey (film), 167–68

UFOs, 62
United States, xiii, 108, 149, 205
"unity of the intellect, the," 165–66
universals, 21–22
unrequited love, 145
Upton, Charles, 188–89
urine, reindeer, 110
utility (utilitarianism), 47, 112–13, 115, 122, 152
Utrecht, Netherlands, 1

values, 47, 57, 72, 108, 150, 164, 201, 218
Varieties of Religious Experience (James), 73
vastu shastra, 150
Vedas, 110, 111, 226
venlafaxine, 10
veridicality, 51, 55–56, 58, 70–71, 131–35, 139, 141–42, 213
vibes, 11, 183
video games, 177, 179, 190–92, 196
Vietnam conflict, 100
Vikings, 111
Virgin Mary, 220
virtual reality (VR), 177, 178, 184, 192

vision(s), 4, 33, 57, 134–35, 158, 166, 185, 193, 195–97, 208–9, 211–313, 217–18, 221; *see also* double vision
visual media, narrative, 176
vitamin C, 95
vodka, 15, 93–94, 224
VR, *See* virtual reality

waking states (waking mind), 59, 60, 72, 74–75, 77, 78, 81, 104–5, 152, 152, 171, 173, 187–88, 218
war, 32, 75–76, 100, 119
Wasson, R. Gordon, 109–11
   Soma: Divine Mushroom of Immortality, 109–10
Wasson, Valentina, 109–11
Wegner, Daniel, 83
Weirdness of the World, The (Schwitzgebel), 77
Weltweisheit, 201
West Indies, 89
Western Europe, 109
Western philosophy, 22, 27, 71–74, 76, 87, 135, 187
Western spiritual traditions, 168
Western world (Western civilization), 81, 187, 210
whales, 117, 121, 143
"What If Psychedelics' Hallucinations Are Just a Side Effect?" (Friedman), 116
"What You Can't Expect When You're Expecting" (Paul), 114–15
whisky, 98
Whitehead, Alfred North, 22
wine (wine tasting), 16–18, 30, 54, 81, 92–94

Wittgenstein, Ludwig, 74
wordiness, 3–4
works of God, 222
World War I, 12
World War II, 100, 210
world-disclosure, 27, 35
worldly accomplishment, 18
world(s), 24–28, 31, 35–37, 49, 52, 54, 55, 57, 59, 60, 63, 64, 70, 74–78, 82, 85, 106, 128–32, 141–43, 146–58, 164, 165, 178–81, 183–87, 191–92, 196, 213

X (Twitter), 123
Xanax, 10

YouTube, 8, 196

Zaehner, R. C., 98, 208–14, 219–21, 223
  "The Menace of Mescalin," 210
Zen Buddhism, 209
zoopharmacognosy, 110
Zoroastrianism, 211